Solving Problems using Dynamic Programming

A Hackers' Perspective

By

Chandra Shekhar Kumar
Integrated M. Sc. in Physics, IIT Kanpur, India
Co-Founder, Ancient Science Publishers
Founder, Ancient Kriya Yoga Mission

Ancient Science Publishers

For comments, suggestions and or feedback, send mail to : *ancientsciencepublishers@gmail.com*

ISBN-13: 978-9354081736
ISBN-10: 9354081738

Preface

A hacker's approach to a coding problem is beyond the foundational aspect of underlying genetic and computational structures, often termed as π^∞.

A concept becomes *not difficult* because the *complexities* built into it are clarified. In a bid to reach the *core* of the problem, the concept is split-broken into fragments, *complexities* are exposed and *delicate* points are examined. Then the concept is *recomposed* to make it integral and as a result, this reintegrated concept becomes sufficiently simple and comprehensible.

This helps build a hacker's insight to reveal the internal structure and internal logic of the concepts, algorithms and mathematical theorems.

This book provides a hacker's perspective to solving problems using dynamic programming. Written in an extremely lively form of problems and solutions (including code in modern C++ and pseudo style), this leads to extreme simplification of optimal coding with great emphasis on unconventional and integrated science of dynamic Programming. Tho-ugh aimed primarily at serious programmers, it imparts the knowledge of deep internals of underlying concepts and beyond to computer scientists alike.

Ancient Science Publishers *Chandra Shekhar Kumar*
July, 2020.

Beautiful (C++) code snippets. Unique yogic exposition to coding.

Ancient Science Hackers

List of Chapters

List of Algorithms

Part I

Genesis

Chapter 1

Optimal Loot Partition

1.1 Deterministic

§ Problem 1. *The head of a gang of robbers embarks on distribution of the looted amount $l(>0)$, starting with division into two parts : x and $l-x$ for $0 \leq x \leq l$. From x : they get a return of $u(x)$ such that they are left with a lesser amount αx : $0<\alpha<1$ and from $l-x$: a return of $v(l-x)$ such that they are left with a lesser amount $\beta(l-x)$: $0<\beta<1$. So the total amount left after the first step of division is $\alpha x+\beta(l-x)$ and the process continues. Devise the partition strategy to help them maximize the return obtained in a finite n or infinite number of steps.* ◊

§§ Solution. Let $y(x)$ denote the return after the first step:

$$\therefore y(x) = u(x) + v(l-x)$$

Assuming u and v to be continuous functions, it is trivial to find the maximum of $y(x)$ over $x \in [0,l]$ using calculus (or graphical approach) :

$$\frac{dy}{dx} = \frac{d}{dx}u(x) + \frac{d}{dx}v(l-x) = 0 \text{ (for extrema).}$$

Solve for x and $y(x)$ is maximum for that x for which $\dfrac{d^2y}{dx^2} < 0$.

Suppose $u(x) = x$ and $v(l-x) = -(l-x)^2$, then

$$y = x - (l-x)^2$$

$$\therefore \frac{dy}{dx} = 1 + 2(l-x) = 0,$$

$$\therefore x = l + \frac{1}{2}.$$
$$\frac{d^2y}{dx^2} = -2 < 0.$$
$$\therefore y_{max} = l + \frac{1}{2} - \frac{1}{4} = l + \frac{1}{4}.$$

After the first step, the initial amount l is reduced to l_1(say):

$$\therefore l_1 = \alpha x + \beta(l - x)$$

In the second step, l_1 is partitioned into x_1 (say) and $(l_1 - x_1)$ for $0 \leq x_1 \leq l_1$. Hence, the return from the second step is $u(x_1) + v(l_1 - x_1)$. Therefore, the total return after the two steps is:

$$\therefore y(x, x_1) = u(x) + v(l - x) + u(x_1) + v(l_1 - x_1).$$

Maximum of the function $y(x, x_1)$ over the 2-dimensional space (x, x_1) yields the maximum return, such that $x \in [0, l]$ and $x_1 \in [0, l_1]$.

Similarly, the total return after n steps is :

$$\therefore y(x, x_1, x_2, \ldots, x_{n-1}) = u(x) + v(l - x) + \sum_{i=1}^{n-1} \left[u(x_i) + v(l_i - x_i)\right]. \tag{1.1}$$

Here $x_i \in [0, l_i]$.

Using this *enumerative* approach to maximize the n-dimensional return, the computation procedure soon becomes cumbersome, error-prone and exponential in nature.

Any choice of $x, x_1, x_2, \ldots$ is a *policy*.
The policy maximizing $y(x, x_1, x_2, \ldots)$ is an *optimal policy*.

It can be noted that each step depends on the respective policy only. Hence at the $(i+1)^{th}$ step, the corresponding *one-dimensional* choice is made : a choice of $x_i \in [0, l]$.

Hence an optimal policy leads to the corresponding maximum return.

Let $y_n(l)$ denote the maximum total return, given the initial amount l and n steps.

$$\therefore y_1(l) = \operatorname*{Max}_{x \in [0,l]} \left[u(x) + v(l - x)\right].$$

After the first step, l becomes $\alpha x + \beta(l - x)$:

$$\therefore y_2(l) = \operatorname*{Max}_{x \in [0,l]} \left[u(x) + v(l - x) + y_1\left(\alpha x + \beta(l - x)\right)\right].$$

This leads to a recurrence relation :

$$\therefore y_n(l) = \operatorname*{Max}_{x \in [0,l]} \left[u(x) + v(l - x) + y_{n-1}\left(\alpha x + \beta(l - x)\right)\right]. \tag{1.2}$$

Hence a single n-dimensional problem is reduced to a sequence of n one-dimensional problems.

Here, the optimal return depends on the initial amount l and initial decision of division into the parts l and $l - x$ only.

This is possible due to *the Principle of Optimality* :

> An optimal policy has the property that whatever the initial state and initial decision are, the remaining decisions must constitute an optimal policy with regard to the state resulting from the first decision.

Hence Eq. (1.2) is the required optimal strategy. ■

1.2 Stochastic

§ **Problem 2.** *The head of a gang of robbers embarks on distribution of the looted amount $l(>0)$, starting with division into two parts : x and $l-x$ for $0 \leq x \leq l$. From x : they get a return of $u_1(x)$ with a probability p_1 such that they are left with a lesser amount $\alpha_1 x : 0 < \alpha_1 < 1$ and a return of $u_2(x)$ with a probability $p_2 = 1 - p_1$ such that they are left with a lesser amount $\alpha_2 x : 0 < \alpha_2 < 1$. Similarly from $l-x$: a return of $v_1(l-x)$ with probability p_1 such that they are left with a lesser amount $\beta_1(l-x) : 0 < \beta_1 < 1$ and a return of $v_2(l-x)$ with probability $p_2 = 1 - p_1$ such that they are left with a lesser amount $\beta_2(l-x) : 0 < \beta_2 < 1$. So the total amount left after the first step of division is $\alpha_1 x + \beta_1(l-x)$ with probability p_1 and $\alpha_2 x + \beta_2(l-x)$ with probability p_2 and the process continues. Devise the partition strategy to help them maximize the return obtained in a finite n or infinite number of steps.* ◊

§§ **Solution**. Let $y_n(l)$ denote the *expected* total return of an n-stage process, obtained using an *optimal* policy, starting with an initial amount l.

Then, the equations are obtained as before :

$$y_1(l) = \underset{x\in[0,l]}{\text{Max}} \left[p_1 \left[u_1(x) + v_1(l-x)\right] + p_2 \left[u_2(x) + v_2(l-x)\right]\right],$$

$$\begin{aligned} y_n(l) = \underset{x\in[0,l]}{\text{Max}} &\left[p_1 \left[u_1(x) + v_1(l-x) + y_{n-1}\left(\alpha_1 x + \beta_1(l-x)\right)\right]\right. \\ &\left.+ p_2 \left[u_2(x) + v_2(l-x) + y_{n-1}\left(\alpha_2 x + \beta_2(l-x)\right)\right]\right]. \end{aligned}$$

As can be noted, using the *expected value* as the measure of the value of a policy, the stochastic process is structurally reduced to the deterministic counterpart. ■

§ **Problem 3.** *With the looted amount $l(>0)$ at his disposal, the leader of a gang of robbers decides to buy a sophisticated weapon, which is not readily available. The probability of buying it is $p(x)$ at the expense of amount x, where $x \in [0,l]$. If he is not able to buy the weapon at his first attempt, he continues with the remaining amount $l-x$. How should he proceed in order to maximize his over-all chance of success ?* ◊

§§ **Solution**. Let $y_n(l)$ be the maximum over-all probability of success, given : the initial amount l and n trials.

After utilizing the amount x on the first try, the probability of buying is $p(x)$. So the probability of not buying will be $1-p(x)$. Then the leader uses an optimal policy starting with the remaining amount $l - x$. Hence, the required optimal procedure is

$$\therefore y_n(l) = \underset{x\in[0,l]}{\text{Max}} \{p(x) + [1 - p(x)]\, y_{n-1}(l - x)\}.$$

Hence it is relatively easy to formulate the problem if the probability of failure is considered than the probability of success. ■

Chapter 2

Exam Prep

§ Problem 4. *School board decides to declare the final exam's result in such a way that a student, named Ram, is either pass or fail. Initially the probability of his failure is given as p. Proper study will reduce this probability to αp, where $\alpha \in [0, 1]$. Mock test will help him know exactly whether he is fail or pass. Ram wants to pass the exam in a minimum time. What is the optimal procedure he should follow ?* ◊

§§ Solution. Let $f(p)$ be the expected minimum time to pass the exam given the initial probability of failing the same is p.

If Ram appears in the mock test, it is known that he is fail with initial probability p and he continues with that knowledge. If he is pass then the process is over.

So if he appears for the mock test as a first step, the expected minimum time is given by

$$1 + pf(1).$$

Otherwise if he follows the proper study plan, then the expected minimum time is given by

$$1 + f(\alpha p).$$

Combining these two results, the required optimal procedure is

$$f(p) = \underset{p\in[0,1]}{\text{Min}} \left[1 + pf(1),\ 1 + f(\alpha p)\right],$$
$$f(0) = 0.$$

■

§ **Problem 5.** *Ram (a student) plans to prepare for the final exams using any of two exam-guides where he is allowed to refer one of these two guides at a given stage. There is a probability p_1 of scoring one mark, a probability p_2 of scoring two marks and a probability p_3 of finishing the study plan with the first guide. The second guide has a similar set of probabilities p_1', p_2' and p_3'. Chalk out the optimal study plan to help him maximize the probability of scoring at least n marks.* ◊

§§ **Solution**. Let $f(n)$ be the probability of scoring at least n marks following an optimal study plan.

If Ram scores k marks on the first step, then he continues so as to maximize the probability of scoring at least $n-k$ marks on the following steps. Notice with p_3 or p_3', there is no gain because the process is terminated. This leads to the following optimal study plan :

$$f(n) = \operatorname*{Max}_{n\geq 2}\left[p_1 f(n-1) + p_2 f(n-2),\ p_1' f(n-1) + p_2' f(n-2)\right].$$

This holds even for $n = 0, 1$ with the convention that $f(-k) = 1$ for $k \geq 0$. ■

§ **Problem 6.** *Ram purchased two sample question papers to help him practice for the final exam. The first paper has m questions while the second has n questions. There is only one solution bank available with him. The probability of solving α percent of the questions of the first paper with this solution bank is p_1, the bank still being useful. There is a probability $(1-p_1)$ that the bank doesn't help in solving any question and will be of no further use. Similarly, the second question paper has the probabilities p_2 and $(1-p_2)$ associated with it with solving β percent of the questions. How does Ram proceed in order to maximize the total number of questions solved before the solution bank is rendered useless.* ◊

§§ **Solution**. Let $f(x, y)$ be the expected number of questions solved using an optimal sequence of choices, when the first paper L has the number of questions x and the second paper B has the number of questions y. $x,\ y \geq 0$.

Let $\alpha_1 = \dfrac{\alpha}{100}$ and $\beta_1 = \dfrac{\beta}{100}$.

If Ram chooses the first paper L (say), then :

$$f_L(x, y) = p_1\left\{\alpha_1 x + f\left[(1-\alpha_1)\,x,\ y\right]\right\}$$

If Ram chooses the second paper M (say), then :

$$f_M(x, y) = p_2\left\{\beta_1 y + f\left[x, (1-\beta_1)\,y\right]\right\}$$

Hence, the optimal procedure is :

$$f(x, y) = \operatorname*{Max}_{x,y\geq 0}\left[f_L(x, y),\ f_M(x, y)\right].$$ ■

§ Problem 7. *In the § Problem 6, it is desired to maximize the expected number of the total solved questions, N. Devise the optimal procedure for maximizing the expected value of $\delta(N)$, where δ is a given function.* ◊

§§ Solution. Let z be the number of questions already solved.
Let $f(x,y,z)$ be the expected $\delta(N)$, using an optimal policy.
Let $\alpha_1 = \dfrac{\alpha}{100}$ and $\beta_1 = \dfrac{\beta}{100}$.
If Ram chooses the first paper L (say), then :

$$f_L(x,y,z) = p_1 f\left[(1-\alpha_1)\,x,\ y,\ z+\alpha_1 x\right] + (1-p_1)\,\delta(z).$$

If Ram chooses the second paper M (say), then :

$$f_M(x,y,z) = p_2 f\left[x, (1-\beta_1)\,y,\ z+\beta_1 y\right] + (1-p_2)\,\delta(z).$$

Hence, the optimal procedure is :

$$f(x,y) = \underset{x,y\geq 0}{\text{Max}}\left[f_L(x,y,z),\ f_M(x,y,z)\right],$$
$$f(0,0,z) = \delta(z).$$

■

§ Problem 8. *Reconsider the § Problem 6 in the case in which Ram knows only the expected number of questions in each paper and the expected number of questions solved each time, without being able to observe the results of individual operations.* ◊

§§ Solution. Let $f(x,y)$ be the expected number of questions solved using an optimal sequence of choices when the first paper L has expected number of questions x and the second paper B has expected number of questions y.
Let $\alpha_1 = \dfrac{\alpha}{100}$ and $\beta_1 = \dfrac{\beta}{100}$.
If Ram chooses the first paper L (say), then :

$$f_L(x,y) = p_1\left\{\alpha_1 x + f\left[(1-\alpha_1)\,x,\ y\right]\right\}$$

If Ram chooses the second paper M (say), then :

$$f_M(x,y) = p_2\left\{\beta_1 y + f\left[x, (1-\beta_1)\,y\right]\right\}$$

Hence, the optimal procedure is :

$$f(x,y) = \underset{n\geq 2}{\text{Max}}\left[f_L(x,y),\ f_M(x,y)\right].$$

Note that this solution is same as in § Problem 6 though the problems are quite different in structure. ■

Chapter 3

Optimal Coin Tossing

§ Problem 9. *Two brothers, Ram and Shyam, Ram possessing an amount x and Shyam possessing an amount y, play a modified coin-tossing game described by the matrix :*

$$M = \begin{vmatrix} m_{11} & m_{12} \\ m_{21} & m_{22} \end{vmatrix}.$$

Assuming that each player is motivated by a desire to ruin the other, how does each play ? ◊

§§ Solution. Let l be the total amount of money, which remains constant in the game. Hence it is sufficient to specify the amount of money x held by Ram.

Let $f(x)$ be the probability that Shyam is ruined before Ram when Ram has x and Shyam has $l - x$ and when both use the optimal strategies.

Let Ram's strategy be $p = (p_1,\ p_2)$, where p_1 and p_2 represent the respective frequencies with which the first and second rows of M are played.

Let Shyam's strategy be $q = (q_1,\ q_2)$, where q_1 and q_2 represent the respective frequencies with which Shyam chooses the first and second columns of M.

$$\begin{aligned} \therefore f(x) &= p_1 q_1 f(x + m_{11}) + p_1 q_2 f(x + m_{12}) \\ &\quad + p_2 q_1 f(x + m_{21}) + p_2 q_2 f(x + m_{22}) \\ &= g[p, q, f(x)] \text{ (say), where } x \in (0, l). \end{aligned}$$

If both play optimally, then

$$\therefore f(x) = \underset{p}{\text{Max}}\, \underset{q}{\text{Min}}\, g[p, q, f(x)]$$

$$= \underset{q}{\text{Min}}\,\underset{p}{\text{Max}}\, g\left[p, q, f(x)\right], \; x \in (0, l)$$

$$f(0) = 0, \; x \le 0,$$
$$f(x) = 1, \; x \ge l.$$

Hence $f(x)$ is the value of the game with the payoff matrix as

$$\begin{vmatrix} f\left(x + m_{11}\right) & f\left(x + m_{12}\right) \\ f\left(x + m_{21}\right) & f\left(x + m_{22}\right) \end{vmatrix}.$$

■

Chapter 4

Proving Optimality Principle

As noted earlier, the principle of optimality helps in transforming a single N-dimensional problem at hand to a sequence of N one-dimensional problems in *a specified order* (i.e. a time-like concept is introduced here : rendering this approach as a *dynamic* one). The functional equation has recurrent yet independent structure. This in turn establishes the transformation from optimal to functional and vice versa.

Typical optimization problem at hand is finding the maximum of a function ϕ of n variables $x_i : i \in [1, n]$:

$$\phi\left(x_1,\ x_2,\ \ldots,\ x_n\right) = \sum_{i=1}^{n} \delta_i\left(x_i\right) \tag{4.1}$$

taken over the region of values determined by the relations:

$$\sum_{i=1}^{n} x_i = c \tag{4.2}$$

$$x_i \geq 0 \tag{4.3}$$

where c is a positive constant.

This problem can be modeled as an optimal resource allocation one, where c is a fixed quantity of an economic *resource*. Each potential usage of the resource is an *activity*. As a result of using all or part of this resource in any single activity, a certain *return* is derived. Assuming that the return from any activity is independent of the allocations to the other activities and the total return can be obtained as the sum of the individual returns, divide the resources so as to maximize the total return.

Here x_i represents the quantity of the resource assigned to the ith activity and $\delta_i(x_i)$ represents the return from the ith activity. The allocations are done one at a time, i.e. first a quantity of resources is assigned to the nth activity, then to the $(n-1)^{th}$ activity and so on. Due to this time-like ordering constraint, this is indeed a *dynamic* allocation process.

Since the maximum of $\phi(x_1, x_2, \ldots, x_n)$ over the designated region depends upon c and n, a sequence of functions $f_1(c)$, $f_2(c)$, …, $f_n(c)$ is defined as :

$$f_n(c) = \underset{\{x_i\}}{\text{Max}}\, \phi(x_1, x_2, \ldots, x_n),\ \sum_{i=1}^{n} x_i = c,\ x_i \geq 0 \tag{4.4}$$

$$f_n(0) = 0\ (\because \delta_i(0) = 0) \tag{4.5}$$

$$f_1(c) = \delta_1(c),\ c \geq 0. \tag{4.6}$$

The function $f_n(c)$ is then the optimal return from an allocation of the quantity of resources c to n activities.

Since x_n is allocated to the nth activity, where $x_n \in [0, c]$, the remaining quantity of resources, $c - x_n$, will be used to obtain a maximum return from the remaining $(n-1)$ activities.

Since the optimal return for $n-1$ activities starting with quantity $c - x_n$ is, by definition, $f_{n-1}(c - x_n)$, hence the initial allocation of x_n to the nth activity results in a total return of $\delta_n(x_n) + f_{n-1}(c - x_n)$ from the n-activity process.

An optimal choice of x_n is obviously one which maximizes this function. Hence this results into the following recurrence :

$$f_n(c) = \underset{x_n \in [0,\, c]}{\text{Max}} \left[\delta_n(x_n) + f_{n-1}(c - x_n)\right],\ n \geq 2,\ c \geq 0 \tag{4.7}$$

$$f_1(c) = \delta_1(c). \tag{4.8}$$

With the known value of $f_1(c)$, it is easy to compute the sequence $\{f_n(c)\}$ inductively because $f_2(c)$ is computed from $f_1(c)$ and so on.

It can be noted that :

$$\underset{\sum_{i=1}^{n} x_i = c,\ x_i \geq 0}{\text{Max}} = \underset{x_n \in [0,\, c]}{\text{Max}} \left[\underset{\sum_{i=1}^{n-1} x_i = c - x_n,\ x_i \geq 0}{\text{Max}} \right] \tag{4.9}$$

Hence Eq. (4.4) translates as follows

$$\begin{aligned} f_n(c) &= \underset{\sum_{i=1}^{n} x_i = c,\ x_i \geq 0}{\text{Max}} \left[\sum_{i=1}^{n} \delta_i(x_i) \right] \\ &= \underset{x_n \in [0,\, c]}{\text{Max}} \left[\underset{\sum_{i=1}^{n-1} x_i = c - x_n,\ x_i \geq 0}{\text{Max}} \left[\sum_{i=1}^{n} \delta_i(x_i) \right] \right] \end{aligned}$$

$$= \underset{x_n \in [0,\, c]}{\text{Max}} \left[\delta_n \left(x_n \right) + \underset{\sum_{i=1}^{n-1} x_i = c - x_n,\; x_i \geq 0}{\text{Max}} \left[\sum_{i=1}^{n-1} \delta_i \left(x_i \right) \right] \right]$$

$$= \underset{x_n \in [0,\, c]}{\text{Max}} \left[\delta_n \left(x_n \right) + f_{n-1} \left(c - x_n \right) \right]. \tag{4.10}$$

Note that the functional equation Eq. (4.7) is derived (earlier using the principle of optimality) again as in Eq. (4.10) using elementary mathematics. This establishes the *Principle of Optimality*. The proof is in the pudding. The functional equation technique is more like a search procedure which is much better compared to the enumeration of all cases.

It is the *Principle of Optimality* that furnishes the key. According to this principle, once some initial x_n is chosen, then there is no need to examine *all* policies involving that particular choice of x_n, but rather only those policies which are *optimal* for an $n - 1$ stage process with resources $c - x_n$. In this magical way, the additive operations are in force than multiplicative ones. For example, the time required for a n^2-stage process is now almost precisely n-times the time required for a n-stage process.

This computing paradigm greatly reduce the time required to solve the original problem. Note that this is possible due to combination of two procedures : the utilization of structural properties of the solution and reduction in dimension.

Additionally, though the maximum return is uniquely determined but there may be many optimal policies which yield this return. Determination of these optimal policies require creativity and insight into the problem space.

Part II

Computation

Chapter 5

Ascension to Heaven

§ Problem 10. *Once upon a time, a certain group of daemons and humans on the earth performed together some tantric rituals in a bid to go to heaven. Pleased with their devotion,* Indra, *the Lord of Heaven, provided his white flying majestic elephant,* Airawat, *for that purpose. But certain constraints were imposed throughout the process of ascension. Anyone could cling to the tail of Airawat, while allowing others to cling to him and so on, thus forming a chain. Ordering was not important. Airawat continued flying back and forth from earth to heaven with at least one being.*

Initially, the number of daemons and humans on the earth were d_e *and* h_e *respectively and the number of daemons and humans in the heaven were* d_h *and* h_h *respectively.*

In order to prevent the humans from being devoured by the daemons On the earth, the following constraints were imposed :

(a). $\delta_e\left(d_e, h_e\right) \geq 0$ *on the earth,*
(b). $\delta_h\left(d_h, h_h\right) \geq 0$ *in the heaven, and*
(c). $\delta_a\left(d, h\right) \geq 0$ *on Airawat who would not allow more than* $\gamma \geq 1$ *beings for a ride.*

Find the maximum number of beings ascended to heaven without any human sacrifice. ◊

§§ Solution. Due to prohibition of human sacrifice by the daemons, the total number of beings remains constant throughout the process of ascension : namely, $d_e + h_e + d_h + h_h$.

Hence at any time, the state of system is completely specified by the numbers d_e and h_e.

Let the function $f_n(d_e, h_e)$ represent the maximum number of beings in the heaven at the end of n stages, starting with d_e daemons and h_e humans on the earth and d_h daemons and h_h humans in the heaven.

It is assumed that once everyone has ascended to the heav-en then Airawat goes back to Indra. Hence the process is terminated, i.e. there is no need for anyone to descend back to the earth.

During one stage of the process, the following sequence of actions takes place :

1. Airawat ascends to heaven with $\alpha_1 \in [0, d_e]$ daemons and $\beta_1 \in [0, h_e]$ humans, followed by
2. Airawat descends back to the earth with $\alpha_2 \in [0, d_h + \alpha_1]$ daemons and $\beta_2 \in [0, h_h + \beta_1]$ humans.

Since Airawat would not allow more than $\gamma \geq 1$ beings for a ride, hence

$$\alpha_1 + \beta_1 \leq \gamma, \ \alpha_2 + \beta_2 \leq \gamma$$

Additionally, on Airawat :

$$\delta_a(\alpha_1, \beta_1) \geq 0, \ \delta_a(\alpha_2, \beta_2) \geq 0$$

On the earth :

$$\delta_e(d_e - \alpha_1, \ h_e - \beta_1) \geq 0$$
$$\delta_e(d_e - \alpha_1 + \alpha_2, \ h_e - \beta_1 + \beta_2) \geq 0.$$

In the heaven :

$$\delta_h(d_h + \alpha_1, \ h_h + \beta_1) \geq 0$$
$$\delta_h(d_h + \alpha_1 - \alpha_2, \ h_h + \beta_1 - \beta_2) \geq 0$$

Using the principle of optimality, the functional equation approach leads to the following recurrence relation :

$$f_n(d_e, h_e) = \max_{\alpha, \beta} f_{n-1}(d_e - \alpha_1 + \alpha_2, \ h_e - \beta_1 + \beta_2), \ n \geq 2$$

For $n = 1$:

$$f_1(d_e, h_e) = \max_{\alpha, \beta} [(d_h + \alpha_1) + (h_h + \beta_1)].$$

where α_1 and β_1 are subject to the foregoing constraints. ■

§ Problem 11. *In § Problem 10, find the minimum number of round-trips required by Airawat to bring all the beings to heaven (if feasible).* ◊

§§ Solution. Let n be the required minimum number of round-trips.

Once all the beings are brought to heaven then total number of beings in heaven is $[(d_e + d_h) + (h_e + h_h)]$. Hence as soon as f_n attains this value, the corresponding n is the required minimum. ■

§ Problem 12. *Once upon a time, a group of three daemons and three humans on the earth performed together some* *tantric rituals in a bid to go to heaven. Pleased with their devotion,* Indra, *the Lord of Heaven, provided his white flying majestic elephant,* Airawat, *for that purpose. Airawat would not allow more than two beings for a ride. Anyone could cling to the tail of Airawat, while allowing others to cling to him and so on, thus forming a chain. Ordering was not important. Airawat continued flying back and forth from earth to heaven with at least one being. As soon as the number of daemons was higher than that of humans, even momentarily, the daemons would devour the humans, whether on the earth or with Airawat or in the heaven. Determine an optimal strategy of ascension of everyone to the heaven without any human sacrifice.* ◊

§§ Solution. A generic algorithmic approach to the stated problem, using functional equation technique resulting from the principle of optimality, is already chalked out in the solutions of § Problem 10 and § Problem 11.

For the n-stage process, choice of the possible initial states is dictated by the specified constraints. Others lead to the human sacrifice which in undesired for the process.

Let (d, h) represent the following state :

- there are d daemons and h humans on the earth, hence
- there are $3-d$ daemons and $3-h$ humans in the heaven.

Here $d \in [0, 3]$ and $h \in [0, 3]$. Since both d and h can take any of the four values : (0, 1, 2, 3), hence the total number of initial states is 16. To avoid human sacrifice, the number of daemons, either on the earth or in the heaven, should not be greater than that of the humans except when there in no human.

$d_e(= d)$	$h_e(= h)$	$d_h(= 3-d)$	$h_h(= 3-h)$	human sacrifice
0	0	3	3	N
0	1	3	2	$Y(d_h > h_h)$
0	2	3	1	$Y(d_h > h_h)$
0	3	3	0	$N(d_h > h_h = 0)$
1	0	2	3	N
1	1	2	2	N
1	2	2	1	$Y(d_h > h_h)$
1	3	2	0	$N(d_h > h_h = 0)$
2	0	1	3	N
2	1	1	2	$Y(d_e > h_e)$
2	2	1	1	N
2	3	1	0	$N(d_h > h_h = 0)$
3	0	0	3	$N(d_e > h_e = 0)$
3	1	0	2	$Y(d_e > h_e)$
3	2	0	1	$Y(d_e > h_e)$
3	3	0	0	N

The state $(0, 0)$ implies that everyone is the heaven in which case nothing needs to be done.

The state $(0, 3)$ implies that since all the three daemons are already in heaven, hence they are higher in number leading to human sacrifice in the heaven in the next step.

Hence only the following initial states are feasible (no human sacrifice):

(1, 0), (1, 1), (1, 3), (2, 0), (2, 2), (2, 3), (3, 0) and (3, 3).

With these initial states, computation using the algorithmic solution of § Problem 10 can be done as follows.

$$\because f_1\,(d_e, h_e) = \underset{\alpha,\beta}{\text{Max}}\,[(d_h + \alpha_1) + (h_h + \beta_1)]$$

$$\therefore f_1(1,0) = 6,\ f_1(1,1) = 6,\ f_1(1,3) = 2,\ f_1(2,0) = 6,$$
$$f_1(2,2) = 3,\ f_1(2,3) = 2,\ f_1(3,0) = 4, f_1(3,3) = 1.$$

For example : to compute $f_1(1,3)$: the only feasible moves, satisfying the constraints, are : Airawat flies with 2 humans to the heaven and flies back to earth with 1 daemon and 1 human. $\therefore \alpha_1 = 0,\ \beta_1 = 2,\ \alpha_2 = 1,\ \beta_2 = 1.$

Similarly with $f_1(2,3)$: Airawat flies with 2 daemons to the heaven and flies back to earth with 1 daemon.

Note that the six-valued functions repeat themselves, i.e, if $f_k(i,j) = 6$ then $f_{k+l} = 6$ for $l = 1, 2, \ldots$.

Hence computations using the recurrence relation is done for all non-six values :

$\therefore f_2(1,3) = 3,\ f_2(2,2) = 4,\ f_2(2,3) = 2,\ f_2(3,0) = 6, f_2(3,3) = 1.$

For example :

$$f_2(1,3) = f_1\,(1 - \alpha_1 + \alpha_2, 3 - \beta_1 + \beta_2)$$
$$= f_1(1 - 0 + 1, 3 - 2 + 1) = f_1(2,2) = 3.$$

Similarly

$$\therefore f_3(1,3) = 4,\ f_3(2,2) = 6,\ f_3(2,3) = 3,\ f_3(3,3) = 2.$$
$$\therefore f_4(1,3) = 6,\ f_4(2,3) = 4,\ f_4(3,3) = 3.$$
$$\therefore f_5(2,3) = 6,\ f_5(3,3) = 4.$$
$$\therefore f_6(3,3) = 6.$$

Note that, at sixth stage, the process is over, i.e., everyone is in the heaven. Therefore, the required number of crossings is 6.

Recording the maximizing decision at each stage will determine the optimal policy. ■

Chapter 6

Fibonacci Line Search

A real-valued continuous function $f(x)$ is called a *convex* function over $x \in [a, b]$, if its value at the mid-point of every interval in $[a, b]$ never exceeds the arithmetic mean of its values at the ends of the interval. For example : x^2 and e^x.

Therefore, for any interval $[x_1, x_2] \in [a, b]$, the following inequality holds :

$$f\left(\frac{x_1 + x_2}{2}\right) \leq \frac{f(x_1) + f(x_2)}{2}.$$

Note that, the graph of a convex function lies below the line segment between any two points $[x_1, x_2] \in [a, b]$.

A real-valued continuous function $f(x)$ is called a *concave* function over $x \in [a, b]$, if its value at the mid-point of every interval in $[a, b]$ always exceeds the arithmetic mean of its values at the ends of the interval.

$$\therefore f\left(\frac{x_1 + x_2}{2}\right) \geq \frac{f(x_1) + f(x_2)}{2}.$$

Note that, the graph of a concave function lies above the line segment between any two points $[x_1, x_2] \in [a, b]$.

$$\therefore \text{concave function} = -\text{convex function}.$$

A real-valued continuous function $f(x)$ is called a *unimodal* function over $x \in [a, b]$, if $\exists \alpha \in [a, b]$, such that the following holds :

1. $x \leq \alpha$: $f(x)$ is monotonically increasing, and
2. $x > \alpha$: $f(x)$ is monotonically decreasing.

or, the following holds :

1. $x < \alpha$: $f(x)$ is monotonically increasing, and
2. $x \geq \alpha$: $f(x)$ is monotonically decreasing.

Note that, concave functions are unimodal functions too. Finding the maximum of a concave function $f(x)$ is same as finding the minimum of the convex function $-f(x)$.

§ Problem 13. *Fibonacci line search is an optimal search algorithm for determining the location of the point α of a unimodal function as defined earlier.*

Let $f(x)$ be a unimodal function over $x \in [0, C_n]$. Assuming that the number C_n possesses a property that the point, at which $f(x)$ is maximum, can be located within a unit-length sub-interval by calculating at most n values of the function $f(x)$ and making comparisons.

If $F_n = \text{Max}\, C_n$, then prove that F_n is the nth Fibonacci number, *i.e.:*

$$F_0 = 1 = F_1$$
$$F_n = F_{n-1} + F_{n-2}, \; n \geq 2. \qquad \Diamond$$

§§ Solution. If $n = 0$, then the domain of $f(x)$ is $[0, C_0]$. Since no value of $f(x)$ is given and the sub-interval is of unit length,

$$\therefore F_0 = \text{Max}\, C_0 = 1.$$

For $n = 1$, the domain of $f(x)$ is $[0, C_1]$. Since only one value of $f(x)$ is given, this is not sufficient to locate the maximum value,

$$\therefore F_1 = \text{Max}\, C_1 = 1.$$

For $n \geq 2$: for $(x_1, x_2) \in (0, C_n)$, the values of $f(x_1)$ and $f(x_2)$ are computed.

If $f(x_1) > f(x_2)$, then $f_{max} \in (0, x_2)$.

If $f(x_2) > f(x_1)$, then $f_{max} \in (x_1, C_n)$.

If $f(x_1) = f(x_2)$, then $f_{max} \in (x_1, x_2)$. Still either of the previous two intervals is chosen for the sake of simplicity.

Thus, at each stage after the first computation, the process yields a sub-interval of $[0, C_n]$ and the value of $f(x)$ at an interior point within that sub-interval.

Note that, values at the ends of an interval is of no use for the intended purpose.

For $n = 2$: $C_n = C_2 = 2 - \delta$, $x_1 = 1 - \delta$, $x_2 = 1$, for an infinitesimal $\delta > 0$. $\therefore \text{Max}\, C_2 \geq 2$. But as per the foregoing analysis : $\text{Max}\, C_2 < 2 + \gamma$ for any $\gamma > 0$.

$$\therefore F_2 = \text{Max}\, C_2 = 2 = F_1 + F_0.$$

For $n > 2$: inductive approach will be used.

Assume that $F_k = F_{k-1} + F_{k-2}$ for $k \in [2, n-1]$.
To prove : $F_n = F_{n-1} + F_{n-2}$.

Assume $[x_1, x_2] \in [0, C_n]$.

If $f(x_1) > f(x_2)$, then $f_{max} \in (0, x_2)$.

Note that for $k = n-1$, i.e. when $n-1$ calculations are allowed, since x_1 is already chosen as the first choice, there are only $n-2$ more choices are allowed. $\therefore x_2 < F_{n-1}$.

Additionally, since $f_{max} \in (0, x_1)$ with only $n-2$ choices left, $\therefore x_1 < F_{n-2}$.

Similarly, if $f(x_2) > f(x_1) : C_n - x_1 < F_{n-1}$.

$$\therefore C_n < x_1 + F_{n-1} < F_{n-1} + F_{n-2}$$

$$\therefore F_n = \text{Max}\, C_n \le F_{n-1} + F_{n-2}. \tag{6.1}$$

Note that, the choice of C_n, x_1 and x_2 can be made arbitrarily close to their respective upper bounds, namely : $F_{n-1} + F_{n-2}$, F_{n-2} and F_{n-1} as follows :

$$C_n = \left(1 - \frac{\delta}{2}\right)(F_{n-1} + F_{n-2})$$

$$x_1 = \left(1 - \frac{\delta}{2}\right)F_{n-2}$$

$$x_2 = \left(1 - \frac{\delta}{2}\right)F_{n-1}.$$

Since δ can be made arbitrarily small,

$$\therefore F_n \ge F_{n-1} + F_{n-2}. \tag{6.2}$$

From Eq. (6.1) and Eq. (6.2), it follows :

$$F_n = F_{n-1} + F_{n-2}.$$

Note that, after comparing $f(x_1)$ and $f(x_2)$, length of the interval left is $C_{n-1} = \left(1 - \frac{\delta}{2}\right)F_{n-1}$. Additional there is a value calculated at an optimal first position for the smaller interval.

Similarly, $C_k = \left(1 - \frac{\delta}{2}\right)F_k$ for $k \in [2, n]$.

$\therefore C_2 = \left(1 - \frac{\delta}{2}\right)F_2 = 2 - \delta$, so that the final interval is of unit length.

■

§ Problem 14. *Let $f(x)$ be a unimodal function defined only for discrete values of x, say, a set of C_n points. Assume that the integer C_n possesses a property that the maximum of $f(x)$ can always be identified in n computations and subsequent comparisons.*

If $D_n = \text{Max}\, C_n$, then prove that

$$D_n = -1 + F_{n+1},\ n \ge 1.$$

where F_n is the nth Fibonacci number, *i.e.:*

$$F_0 = 1 = F_1$$

$$F_n = F_{n-1} + F_{n-2},\ n \ge 2.$$

◊

§§ Solution. For the sake of simplicity, let the discrete points be in ascending order in units of one, i.e. $x \in [1, 2, 3, \ldots, C_n]$.

It is easy to observe that $D_1 = 1 = -1 + F_2,\ D_2 = 2 = -1 + F_3,\ D_3 = 4 = -1 + F_5$.

As earlier, the proof by induction will be adopted for $n > 3$.
Assume that $D_k = -1 + F_{k-1}$ for $k \in [4, n-1]$.
To prove that $D_n = -1 + F_{n+1}$.

Assume $[x_1, x_2] \in [4, C_n]$.
In the light of similar logic as in § Problem 13, it can be deduced that

$$x_1 \leq D_{n-2} + 1$$
$$C_n - x_1 \leq D_{n-1}$$
$$\begin{aligned}\therefore C_n &\leq x_1 + D_{n-1}\\ &\leq D_{n-2} + 1 + D_{n-1}\\ &= (-1 + F_{n-1}) + 1 + (-1 + F_n)\\ &= -1 + F_{n+1}.\end{aligned}$$

■

Chapter 7

Coin Change

§ Problem 15. *Given a list of denominations for $k > 0$ coins, $c_i \ : i \in [0..k-1]$ and an unlimited supply of any denomination, determine the minimum number of coins needed to make change for a given amount $s \geq 0$.* ◊

§§ Solution. Let $f_n(s)$ be the minimum number of coins needed to make change for a given amount s, obtained using an optimal policy and n steps.

Let c_i be the denomination of the first or last coin, i.e. c_i is used at the 1st or n^{th} step respectively. Then we can use an optimal policy starting with the remaining amount $s - c_i \geq 0$.

Hence the required optimal procedure is

$$\therefore f_n(s > 0) = \underset{\substack{i \in [0,\ k-1] \\ s - c_i \geq 0}}{\text{Min}} [f_{n-1}(s - c_i) + 1]$$

$$f_n(0) = 0$$

$$f_n(s < 0) = 0$$

i.e. if c_i is the first (or last) coin in the optimal solution to making change for amount s, then one c_i coin plus $f_{n-1}(s - c_i)$ coins to make change for the remaining amount $s - c_i$ is the optimal procedure to make change for the total amount s.

Intuitive Proof : Let us prove that the optimal solution $f_n(s)$ for the amount s contains within it an optimal solution $f_{n-1}(s - c_i)$ for the amount $s - c_i$. Let us assume that the optimal solution $f_n(s)$ uses m coins and it is known that this optimal solution uses a coin c_i. Then there are $m - 1$ coins in the solution $f_{n-1}(s - c_i)$ used within the optimal solution

$f_n(s)$. If $f_{n-1}(s - c_i)$ used fewer than $m - 1$ coins, then this solution can be used to produce a solution $f_n(s)$ that uses less than k coins, which contradicts the optimality of our solution. Hence the solution $f_{n-1}(s - c_i)$ is also an optimal one.

Algorithm 1 Minimum Coin Change : Iterative (Bottom-up) Approach

```
function min-coin-change(c[0..k − 1], s)
    f[0] ← 0        ▷ 0 coins needed to make change for the amount 0
    for i ← 1, s do
        f[i] ← ∞
        for j ← 0, k − 1 do
            if c[j] ≤ i then
                f[i] ← Min (f[i − c[j]]) + 1
            end if
        end for
    end for
    return f[s]
end function
```

This is also known as **forward dynamic programming**.

We need to try k denominations of coins per state in the amount s, hence the time complexity is $\mathcal{O}(ks)$. We are using a storage of size $s + 1$ to store (and possibly reuse)* the optimally computed states, therefore the space complexity is $\mathcal{O}(s)$.

```
int min_coin_change(std::vector<int> & coins, int
    amount)
{
    std::vector<int> f(amount + 1, std::
        numeric_limits<int>::max()/2);

    f[0] = 0;

    for(int i = 1; i <= amount; ++i)
    {
        for(int c : coins)
        {
            if(c <= i)
            {
                f[i] = std::min(f[i], f[i-c] + 1);
            }
        }
    }
    return f[amount] > amount ? -1 : f[amount];
}
```

*Memoization

Algorithm 2 Minimum Coin Change : Recursive (Top-down) Approach

$f[0..s+1] \leftarrow 0$
function min-coin-change($c[0..k-1]$, s)
    if $f[s] \neq 0$ **then**
        return $f[s]$
    end if
    $min \leftarrow \infty$
    for $i \leftarrow 0, k-1$ **do**
        $res \leftarrow$ min-coin-change($c[0..k-1]$, $s-i$)
        if $res \geq 0$ **and** $res < min$ **then**
            $min \leftarrow 1 + res$
        end if
    end for
    $f[s] \leftarrow min$
    return $f[s]$
end function

This is also known as **backward dynamic programming**.

```
int min_coin_change(std::vector<int> & coins, int amount, std::vector<int> & f)
{
    if(amount < 0) return -1;

    if(amount == 0) return 0;

    if(f[amount] != 0) return f[amount];

    int min = std::numeric_limits<int>::max()/2;

    int res = 0;

    for(int c : coins)
    {
        res = min_coin_change(coins, amount - c, f);

        if(res >= 0 and res < min)
        {
            min = 1 + res;
        }
    }

    f[amount] = (min == std::numeric_limits<int>::max()/2) ? -1 : min;

    return f[amount];
}


int min_coin_change(std::vector<int> & coins, int amount)
{
```

```
    std::vector<int> f(amount + 1, 0);

    return min_coin_change(coins, amount, f);
}
```
■

§ Problem 16. *In § Problem 15, identify the optimal set of coins for making the change for the amount s.* ◊

§§ Solution. In § Problem 15, we need to construct the optimal solution from the computed information.

Algorithm 3 Minimum Coin Change : Optimal set of coins

```
function min-coin-change(c[0..k − 1], s)
    f[0] ← 0
    for i ← 1, s do
        f[i] ← ∞
        for coin ∈ c[0..k − 1] do
            if coin ≤ i then
                if f[i − coin] + 1 < f[i] then
                    f[i] ← f[i − coin] + 1
                    coinset[i] ← coin
                end if
            end if
        end for
    end for    ▷ coinset[s] is the first coin in the optimal solution for amount s

    changes ← ∅

    if f[s] > s then
        return changes                    ▷ No solution
    end if

    j ← s
    while j > 0 do
        changes.add(coinset[j])
        j ← j − coinset[j]
    end while
    return changes
end function
```

```
std::vector<int> min_coin_change(std::vector<int>
    & coins, int amount)
{
    std::vector<int> f(amount + 1, std::
        numeric_limits<int>::max()/2);
    std::vector<int> coinset(amount + 1, 0);
    std::vector<int> changes;

```

```
    f[0] = 0;

    for(int i = 1; i <= amount; ++i)
    {
        for(int c : coins)
        {
            if(c <= i)
            {
                if(f[i-c] + 1 < f[i])
                {
                    f[i] = f[i-c] + 1;
                    coinset[i] = c;
                }
            }
        }
    }

    if(f[amount] > amount) return changes;

    int j = amount;

    while(j > 0)
    {
        changes.push_back(coinset[j]);
        j -= coinset[j];
    }

    return changes;
}
```

There is an additional time complexity of $\mathcal{O}(s)$ due to while loop and an additional space complexity of $\mathcal{O}(s)$ for the additional storage.

Hence total time complexity is $\mathcal{O}(ks)$ and space complexity is $\mathcal{O}(s)$.

coins	amount	changes
25, 10, 5	30	25, 5
2,3,5,6,7,8	10	2,8
1,2,5	11	1,5,5
1,2,3	4	1,4
2,5,3,6	10	5,5
9,6,5,1	11	6,5
3	5	
1	3	1,1,1

■

§ Problem 17. *In § Problem 15, determine total number of ways to make change for the amount s.* ◊

§§ Solution. Required number of ways :

Algorithm 4 Coin Change : No of Ways

```
function ways-coin-change(c[0..k − 1], s)
    f[0] ← 1    ▷ 1 way (empty set) to make change for the amount 0
    for coin ∈ c[0..k − 1] do
        for i ← coin, s do
            f[i] ← f[i] + f[i − coin]
        end for
    end for
    return f[s]
end function
```

Time complexity is $\mathcal{O}(ks)$ and space complexity is $\mathcal{O}(s)$.

```cpp
int ways_coin_change(std::vector<int> & coins, int amount)
{
    std::vector<int> f(amount + 1, 0);

    f[0] = 1;

    for(int coin : coins)
    {
        for(int i = coin; i <= amount; ++i)
        {
            f[i] += f[i-coin];
        }
    }
    return f[amount];
}
```

There are 4 number of ways to make change for amount = 5 with the coins = {1, 2, 5}

[5, [2,2,1], [2,1,1,1], [1,1,1,1,1]]. ■

Chapter 8

Constrained Subsequence

8.1 Maximum Sum

§ Problem 18. *Given a sequence of* $n \in (-\infty, \infty)$ *integers, determine the largest possible sum of the contiguous subsequence.* ◊

§§ Solution. Let $f_n(i)$ be the maximum sum of a contiguous subsequence ending at index i, obtained using an optimal policy and n steps.

Let s_i be the value of the element at index i, i.e. s_i is used at the nth step. The we can use an optimal policy starting with previously accumulated maximum sum of a contiguous subsequence ending at index $i - 1$.

Hence the required optimal procedure is

$$\therefore f_n(i) = \underset{i \in [0,\, n-1]}{\text{Max}} \left[f_{n-1}(i-1) + s_i \right]$$

At each step (with addition of s_i), there are 2 options :

1. leverage the previous accumulated maximum sum if $f_{n-1}(i-1) + s_i > 0$, because it is better to continue with a positive running sum or
2. start afresh with a new range (with the starting sum as 0) if $f_{n-1}(i-1) + s_i < 0$, because it is better to start with 0 than continuing with a negative running sum.

Also note that:

- If all the elements are negative, then there is no such subsequence, i.e. the required sum is 0.
- If all the elements are positive, then the entire sequence is the required subsequence, i.e. the required sum is the sum of all the elements of the sequence.
- The required subsequence (if any) starts at and ends with a positive value.

Algorithm 5 Maximum sum contiguous subsequence : compute sum

```
function maxseq(s[0..n − 1])
    currentsum ← 0
    maxsum ← 0
    for x ∈ s[0..n − 1] do
        currentsum ← max(currentsum + x, 0)
        maxsum ← max(maxsum, currentsum)
    end for
    return maxsum
end function
```

Time complexity is $\mathcal{O}(n)$. Space complexity is $\mathcal{O}(1)$.

```cpp
int maxseq(std::vector<int> & s)
{
    int current_sum = 0;
    int max_sum = 0;

    for(int x : s)
    {
        current_sum = std::max(current_sum + x, 0)
        ;
        max_sum = std::max(max_sum, current_sum);
    }
    return max_sum;
}
```

■

§ Problem 19. *In § Problem 18, identify the start and end indices of the contiguous subsequence having the largest possible sum..* ◊

§§ Solution. We need to construct the optimal solution from the computed information, i.e. identify the indices i and j such that $\underset{i \le j}{\text{Max}}(s_i + .. + s_j)$.

Algorithm 6 Maximum sum contiguous subsequence : compute indices

```
function maxseq(s[0..n − 1])
    currentsum ← 0
    maxsum ← 0

    currentsumstart ← 0
    maxsumstart ← 0
    maxsumend ← 0

    for i ∈ [0, n) do
        currentsum ← currentsum + s[i]
        if currentsum < 0 then
            currentsum ← 0
            currentsumstart ← i + 1
        else if currentsum > maxsum then
            maxsum ← currentsum
            maxsumstart ← currentsumstart
            maxsumend ← i
        end if
    end for
    return maxsumstart, maxsumend
end function
```

Time complexity is $\mathcal{O}(n)$. Space complexity is $\mathcal{O}(1)$.

```cpp
std::pair<int, int> maxseq(std::vector<int> & s)
{
    int current_sum = 0;
    int max_sum = 0;

    int current_sum_start = 0;
    int max_sum_start = 0;
    int max_sum_end = 0;

    int n = s.size();

    for(int i = 0; i < n; i++)
    {
        current_sum = current_sum + s[i];

        if(current_sum < 0)
        {
            current_sum = 0;
            current_sum_start = i + 1;
        }
        else
        if(current_sum > max_sum)
        {
            max_sum = current_sum;
            max_sum_start = current_sum_start;
            max_sum_end = i;
        }
    }

    if(max_sum != 0) return {max_sum_start,
```

```
        max_sum_end};
    else return {-1, -1};
}
```

Sequence	<Start Index, End Index>	Max Subsequence	Max Sum
34, -50, 42, 14, -5, 86	<2, 5>	42, 14, -5, 86	137
-5, -1, -8, -9	<-1, -1>		0
-2, 1, -3, 4, -1, 2, 1, -5, 4	<3, 6>	4, -1, 2, 1	6
4, -1, 2, 1	<0, 3>	4, -1, 2, 1	6
4	<0, 0>	4	4

■

§ Problem 20. *Given a sequence of $n \in (-\infty, \infty)$ integers, determine a non-contiguous subsequence having the largest possible sum.* ◊

§§ Solution. Let $f_n(i)$ be the maximum sum of a non-contiguous subsequence ending at index i, obtained using an optimal policy of a n-stage process.

Let s_i be the value of the element at index i. Since no two elements are adjacent, there are 2 options:

1. s_i is included : $\therefore f_n^{inclusive}(i) = f_n(i-2) + s_i$
2. s_i is excluded : $\therefore f_n^{exclusive}(i) = f_n(i-1)$

Hence the required optimal procedure is

$$f_n(i) = \text{Max}\{f_n(i-2) + s_i,\ f_n(i-1)\}$$
$$f_n(0) = s_0$$
$$f_n(1) = \text{Max}(s_0,\ s_1)$$

Algorithm 7 Maximum sum non-contiguous subsequence : compute sum

```
function maxncseq(s[0..n − 1])
    f[0..n − 1] ← {0}
    f[0] ← s[0]
    f[1] ← max(s[0], s[1])

    for i ∈ [2, n) do
        f[i] ← max(f[i − 2] + s[i], f[i − 1])
    end for

    return f[n − 1]
end function
```

Time complexity is $\mathcal{O}(n)$. Space complexity is $\mathcal{O}(n)$.

```
int maxncseq(std::vector<int> & s)
{
    if(s.empty()) return 0;

    int n = s.size();

```

```
    std::vector<int> f(n, 0);

    f[0] = s[0];
    f[1] = std::max(s[1], s[0]);

    for(int i = 2; i < n; ++i)
    {
        f[i] = std::max(f[i-2] + s[i], f[i-1]);
    }
    return f[n-1];
}
```

Algorithm 8 Maximum sum non-contiguous subsequence : compute sum : space optimized

```
function maxncseq(s[0..n − 1])
    f2 ← 0                                   ▷ sum till i − 2
    f1 ← 0                                   ▷ sum till i − 1
    f ← 0                                    ▷ sum till i

    for e ∈ s[0..n − 1] do
        f ← max(f2 + e, f1)
        f2 ← f1
        f1 ← f
    end for

    return f1
end function
```

Time complexity is $\mathcal{O}(n)$. Space complexity is $\mathcal{O}(1)$.

```
int maxncseq(std::vector<int> & s)
{
    if(s.empty()) return 0;

    int f2 = 0, f1 = 0;

    for(int e : s)
    {
        int f = std::max(f2 + e, f1);
        f2 = f1;
        f1 = f;
    }
    return f1;
}
```

Or,

```
int maxncseq(std::vector<int> & s)
{
    if(s.empty()) return 0;

    int lastsum = 0, prev_maxsum = 0, maxsum = 0;

```

```
    for(int e : s)
    {
        prev_maxsum = maxsum;
        maxsum = std::max(lastsum + e, maxsum);
        lastsum = prev_maxsum;
    }
    return maxsum;
}
```

Sequence	Non Contiguous Subsequence	Max Sum
1,2,5,2	1,5	6
1,7,8,4,2	1,8,2	11

■

8.2 Minimum Sum

§ Problem 21. *Given a sequence s of $n \in (-\infty, \infty)$ integers, find a contiguous subsequence of s having the smallest possible sum.* ◊

§§ Solution. The solution is similar to § Problem 18. Let $f_n(i)$ be the minimum sum of a contiguous subsequence ending at index i, obtained using an optimal policy of a n-stage process.

Let s_i be the value of the element at index i, i.e. s_i is used at the nth step. The we can use an optimal policy starting with previously accumulated maximum sum of a contiguous subsequence ending at index $i-1$.

Hence the required optimal procedure is

$$\therefore f_n(i) = \underset{i \in [0,\ n-1]}{\text{Min}} \left[f_{n-1}(i-1) + s_i\right]$$

At each step (with addition of s_i), there are 2 options :

1. leverage the previous accumulated minimum sum if $f_{n-1}(i-1) + s_i < s_i$, or
2. start afresh with a new range with s_i.

Also note that:

- If all the elements are positive, then the required sum is value of the least +ve element.
- If all the elements are negative, then the entire sequence is the required subsequence, i.e. the required sum is the sum of all the elements of the sequence.

Algorithm 9 Minimum sum contiguous subsequence

function minseq($s[0..n-1]$)

```
    currentmin ← ∞
    minsum ← 0
    for x ∈ s[0..n − 1] do
        currentmin ← min(currentmin + x, x)
        minsum ← min(minsum, currentmin)
    end for
    return minsum
end function
```

Time complexity is $\mathcal{O}(n)$. Space complexity is $\mathcal{O}(1)$.

```
int minseq(std::vector<int> & s)
{
    int current_min = 0;
    int min_sum = std::numeric_limits<int>::max();

    for(int x : s)
    {
        current_min = std::min(current_min + x, x)
            ;
        min_sum = std::min(min_sum, current_min);
    }
    return min_sum;
}
```

After multiplication with a negative element (say -1), maximum becomes minimum and vice versa:

Algorithm 10 Min sum contiguous subsequence : Find max of -ve

```
function minseq(s[0..n − 1])
    currentmax ← −∞
    maxsum ← 0
    for x ∈ s[0..n − 1] do
        currentmax ← max(currentmax + (−x), −x)
        maxsum ← max(maxsum, currentmax)
    end for
    return −maxsum
end function
```

Time complexity is $\mathcal{O}(n)$. Space complexity is $\mathcal{O}(1)$.

```
int minseq(std::vector<int> & s)
{
    int current_max = 0;
    int max_sum = std::numeric_limits<int>::min();

    for(int x : s)
    {
        current_max = std::max(current_max + (−x),
            −x);
        max_sum = std::max(max_sum, current_max);
    }
```

```
    return -max_sum;
}
```
■

§ Problem 22. *In § Problem 21, identify the start and end indices of the contiguous subsequence having the smallest possible sum..* ◊

§§ Solution. We need to construct the optimal solution from the computed information, i.e. identify the indices i and j such that $\underset{i \le j}{\text{Min}}(s_i + .. + s_j)$.

Algorithm 11 Minimum sum contiguous subsequence : compute indices

---

```
function minseq(s[0..n − 1])
    currentmin ← 0
    minsum ← ∞

    curminstart ← 0
    minstart ← 0
    minend ← 0

    for i ∈ [0, n) do
        currentmin ← currentmin + s[i]
        if currentmin > s[i] then
            currentmin ← s[i]
            curminstart ← i
        end if
        if minsum > currentmin then
            minsum ← currentmin
            minstart ← curminstart
            minend ← i
        end if
    end for
    return minstart, minend
end function
```

Time complexity is $\mathcal{O}(n)$. Space complexity is $\mathcal{O}(1)$.

```
std::pair<int, int> minseq(std::vector<int> & s)
{
    int current_min = 0;
    int min_sum = std::numeric_limits<int>::max();

    int curmin_start = 0, min_start = 0, min_end =
        0;

    int n = s.size();

    for(int i = 0; i < n; i++)
```

```
    {
        current_min = current_min + s[i];

        if(current_min > s[i])
        {
            current_min = s[i];
            curmin_start = i;
        }

        if(min_sum > current_min)
        {
            min_sum = current_min;
            min_start = curmin_start;
            min_end = i;
        }
    }
    return {min_start, min_end};
}
```

Sequence	<Start Index, End Index>	Min Subsequence	Min Sum
34, -50, 42, 14, -5, 86	<1, 4>	-50,42,-43,-5	-56
-5, -1, -8, -9	<0, 3>	-5,-1,-8,-9	-23
-2, 1, -3, 4, -1, 2, 1, -5, 4	<7, 7>	-5	-5
4, -3, 2, -5	<1, 3>	-3,2,-5	-6
4,1,5,2,3	<1,1>	1	1

∎

8.3 Circular Sequence

§ Problem 23. *Given a circular sequence s of $n \in (-\infty, \infty)$ integers, find the maximum possible sum of a non-empty contiguous subsequence of s.* ◊

§§ Solution. The end of a circular sequence wraps around the start of the sequence itself, i.e.

$$\because i \equiv (i+n) \textbf{ mod } n \quad \forall i \in [0, n)$$
$$\therefore s_i \equiv s_{(i+n) \textbf{ mod } n} \quad \forall i \in [0, n).$$

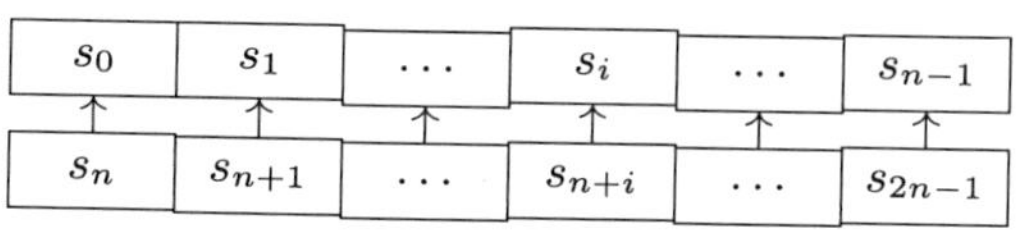

For a maximum contiguous subsequence $[s_i \cdots s_j]$, the solution of § Problem 18 can be used.

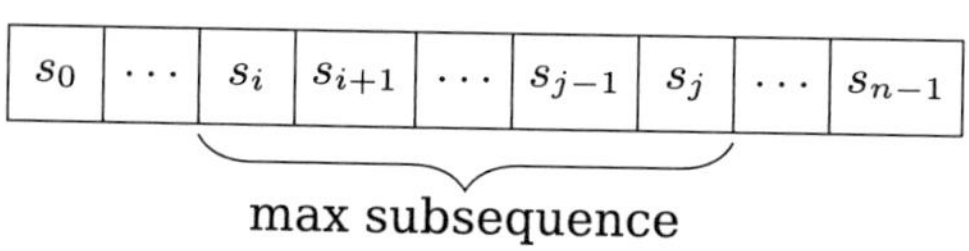

For a maximum contiguous subsequence $[s_j \cdots s_{n-1}, s_0 \cdots s_i]$, the left-over part $[s_{i+1} \cdots s_{j-1}]$ forms a minimum contiguous subsequence.

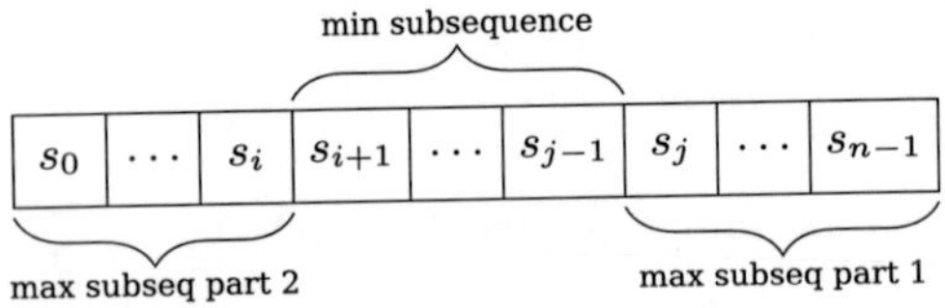

Summation of the contiguous subsequence $[s_j \cdots s_{n-1}, s_0 \cdots s_i]$ is

$$= s_j + \cdots + s_{n-1} + s_0 + \cdots + s_i$$
$$= s_0 + \cdots + s_{n-1} - [s_{i+1} + \cdots + s_{j-1}]$$

This is maximum when $[s_{i+1} + \cdots + s_{j-1}]$ is minimum.

$$\therefore \text{Max}[s_j + \cdots + s_{n-1} + s_0 + \cdots + s_i] = \sum_{k=0}^{k=n-1} s_k - \text{Min} \sum_{k=i+1}^{k=j-1} s_k$$

$$\therefore \text{Maximum sum subsequence} = \text{Total sum of the sequence} - \text{Minimum sum subsequence}$$

Algorithm 12 Maximum sum circular subsequence

```
function maxcircularseq(s[0..n − 1])
    currentmax ← 0
    maxsum ← −∞
    currentmin ← 0
    minsum ← ∞
    totalsum ← 0

    for x ∈ s[0..n − 1] do
        currentmax ← max(currentmax + x, x)
        maxsum ← max(maxsum, currentmax)

        currentmin ← min(currentmin + x, x)
        minsum ← min(minsum, currentmin)

        totalsum ← totalsum + x
    end for

    if totalsum == minsum then        ▷ All elements are -ve
        return maxsum        ▷ Value of the least -ve element
    else
        return max(maxsum, totalsum − minsum)
    end if
end function
```

Time complexity is $\mathcal{O}(n)$. Space complexity is $\mathcal{O}(1)$.

```
int maxsum_circular(std::vector<int> & s)
{
    int current_max = 0, max_sum = std::numeric_limits<int>::min();
    int current_min = 0, min_sum = std::numeric_limits<int>::max();
    int total_sum = 0;

    for(int x : s)
    {
        current_max = std::max(current_max + x, x);
        max_sum = std::max(max_sum, current_max);

        current_min = std::min(current_min + x, x);
        min_sum = std::min(min_sum, current_min);

        total_sum += x;
    }
    // when all elements are -ve => total_sum == min_sum,
    // i.e. total_sum - min_sum becomes 0 => empty subsequence
    // but max_sum still holds the value of the least -ve element,
    // hence return this singleton than an empty one
    return total_sum == min_sum ? max_sum : std::max(max_sum, total_sum - min_sum);
}
```

Circular Sequence	Max Sum Subsequence	Max Sum
1,-2,3,-2	3	3
5,3,-5	5,5	10
3,-1,2,-1	3,-1,2 and 2, -1, 3	4
3,-2,2,-3	3 and 3,-2,2	3
-2,-3,-1	-1	-1
8,-1,3,4	3,4,8	15
5,-3,5,5,-3	5,-3,5,5 and 5,5,-3,5	12

■

§ **Problem 24.** *Given a circular sequence s of $n \in (-\infty, \infty)$ integers, find the minimum possible sum of a non-empty contiguous subsequence of s.* ◊

§§ **Solution**. This is similar to § Problem 23.

For a minimum contiguous subsequence $[s_i \cdots s_j]$, the solution of § Problem 18 can be used.

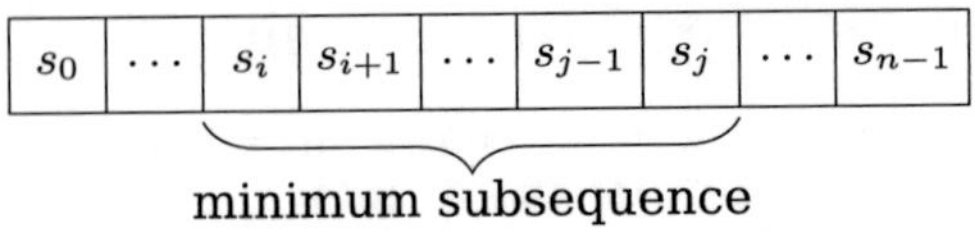

For a minimum contiguous subsequence $[s_j \cdots s_{n-1}, s_0 \cdots s_i]$, the left-over part $[s_{i+1} \cdots s_{j-1}]$ forms a maximum contiguous subsequence.

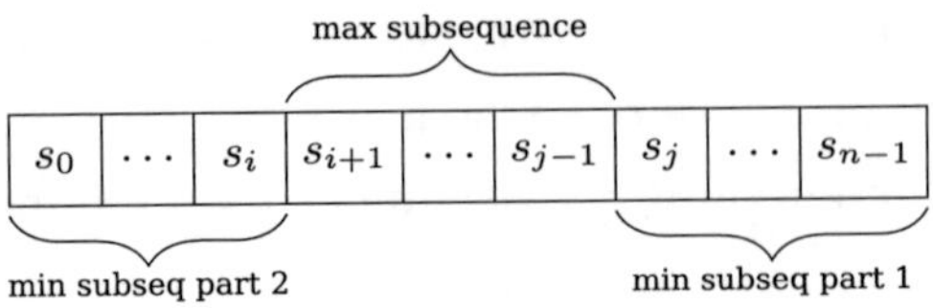

Summation of the contiguous subsequence $[s_j \cdots s_{n-1}, s_0 \cdots s_i]$ is

$$\sum_{k=0}^{k=n-1} s_k - \sum_{k=i+1}^{k=j-1} s_k$$

This is minimum when $\sum_{k=i+1}^{k=j-1} s_k$ is maximum.

$$\therefore \text{Min}[s_j + \cdots + s_{n-1} + s_0 + \cdots + s_i] = \sum_{k=0}^{k=n-1} s_k - \text{Max} \sum_{k=i+1}^{k=j-1} s_k$$

$\therefore$ Minimum sum subsequence = Total sum of the sequence − Maximum sum subsequence

Algorithm 13 Minimum sum circular subsequence

```
function mincircularseq(s[0..n − 1])
    currentmax ← 0
    maxsum ← −∞
    currentmin ← 0
    minsum ← ∞
    totalsum ← 0

    for x ∈ s[0..n − 1] do
        currentmax ← max(currentmax + x, x)
        maxsum ← max(maxsum, currentmax)

        currentmin ← min(currentmin + x, x)
        minsum ← min(minsum, currentmin)

        totalsum ← totalsum + x
```

```
    end for

    if totalsum == maxsum then          ▷ All elements are +ve
        return minsum                   ▷ Value of the least +ve element
    else
        return min(minsum, totalsum − maxsum)
    end if
end function
```

Time complexity is $\mathcal{O}(n)$. Space complexity is $\mathcal{O}(1)$.

```cpp
int minsum_circular(std::vector<int> & s)
{
    int current_max = 0, max_sum = std::numeric_limits<int>::min();
    int current_min = 0, min_sum = std::numeric_limits<int>::max();
    int total_sum = 0;

    for(int x : s)
    {
        current_max = std::max(current_max + x, x);
        max_sum = std::max(max_sum, current_max);

        current_min = std::min(current_min + x, x);
        min_sum = std::min(min_sum, current_min);

        total_sum += x;
    }
    // when all elements are +ve => total_sum == max_sum,
    // i.e. total_sum - max_sum becomes 0 => empty subsequence
    // but min_sum still holds the value of the least +ve element,
    // hence return this singleton than an empty one
    return total_sum == max_sum ? min_sum : std::min(min_sum, total_sum - max_sum);
}
```

Circular Sequence	Min Sum Subsequence	Min Sum
-1,2,-3,2	-3	-3
-5,3,-5	-5,-5	-10
-3,1,-2,1	-3,1,-2 and -2, 1, -3	-4
-3,2,-2,3	-3 and -3,2,-2	-3
2,3,1	1	1
-8,1,-3,-4	-3,-4,-8	-15
-5,3,-5,-5,3	-5,3,-5,-5 and -5,-5,3,-5	-12

■

§ Problem 25. *Given a circular sequence s of $n \in (-\infty, \infty)$ integers, find the minimum possible sum of a non-empty non-contiguous subsequence of s.* ◊

§§ Solution. This is similar to § Problem 20 with the additional constraint that the elements s_0 and s_{n-1} are adjacent, hence both elements together cannot be part of the solution.

Let $f_n(s, i, j)$ be the maximum sum of the sequence s between indices i and j, obtained using an optimal sequence of choices of a n-stage process.

$$\therefore f_n(s, 0, n-1) = \text{Max}\{f_n(s, 0, n-2),\ f_n(s, 1, n-1)\}$$

```
int maxncseq(std::vector<int> & s, int l, int r)
{
    int n = r-l+1;

    std::vector<int> f(n, 0);

    f[0] = s[l];
    f[1] = std::max(s[l], s[l+1]);

    for(int i = 2; i < n; ++i)
    {
        f[i] = std::max(f[i-2] + s[l+i], f[i-1]);
    }
    return f[n-1];
}

int maxncseq_circular(std::vector<int> & s)
{
    if(s.empty()) return 0;

    int n = s.size();

    return std::max(maxncseq(s,0,n-2), maxncseq(s
        ,1,n-1));
}
```

Circular Sequence	Max Sum Subsequence	Max Sum
4,7,4	7	7
4,7,9,1	4,9	13

■

8.4 Maximum Product

§ Problem 26. *Given a sequence s of $n \in (-\infty, \infty)$ integers, find a contiguous subsequence which has the largest possible product.* ◊

§§ Solution. Note that the product of a running minimum with a negative element is also a running maximum so far and the product of a running maximum with a negative element is also a running minimum so far.

Let $f_n(i)$ be the maximum product, ending at index i, obtained using an optimal sequence of choices of a n-stage process and s_i be the ith element.

$$f_n^{max}(i) = \underset{i\in[0,n)}{\text{Max}} \left(s_i,\ f_{n-1}^{max}(i-1)\cdot s_i,\ f_{n-1}^{min}(i-1)\cdot s_i\right)$$
$$f_n^{min}(i) = \underset{i\in[0,n)}{\text{Min}} \left(s_i,\ f_{n-1}^{max}(i-1)\cdot s_i,\ f_{n-1}^{min}(i-1)\cdot s_i\right)$$
$$\therefore f_n(i) = \underset{i\in[0,n)}{\text{Max}} \left[f_n^{max}(i),\ f_n^{min}(i)\right]$$

Algorithm 14 Maximum product contiguous subsequence : compute product

```
function maxprodseq(s[0..n − 1])
    maxprod ← 1
    minprod ← 1
    result ← 1

    for x ∈ s[0..n − 1] do
        prevmaxprod ← maxprod
        prevminprod ← minprod

        maxprod ← max(x, prevmaxprod∗x, prevminprod∗x)
        minprod ← min(x, prevmaxprod∗x, prevminprod∗x)
        result ← max(maxprod, minprod)
    end for

    return result
end function
```

Time complexity is $\mathcal{O}(n)$. Space complexity is $\mathcal{O}(1)$.

```
int maxprodseq(std::vector<int> & s)
{
    if(s.empty()) return 0;

    int maxprod = 1, minprod = 1, result = 1;

    for(int x : s)
    {
        int prev_maxprod = maxprod, prev_minprod =
            minprod;

        maxprod = std::max(std::max(x,
            prev_maxprod * x), prev_minprod * x);
        minprod = std::min(std::min(x,
            prev_maxprod * x), prev_minprod * x);
        result = std::max(maxprod, minprod);
    }
    return result;
}
```

Algorithm 15 Maximum product contiguous subsequence : compute product : modified

```
function maxprodseq(s[0..n − 1])
    maxprod ← 1
    minprod ← 1
    result ← 1

    for x ∈ s[0..n − 1] do
        if x < 0 then        ▷ Multiply with -ve : max becomes min and min becomes max
            swap(maxprod, minprod)
        end if

        maxprod ← max(x, maxprod ∗ x)
        minprod ← min(x, minprod ∗ x)
        result ← max(maxprod, minprod)
    end for

    return result
end function
```

```
int maxprodseq(std::vector<int> & s)
{
    if(s.empty()) return 0;

    int maxprod = 1, minprod = 1, result = 1;

    for(int x : s)
    {
        if(x < 0) std::swap(maxprod, minprod);

        maxprod = std::max(x, maxprod * x);
        minprod = std::min(x, minprod * x);
        result = std::max(maxprod, minprod);
    }
    return result;
}
```

Sequence	Max Product Subsequence	Max Product
2, 4, 5	2, 4, 5	40
-2, -4, -5	-4, -5	20
2, -4, -5	2, -4, -5	40
-1, 0, -3	0	0
0, -4, 0, -2	0	0
-1, 2, -3	-1, 2, -3	6
-3, -5, 0, -6, -5	-6, -5	30
-8	-8	-8
-2, 5, 2, -3	-2, 5, 2, -3	60
-6, -3, 3, -40	-3, 3, -40	360

■

Chapter 9

Stock Trading

§ Problem 27. *There is a sequence p of prices of a given stock over n consecutive days. Determine the maximum profit with the constraint of at most one transaction.* ◊

§§ Solution. Let $f_n(i)$ be the maximum profit for selling the stock on day i, using an optimal policy of a n-stage process.

Let p_i be the price of the stock on day i. In order to maximize the profit, one has to buy at the minimum possible price and sell at the maximum possible price. Of course, a stock has to be bought before it can be sold.

Hence the required optimal procedure is

$$\therefore f_n(i > 1) = \text{Max}\left[f_{n-1}(i-1),\ p_i - \underset{j<i}{\text{Min}}\, p_j\right]$$
$$f_n(i \leq 1) = 0$$

Algorithm 16 Stock Trading : Maximum Profit : One Transaction

```
function max-profit(p[0..n − 1])
    maxprofit ← 0
    buyprice ← ∞

    for price ∈ p[0..n − 1] do
        buyprice ← min(buyprice, price)
        maxprofit ← max(maxprofit, price − buyprice)
```

end for

return $maxprofit$

end function

Time complexity is $\mathcal{O}(n)$. Space complexity is $\mathcal{O}(1)$.

```cpp
int max_profit(std::vector<int> & prices)
{
    // selling price >= buying price to make a profit
    int maxprofit = 0, buyprice = std::numeric_limits<int>::max();

    for(int price : prices)
    {
        buyprice = std::min(buyprice, price);
        // profit => sellingprice - buyprice
        maxprofit = std::max(maxprofit, price - buyprice);
    }
    return maxprofit;
}
```

Assuming that the stock is bought on day k and sold on day i, the profit is

$$p_i - p_k = (p_i - p_{i-1}) + (p_{i-1} - p_{i-2}) + \cdots + (p_{k+1} - p_k)$$

$$\therefore \operatorname*{Max}_{i>k}(p_i - p_k) = \text{Max} \sum_{j=i}^{j=k+1} (p_j - p_{j-1}))$$

$$= \text{Max} \sum_{j=k+1}^{j=i} (p_j - p_{j-1}))$$

So, maximizing the profit is equivalent to the maximum sum contiguous subsequence § Problem 18.

Hence the required optimal procedure is

$$f_n(i) = \text{Max}[f_{n-1}(i-1) + (p_i - p_{i-1})]$$

Algorithm 17 Maximize Profit : Maximum sum contiguous subsequence

function maxprofit($p[0..n-1]$)
  $currentprofit \leftarrow 0$
  $maxprofit \leftarrow 0$
  for $i \in [1, n)$ **do**
    $currentprofit \leftarrow$ **max**$\{currentprofit + (p_i - p_{i-1}),\ 0\}$
    $maxprofit \leftarrow$ **max**$(maxprofit,\ currentprofit)$
  end for
  return $maxprofit$
end function

Time complexity is $\mathcal{O}(n)$. Space complexity is $\mathcal{O}(1)$.

```cpp
int max_profit(std::vector<int> & prices)
{
    int currentprofit = 0, maxprofit = 0;

    int n = prices.size();

    for(int i = 1; i < n; i++)
    {
        currentprofit = std::max(currentprofit +
            prices[i] - prices[i-1], 0);
        maxprofit = std::max(maxprofit,
            currentprofit);
    }
    return maxprofit;
}
```

In order to identify the buying day and the selling day corresponding to the maximum profit, we need to construct the optimal solution from the computed information:

Algorithm 18 Maximize Profit : Buy and Sell Days

function max-profit($p[0..n-1]$)
  $currentprofit \leftarrow 0$
  $maxprofit \leftarrow 0$

  $curbuyday \leftarrow 0$
  $buyday \leftarrow 0$
  $sellday \leftarrow 0$

  for $i \in [0, n)$ **do**
    $currentprofit \leftarrow currentprofit + p[i] - p[i-1]$ ▷ buy at $p[i-1]$, sell at $p[i]$
    if $currentprofit < 0$ **then**
      $currentprofit \leftarrow 0$
      $curbuyday \leftarrow i$ ▷ Move to the next buy day i
    else if $currentprofit > maxprofit$ **then**
      $maxprofit \leftarrow currentprofit$
      $buyday \leftarrow curbuyday$
      $sellday \leftarrow i$
    end if
  end for

  return $buyday$, $sellday$
end function

Time complexity is $\mathcal{O}(n)$. Space complexity is $\mathcal{O}(1)$.

```cpp
std::pair<int, int> max_profit(std::vector<int> &
    prices)
```

```
{
    int currentprofit = 0, maxprofit = 0;
    int curbuyday = 0;
    int buyday = 0, sellday = 0;

    int n = prices.size();

    for(int i = 1; i < n; i++)
    {
        currentprofit = currentprofit + prices[i] - prices[i-1];

        if(currentprofit < 0)
        {
            currentprofit = 0;
            curbuyday = i;
        }
        else
        if(currentprofit > maxprofit)
        {
            maxprofit = currentprofit;
            buyday = curbuyday;
            sellday = i;
        }
    }
    if(maxprofit != 0) return {buyday, sellday};
    else return {-1, -1};
}
```

Prices	<Buy Day Index, Sell Day Index>	<Buy Price, Sell Price>	Max Profit
9,1,7,3,7,5	<1, 2>	<1, 7>	6
9,6,5,3,1	<-1, -1>		
1,3,7,9	<0, 3>	<1, 9>	8

Or

```
// returns <buy price, sell price>
std::pair<int, int> max_profit(std::vector<int> & prices)
{
    int maxprofit = 0, buyprice = std::numeric_limits<int>::max();

    for(int price : prices)
    {
        buyprice = std::min(buyprice, price);
        maxprofit = std::max(maxprofit, price - buyprice);
    }
    if(maxprofit != 0) return {buyprice, buyprice + maxprofit};
    else return {-1, -1};
}
```

■

§ Problem 28. *Determine the maximum profit if at most 2 transactions are allowed in § Problem 27.* ◊

§§ Solution. The logic for the first buy and sell remains the same. For the second transaction, the profit of the first transaction has to be integrated with the second buy to propagate it to the total profit with the second sell.

Algorithm 19 Stock Trading : Maximum Profit : Two Transactions

---

function max-profit($p[0..n-1]$)
  $firstbuyprice \leftarrow \infty$
  $firstmaxprofit \leftarrow 0$
  $secondbuyprice \leftarrow \infty$
  $finalmaxprofit \leftarrow 0$

  for $price \in p[0..n-1]$ **do**
    $firstbuyprice \leftarrow$ **min**$(firstbuyprice, price)$
    $firstmaxprofit \leftarrow$ **max**$(firstmaxprofit, price - firstbuyprice)$
    $secondbuyprice \leftarrow$ **min**$(secondbuyprice, price - firstmaxprofit)$
    $finalmaxprofit \leftarrow$ **max**$(finalmaxprofit, price - secondbuyprice)$
  end for

  return $finalmaxprofit$
end function

Time complexity is $\mathcal{O}(n)$. Space complexity is $\mathcal{O}(1)$.

```cpp
int max_profit(std::vector<int> & prices)
{
    int firstbuyprice = std::numeric_limits<int>::
        max();
    int firstmaxprofit = 0, finalmaxprofit = 0;
    int secondbuyprice = std::numeric_limits<int
        >::max();

    for(int price : prices)
    {
        firstbuyprice = std::min(firstbuyprice,
            price);
        firstmaxprofit = std::max(firstmaxprofit,
            price - firstbuyprice);

        secondbuyprice = std::min(secondbuyprice,
            price - firstmaxprofit);
        finalmaxprofit = std::max(finalmaxprofit,
            price - secondbuyprice);
    }
```

```
    return finalmaxprofit;
}
```

Simplified presentation leads to a case of at most $m < prices.size()$ transactions :

```
int max_profit(std::vector<int> & prices, int m = 2)
{
    std::vector<int> buyprice(m+1, std::numeric_limits<int>::max());
    std::vector<int> maxprofit(m+1, 0);

    for(int price : prices)
    {
        for(int i = 1; i <= m; i++) // m is number of transactions
        {
            buyprice[i] = std::min(buyprice[i], price - maxprofit[i-1]);
            maxprofit[i] = std::max(maxprofit[i], price - buyprice[i]);
        }
    }
    return maxprofit[m];
}
```

Algorithm 20 Stock Trading : Maximum Profit : $m(< n)$ Transactions

```
function max-profit(p[0..n − 1], m)
    buyprice[0..m] ← ∞
    maxprofit[0..m] ← 0

    for price ∈ p[0..n − 1] do
        for i ∈ [1, m] do
            buyprice[i] ← min(buyprice[i], price−maxprofit[i−1])
            maxprofit[i] ← max(maxprofit[i], price − buyprice[i])
        end for
    end for

    return maxprofit[m]
end function
```

Time complexity is $\mathcal{O}(mn)$. Space complexity is $\mathcal{O}(m)$.

If $m > n$ then it can be simplified further (same is the case with unlimited transactions):

Algorithm 21 Stock Trading : Maximum Profit : $m(> n)$ or Unlimited Transactions

```
function max-profit(p[0..n − 1])
    buyprice ← ∞
    maxprofit ← 0

    for price ∈ p[0..n − 1] do
        buyprice ← min(buyprice, price − maxprofit)
        maxprofit ← max(maxprofit, price − buyprice)
    end for

    return maxprofit
end function
```

Time complexity is $\mathcal{O}(n)$. Space complexity is $\mathcal{O}(1)$.

```cpp
int max_profit(std::vector<int> & prices)
{
    int maxprofit = 0, buyprice = std::
        numeric_limits<int>::max();

    for(int price : prices)
    {
        buyprice = std::min(buyprice, price -
            maxprofit);
        maxprofit = std::max(maxprofit, price -
            buyprice);
    }
    return maxprofit;
}
```

Or,

Algorithm 22 Stock Trading : Maximum Profit : $m(> n)$ or Unlimited Transactions : Alternative

```
function max-profit(p[0..n − 1])
    maxprofit ← 0

    for i ∈ [1, p.size()) do
        maxprofit ← maxprofit + max(p[i] − p[i − 1], 0)
    end for

    return maxprofit
end function
```

Time complexity is $\mathcal{O}(n)$. Space complexity is $\mathcal{O}(1)$.

```cpp
int max_profit(std::vector<int> & prices)
{
    int maxprofit = 0;
```

```
    int n = prices.size();

    for(int i = 1; i < n; i++)
    {
        maxprofit += std::max(prices[i] - prices[i
            -1], 0);
    }
    return maxprofit;
}
```

Prices	No of Transactions	<Buy Price, Sell Price>	Max Profit
4,4,6,0,0,3,1,9	2	<0, 3> <1, 9>	11
9,6,5,3,1	2		0
1,3,7,9	2	<1, 9>	8
4,2,9,8,0,7	2	<2, 9> <0, 7>	14
4,2,9,8,0,7,6,9	3	<2, 9> <0, 7> <6, 9>	17

Alternatively :

```
int max_profit(std::vector<int> & prices, int m =
    2)
{
    std::vector<int> curprofit(m+1, 0);
    std::vector<int> maxprofit(m+1, 0);

    int n = prices.size();

    for(int i = 0; i < n-1; i++)
    {
        int dailygain = prices[i+1] - prices[i];

        for(int j = m; j >= 1; j--)
        {
            curprofit[j] = std::max(curprofit[j] +
                dailygain, maxprofit[j-1] + std::
                max(dailygain, 0));
            maxprofit[j] = std::max(maxprofit[j],
                curprofit[j]);
        }
    }

    return maxprofit[m];
}
```

Similarly in case of unlimited transactions with a fee per transaction:

```
int max_profit(std::vector<int> & prices, int fee)
{
    int maxprofit = 0, buyprice = std::
        numeric_limits<int>::max();

    for(int price : prices)
    {
        buyprice = std::min(buyprice, price -
            maxprofit + fee);
```

```
        maxprofit = std::max(maxprofit, price -
            buyprice);
    }
    return maxprofit;
}
```

Prices	Fee	<Buy Price, Sell Price>	Max Profit
1,3,2,7,4,8	2	<1, 7> <4, 8>	6 [(7-1) - 2 + (8-4) - 2]

With a constraint of no buy next day of a sell, unlimited transactions:

```
int max_profit(std::vector<int> & prices)
{
    int prev_maxprofit = 0, prev_buyprice = std::
        numeric_limits<int>::max();
    int maxprofit = 0, buyprice = std::
        numeric_limits<int>::max();

    for(int price : prices)
    {
        prev_buyprice = buyprice;
        buyprice = std::min(prev_buyprice, price -
            prev_maxprofit);

        prev_maxprofit = maxprofit;
        maxprofit = std::max(prev_maxprofit, price
            - prev_buyprice);
    }
    return maxprofit;
}
```

Prices	<Buy Price, Sell Price>	Max Profit
1,3,5,1,9	<1, 3> <1, 9>	10

■

Chapter 10

Binary Tree Mall Loot

§ Problem 29. *In the Binary Tree mall with root as the only entry, all the shops are located in a binary form with a burglar alarm which comes into action in case of loot from any two directly-linked shops. Determine the maximum amount of loot, possible without raising the alarm.* ◊

§§ Solution. Let $f_n(root)$ be the maximum amount of loot with entry at the root, using an optimal policy and n steps.

There are two choices :

1. root is looted : then it is not possible to loot its left and right shops because these two are directly linked, but next level shops can be looted : left->left, left->right, right->left and right->right.

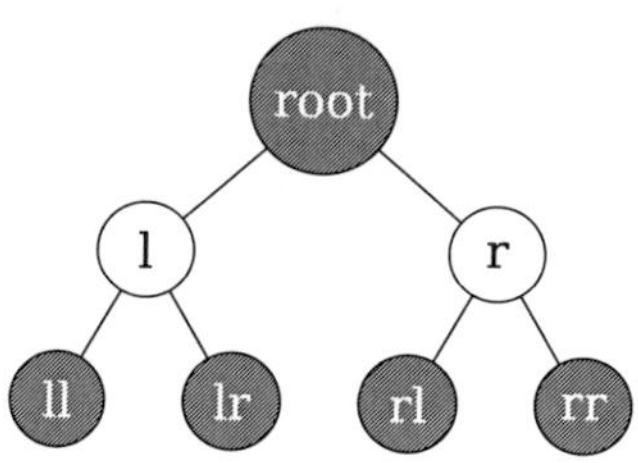

$\therefore f_n^{loot}(root) = amount_{root} + f_n(ll) + f_n(lr) + f_n(rl) + f_n(rr)$

2. root is not looted : its left and right shops can be looted.

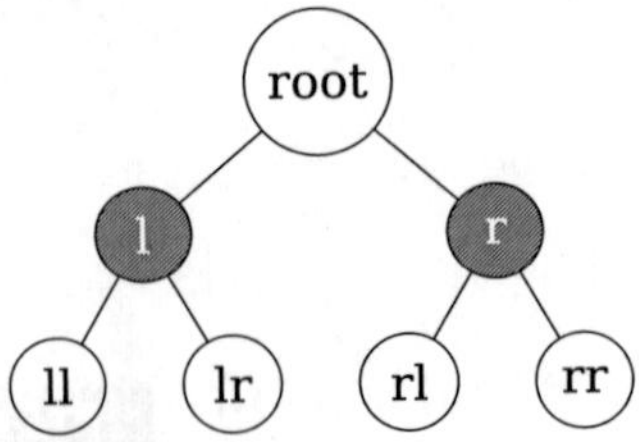

$$\therefore f_n^{no\ loot}(root) = f_n(l) + f_n(r)$$

$$\therefore f_n(root) = \text{Max}\left\{f_n^{loot}(root),\ f_n^{no\ loot}(root)\right\}$$

```cpp
struct Shop
{
    int amount;
    Shop * left;
    Shop * right;

    Shop(int amt) : amount(amt), left(nullptr), right(nullptr) {}
};

std::unordered_map<Shop*, int> cache;

int loot(Shop * shop)
{
    if(not shop) return 0;

    if(cache.find(shop) != cache.end()) return cache[shop];

    int l_plus_r = loot(shop->left) + loot(shop->right);

    int ll_plus_lr = shop->left == nullptr ? 0 : loot(shop->left->left) + loot(shop->left->right);

    int rl_plus_rr = shop->right == nullptr ? 0 : loot(shop->right->left) + loot(shop->right->right);

    cache[shop] = std::max(shop->amount + ll_plus_lr + rl_plus_rr, l_plus_r);

    return cache[shop];
}
```

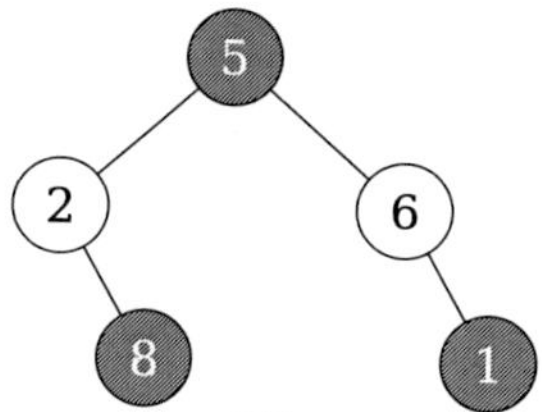

5+8+1=14

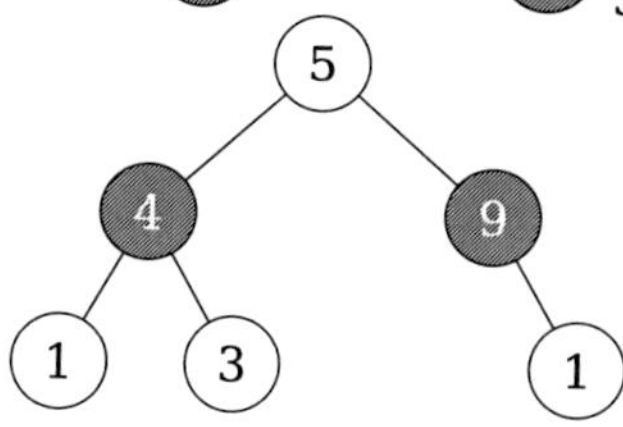

4+9=13

■

Chapter 11

Binary Search Tree Generation

§ Problem 30. *Determine the total number of binary search trees possible with $n \geq 1$ integers as keys.* ◊

§§ Solution. Let $f(i)$ be the total number of binary search trees possible with root holding an integer $i \in [1, n]$ as its key, following an optimal sequence of choices.

Hence total number of unique binary search trees is

$$C_n = \sum_{i=1}^{i=n} f(i) \tag{11.1}$$

When root is i :

1. its left subtree can hold the integers from 1 to $i - 1$, therefore number of left BSTs is C_{i-1}.
2. its right subtree is possible using the integers $i + 1$ to n, hence number of right BSTs is C_{n-i}.

and cartesian product of these two yields $f(i)$:

$$\therefore f(i) = C_{i-1} \times C_{n-i} \tag{11.2}$$

Combining Eq. (11.1) and Eq. (11.2):

$$C_n = \sum_{i=1}^{i=n} C_{i-1} \times C_{n-i}{}^{*}$$

$C_0 = 1$ (Counting the empty BST as 1)
$C_1 = 1$ (Only one BST with only a root)

---

*Also known as Catalan numbers.

Algorithm 23 Count Unique BSTs

```
function countbst(n)
    C[0..n] ← {0}
    C[0] ← 1
    C[1] ← 1

    for i ∈ [2, n] do
        for j ∈ [1, i] do
            C[i] ← C[i] + C[j − 1] · C[i − j]
        end for
    end for

    return C[n]
end function
```

Time complexity is $\mathcal{O}(n^2)$. Space complexity is $\mathcal{O}(n)$.

```cpp
int count_bst(int n)
{
    std::vector<int> c(n+1, 0);
    c[0] = c[1] = 1;

    for(int i = 2; i <= n; i++)
    {
        for(int j = 1; j <= i; j++)
        {
            c[i] += c[j-1] * c[i-j];
        }
    }
    return c[n];
}
```

C[2]	2
C[3]	5
C[4]	14
C[5]	42
C[6]	132

C[2]

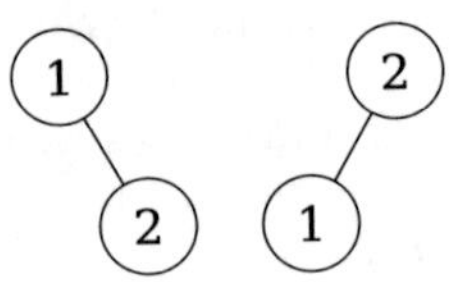

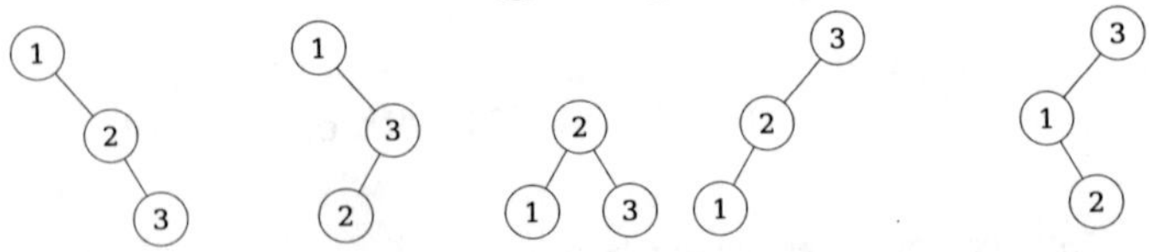

C[3]

For generating the unique BSTs, reconstruction of the optimal solution leads to

Algorithm 24 Generate Unique BSTs

```
function genbst(n)
    C[0..n] ← {list<Node>()}
    C[0].add(null)

    for i ∈ [1, n] do
        for j ∈ [1, i] do
            for l ∈ C[j − 1] do
                for r ∈ C[i − j] do
                    Node tn ← new Node(j)
                    tn.left ← l
                    tn.right ← copyadjust(r, j)  ▷ right subtree is at offset j
                    C[i].add(tn)
                end for
            end for
        end for
    end for

    return C[n]
end function

function copyadjust(root, offset)  ▷ Time Complexity : O(n)
    Node tn ← new Node(root.key + offset)
    tn.left ← copyadjust(root.left, offset)
    tn.right ← copyadjust(root.right, offset)

    return tn
end function
```

Time complexity is $\mathcal{O}(n^5)$. Space complexity is $\mathcal{O}(n^2)$.

```
struct tnode
{
    int key;
    tnode * left;
    tnode * right;

    tnode(int k) : key(k), left(nullptr), right(
        nullptr) {}
};

tnode * copyadjust(tnode * node, int offset)
{
    if(node == nullptr) return nullptr;

    tnode * tn = new tnode(node->key + offset);
```

```
    tn->left = copyadjust(node->left, offset);
    tn->right = copyadjust(node->right, offset);
    return tn;
}

std::vector<tnode*> gen_bst(int n)
{
    std::vector<std::vector<tnode*>> c(n+1);

    c[0].push_back(nullptr);

    for(int i = 1; i <= n; i++)
    {
        for(int j = 1; j <= i; j++)
        {
            for(auto l : c[j-1]) // left subtrees
            {
                for(auto r : c[i-j]) // right subtrees
                {
                    tnode * tn = new tnode(j);
                    tn->left = l; // reuse the left subtree
                    // root of the right subtree is at an offset j
                    tn->right = copyadjust(r, j);
                    c[i].push_back(tn);
                }
            }
        }
    }
    return c[n];
}
```

Chapter 12

Quantify Yogic Effect

§ Problem 31. *Ancient Kriya Yoga Mission, a monastry of realized sages, devised a divine yogic system : Drink Air Therapy, represented as a full binary tree, a path to self-cure and immortality.. Leaf nodes represent the techniques associated with the system. Mastery of a given technique leads to a certain gain in longevity, measured in years. Cumulative gain of a given internal node is measured by the product of the maximum gains associated with the leafs in its left and right subtrees respectively. Given a gain-list representing the years in the leaves in an inorder traversal and considering all the possible binary trees, determine the minimum possible sum of all the non-leaf nodes (i.e. minimum aggregate of the cumulative gains) to help quantify the yogic effect of the system.* ◊

§§ Solution. Let $f_n(l, r)$ be the minimum aggregate of the internal nodes for a given gain-list $g[l, r]$, following an optimal sequence of choices of a n-stage process.

$$\therefore f_n(l, r)$$
$$= \underset{k \in [l,r)}{\text{Min}} [f_{n-1}(l, k) + f_{n-1}(k + 1, r) + \text{Max}\, g[l, k] \cdot \text{Max}\, g[k + 1, r]]$$

Algorithm 25 Quantify Yogic Effect : Drink Air Therapy

```
function drinkairtherapy(a[0..n-1])
```

    for $i \in [0, n)$ **do**
        $g[i][i] \leftarrow a[i]$
        $f[i][i] \leftarrow 0$
    end for
    for $l \in [0, n)$ **do**
        for $i \in [0, n-l]$ **do**
            $j \leftarrow i + l$
            for $k \in [i, j)$ **do**
                $g[i][j] \leftarrow \textbf{max}(g[i][k],\ g[k+1][j]$
                $f[i][j] \leftarrow \textbf{min}(f[i][j],\ f[i][k] + f[k+1][j] + g[i][k] \cdot g[k+1][j])$
            end for
        end for
    end for
    return $f[0][n-1]$
end function

Time complexity is $\mathcal{O}(n^3)$. Space complexity is $\mathcal{O}(n^2)$.

```cpp
int drinkairtherapy(std::vector<int> & v)
{
    int n = v.size(); // number of leaves

    // g[l][r] : maximum years in the leaf-nodes between [l, r]
    std::vector<std::vector<int>> g(n, std::vector<int>(n, 0));

    // f[l][r] : minimum sum of years in internal nodes between [l, r]
    std::vector<std::vector<int>> f(n, std::vector<int>(n, std::numeric_limits<int>::max()));

    for(int i = 0; i < n; i++)
    {
        g[i][i] = v[i];
        f[i][i] = 0;
    }

    for(int l = 0; l < n; l++)
    {
        for(int i = 0; i < n - l; i++)
        {
            int j = i + l;

            for(int k = i; k < j; k++)
            {
                // max years in leaf node
                g[i][j] = std::max(g[i][k], g[k+1][j]);

                int left = f[i][k];
                int right = f[k+1][j];

```

```
                f[i][j] = std::min(f[i][j], left +
                    right + g[i][k] * g[k+1][j]);
            }
        }
    }
    return f[0][n-1];
}
```

gain-list : [4, 3, 6]

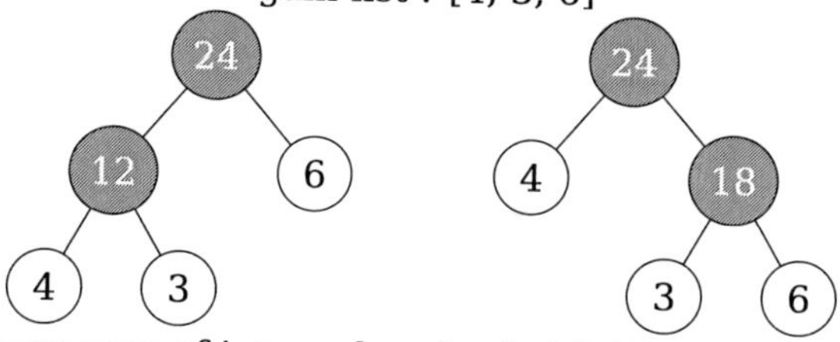

Minimum sum of internal nodes is 36 (12+24 < 24+18). ■

§ **Problem 32.** *Khechari Kriya is a mysterious and divine yogic system to attain immortality. There is an ordered sequence of n sub-kriyas in the system, each bearing a specific number of years. After practicing a given sub-kriya, longevity of the practitioner is increased by the product of the years associated with that sub-kriya and its left and right adjacent sub-kriyas. Moreover that sub-kriya after practice is marked out of the sequence because it is not available for practice any further, making its left and right sub-kriyas as adjacent to each other. Determine the maximum possible number of years gained after practicing all sub-kriyas assuming that a year is associated in the absence of adjacent sub-kriya(s).* ◊

§§ **Solution**. Let $f_n(l, r)$ be the maximum possible number of years gained for a given sequence of sub-kriyas $g[l, r]$, following an optimal sequence of choices of a n-stage process.

Let the sub-kriya i be the last one available for practice. There is no adjacent sub-kriyas per se because all except the ith one were already put to practice. For simplicity, we can add one sub-kriya at the very start (i.e. l-1) and another one at very end (i.e. r+1), associating each with 1 year respectively. Hence the years gained, after practicing the last sub-kriya i, is

$$g[l-1] \cdot g[i] \cdot g[r+1] = 1 \cdot g[i] \cdot 1 = g[i]$$

Note that the sentinel entries : $g[l-1]$ and $g[r+1]$: holding 1 year each respectively, doesn't depend further on any sub-kriya as well as doesn't affect the final outcome, thus making the start of the computation easier and so on.

Hence, the optimal procedure to maximized longevity is given by :
$f_n(l, r) = \underset{i \in [l,r]}{\text{Max}}[f_{n-1}(l, i-1) + f_{n-1}(i+1, r) + g[l-1] \cdot g[i] \cdot g[r+1]]$

Algorithm 26 Quantify Yogic Effect : Khechari Kriya

---

function khechari(g[0..n-1])
    $g[0..n+1] \leftarrow 1, g[0..n-1], 1$ ▷ Sentinels
    $f[0..n+1][0..n+1] \leftarrow \{0\}$

    for $l \in [1, n]$ **do**
        for $i \in [1, n-l+1]$ **do**
            $j \leftarrow i + l - 1$
            for $k \in [i, j]$ **do**
                $f[i][j] \leftarrow$ **max**$(f[i][j],\ f[i][k-1] + f[k+1][j] + g[i-1] \cdot g[k] \cdot g[j+1])$
            end for
        end for
    end for

    return $f[1][n]$
end function

Time complexity is $\mathcal{O}(n^3)$. Space complexity is $\mathcal{O}(n^2)$.

```
int khechari(std::vector<int> & g)
{
    int n = g.size(); // total number of sub-kriyas in khechari kriya

    // Add sentinels worth 1 year each
    g.insert(g.begin(), 1);
    g.push_back(1);

    std::vector<std::vector<int>> f(n+2, std::vector<int>(n+2, 0));

    for(int l = 1; l <= n; l++)
    {
        for(int i = 1; i <= n-l+1; i++)
        {
            int j = i+l-1;

            for(int k = i; k <= j; k++)
            {
                f[i][j] = std::max(f[i][j], f[i][k-1] + f[k+1][j] + g[i-1] * g[k] * g[j+1]);
            }
        }
    }
    return f[1][n];
```

```
}
```

khechari list : [4, 1, 5, 6]

modified list	4, 1, 5, 9	4, 5, 9	4, 9	9	[]
years	$4 \cdot 1 \cdot 5$	$4 \cdot 5 \cdot 9$	$1 \cdot 4 \cdot 9$	$1 \cdot 9 \cdot 1$	$= 245$

f-matrix

$$
\begin{matrix}
0 & 0 & 0 & 0 & 0 & 0 \\
0 & 4 & 40 & 236 & \mathbf{245} & 0 \\
0 & 0 & 20 & 200 & 236 & 0 \\
0 & 0 & 0 & 45 & 54 & 0 \\
0 & 0 & 0 & 0 & 45 & 0 \\
0 & 0 & 0 & 0 & 0 & 0
\end{matrix}
$$

khechari list : [1, 2, 3, 4, 5]

modified list	1, 2, 3, 4, 5	1, 2, 3, 5	1, 2, 5	1, 5	5	[]
years	$3 \cdot 4 \cdot 5$	$2 \cdot 3 \cdot 5$	$1 \cdot 2 \cdot 5$	$1 \cdot 1 \cdot 5$	$1 \cdot 5 \cdot 1$	$= 110$

f-matrix

$$
\begin{matrix}
0 & 0 & 0 & 0 & 0 & 0 & 0 \\
0 & 2 & 9 & 36 & 105 & \mathbf{110} & 0 \\
0 & 0 & 6 & 32 & 100 & 105 & 0 \\
0 & 0 & 0 & 24 & 90 & 100 & 0 \\
0 & 0 & 0 & 0 & 60 & 75 & 0 \\
0 & 0 & 0 & 0 & 0 & 20 & 0 \\
0 & 0 & 0 & 0 & 0 & 0 & 0
\end{matrix}
$$

■

§ Problem 33. *Mool Kriya is a fundamental yet subtle ancient yogic process to attain divinity by unblocking the breath channels. Each sub-kriya is identified by a unique integral id. Given an ordered sequence of sub-kriyas, potentially repetitive, the number of breath channels unblocked after practicing a contiguous sequence of $\alpha \geq 0$ identical sub-kriyas is α^2. After practice, the particular instance(s) of sub-kriya is(are) removed from the ordered sequence. Determine the maximum possible number of breath channels unblocked by practicing wisely.* ◊

§§ Solution. Let $f(l, r, \alpha)$ be the maximum number of breath channels unblocked by practicing the sub-kriya-list $[l, r]$ such that there is a contiguous sequence of $\alpha \in [0,\ l]$ identical sub-kriyas, to the adjacent left of the sub-kriya l, with ids being the same as that of the sub-kriya l.

There are two choices with the sub-kriya l :

1. practicing it now leads to the maximal possible number of breath channels as
$$(\alpha+1)^2 + f(l+1,\ r,\ 0)$$
2. practicing it later with a identical sub-kriya $k \in (l, r]$ leads to
$$f(l+1,\ k-1,\ 0) + f(k,\ r,\ \alpha+1)$$

$$\therefore f(l,\ r,\ \alpha) = \underset{\alpha\in[0,\ l]}{\text{Max}} \begin{cases} (\alpha+1)^2 + f(l+1,\ r,\ 0) & \\ f(l+1,\ k-1,\ 0) + f(k,\ r,\ \alpha+1) & k \in (l, r] \text{ and } l \equiv k \end{cases}$$

Sentinels :

$$f(l,\ l-1,\ \alpha) = 0 \quad \text{(no sub-kriya : no unlocking)}$$

$$f(l,\ l,\ \alpha) = (\alpha+1)^2 \quad \text{(one sub-kriya left)}$$

Algorithm 27 Quantify Yogic Effect : Mool Kriya

function mool($s[0..n-1]$)
  $f[0..n-1][0..n-1][0..n-1] \leftarrow \{0\}$

  for $l \in [0, n)$ **do**
    for $\alpha \in [0, l]$ **do**
      $f[l][l][\alpha] \leftarrow (\alpha+1)^2$
    end for
  end for

  for $i \in [1,\ n)$ **do**
    for $r \in [i,\ n)$ **do**
      $l \leftarrow r - i$
      for $\alpha \in [0,\ l]$ **do**
        $maxbreaths \leftarrow (\alpha+1)^2 + f[l+1][r][0]$
        for $k \in [l+1,\ r]$ **do**
          if $s[k] == s[l]$ **then**
            $maxbreaths \leftarrow$ **max**$(maxbreaths, f[l+1][k-1][0] + f[k][r][\alpha+1])$
          end if
        end for

        $f[l][r][\alpha] \leftarrow maxbreaths$
      end for
    end for
  end for

  return $f[0][n-1][0]$
end function

Time complexity is $\mathcal{O}(n^4)$. Space complexity is $\mathcal{O}(n^3)$.

```
int mool(std::vector<int> & s)
{
    int n = s.size(); // total number of sub-kriyas in Mool Kriya

    int f[n][n][n] = {0};

    for(int l = 0; l < n; l++)
    {
        for(int alpha = 0; alpha <= l; alpha++)
        {
```

```
                f[l][l][alpha] = (alpha + 1) * (alpha + 1);
            }
        }

        for(int i = 1; i < n; i++)
        {
            for(int r = i; r < n; r++)
            {
                int l = r - i;

                for(int alpha = 0; alpha <= l; alpha++)
                {
                    int maxbreaths = (alpha + 1) * (alpha + 1) + f[l + 1][r][0];

                    for(int k = l + 1; k <= r; k++)
                    {
                        if(s[k] == s[l])
                        {
                            maxbreaths = std::max(maxbreaths, f[l+1][k-1][0] + f[k][r][alpha+1]);
                        }
                    }

                    f[l][r][alpha] = maxbreaths;
                }
            }
        }

        return (n == 0 ? 0 : f[0][n-1][0]);
}
```

Mool Kriya Sequence : $\{1, 5, 4, 4, 4, 4, 5, 6, 5, 3, 2, 2, 2, 3, 2, 1\}$

Modified Sequence	Unlocked Breath Count
1, 5, 5, 6, 5, 3, 2, 2, 2, 3, 2, 1	4^2
1, 5, 5, 5, 3, 2, 2, 2, 3, 2, 1	1^2
1, 3, 2, 2, 2, 3, 2, 1	3^2
1, 3, 2, 2, 2, 2, 1	1^2
1, 3, 1	4^2
1, 1	1^2
[]	2^2

$\sum$ Unlocked Breath Count = **48** ■

§ **Problem 34.** *Tandav Kriya is a path to attain the state of Lord Shiva. The practitioner passes through intermediate states of attaining to respective gods during the course of Sadhana. Given a contiguous sequence of years of completion of the participating sub-kriyas respectively, attainment* *of a given state β is possible by practicing all sub-kriyas in a specific way : only a contiguous subsequence of β sub-kriyas needs to be practiced together at a time and so on. After practice, β sub-kriyas are replaced by a sub-kriya of equivalent number of years and the Sadhak continues to practice the transformed sequence subsequently. Determine the minimum possible number of years to attain a given godliness.* ◇

§§ Solution. Let $f_n(l,\ r)$ be the minimum possible number of years to attain the state of god β after practicing a contiguous sequence of years of completion of the participating sub-kriyas $y[l,\ r]$, following an optimal policy with n-steps.

Note that after the practice, β is reduced to 1, i.e. $\beta - 1$ is vanished corresponding to $r - l$, i.e. length of the subsequence is now $(r-l)\ mod\ (\beta-1)+1$, which is less than β and no more vanishing is possible further. Hence the reduction of the length of $[l,\ r]$ to 1 is possible when $(r - l)\ mod\ (\beta - 1) == 0$. Note that number of reductions possible is $p = \dfrac{r-l}{\beta-1}$.

$$\therefore f_n(l,\ r) = \underset{\substack{m\in[l,\ r) \\ m=l+p(\beta-1) \\ p\in\left[0,\ \frac{r-l}{\beta-1}\right]}}{\text{Min}} \left\{ f_{n-1}(l,\ m) + f_{n-1}(m+1,\ r) + \sum_{\substack{i\in[l,\ r] \\ (r-l)\ mod\ (\beta-1)==0}} y_i \right\}$$

$$f_n(l,\ l) = 0$$

Algorithm 28 Quantify Yogic Effect : Tandav Kriya

```
function tandav(y[0..n − 1], β)
    if (n − 1) mod (β − 1) ≠ 0 then          ▷ Infeasible Solution
        abort
    end if
    prefixsum[0..n] ← {0}                    ▷
  sum[i, j] ≡ prefixsum[j + 1] − prefix[i]
    for i ∈ [0, n) do
        prefixsum[i + 1] ← prefixsum[i] + y[i]
    end for
    f[0..n − 1][0..n − 1] ← {∞}
    for l ∈ [0, n) do
        f[l][l] ← 0                          ▷ Singletons
    end for

    for i ∈ [2, n] do
        for l ∈ [0, n − i] do
            r ← l + i − 1
            for m ← l, m < r; m ← m + β − 1 do
                f[l][r] ← min(f[l][r], f[l][m] + f[m + 1][r])
```

end for

if $(r-l)$ **mod** $(\beta-1) \equiv 0$ **then**
$f[l][r] \leftarrow f[l][r] + prefixsum[r+1] - prefixsum[l]$
end if
end for
end for

return $f[0][n-1]$
end function

Time complexity is $\mathcal{O}\left(\frac{n^3}{\beta}\right)$. Space complexity is $\mathcal{O}(n^2)$.

```cpp
int tandav(std::vector<int> & y, int beta)
{
    int n = y.size(); // total number of sub-kriyas

    // no feasible solution
    if((n-1) % (beta - 1) != 0) return -1;

    // handy to compute the sum of y[i, j] as prefixsum[j+1] - prefix[i]
    std::vector<int> prefixsum(n+1, 0);

    for(int i = 0; i < n; i++)
    {
        prefixsum[i+1] = prefixsum[i] + y[i];
    }

    // min years to transform y[l,r] to a length of (r-l)%(beta - 1) + 1
    std::vector<std::vector<int>> f(n, std::vector<int>(n, std::numeric_limits<int>::max()));

    for(int l = 0; l < n; l++)
    {
        f[l][l] = 0;
    }

    for(int i = 2; i <= n; i++)
    {
        for(int l = 0; l <= n-i; l++)
        {
            int r = l + i -1;

            for(int m = l; m < r; m += beta-1)
            {
                f[l][r] = std::min(f[l][r], f[l][m] + f[m+1][r]);
            }

            if((r-l) % (beta-1) == 0)
            {
```

```
                f[l][r] += prefixsum[r+1] -
                    prefixsum[l];
            }
        }
    }

    return f[0][n-1];
}
```

Tandav Kriya Sequence : [6, 2, 8, 3]

$\beta = 2$

modified sequence	8, 8, 3	8, 11	19	[]
years	6 + 2	8 + 3	8 + 11	

$\sum$ years = 38

Tandav Kriya Sequence : [6, 2, 8, 3, 7]

$\beta = 3$

modified sequence	6, 13, 7	26	[]
years	2 + 8 + 3	6 + 13 + 7	

$\sum$ years = 39

■

§ Problem 35. *Guru selects a kriya out of n ordered ones in the range $[1, n]$, suitable for her disciple where there is n pranayams associated with the nth kriya and so on. The disciple needs to guess the selected one. Guru hints whether the guessed kriya is higher or lower. Each wrong guess costs the associated pranayams. Guru is happy if guessed right and grants a boon. Determine the pranayams needed to guarantee the boon.* ◊

§§ Solution. Let $f_n(l, r)$ be the minimum pranayams to guarantee the boon for kriyas in the range $[l, r]$, following an optimal sequence of n-steps.

If the Sadhak selects the kriya m as her guess, then m pranayams are needed and now the next guess is either from $[l, m-1]$ or $[m+1, r]$ based on the hint from the Guru. She needs to account for the worst case to guarantee the boon. *.

Note that :

For $[1, 2]$: guessing 1 leads to minimum pranayams even if it is wrong because it is still smaller than guessing 2. So minimum pranayams = 1.

For $[1, 2, 3]$: guessing 2 first helps determine the correct kriya based on hint from Guru. So minimum pranayams = 2.

*Minimax Algorithm

For [1, 2, 3, 4] : optimal strategy is to use $m \in [1,\ 4]$ to iterate over the entire sequence, then divide the left and right sequences based on m, selecting the higher pranayams plus m :

1. $m = 1$: left sequence is empty [] : 0 pranayam, right sequence is [2, 3, 4] : 3 is selected as before : total pranayams $= 1 + 3 = 4$.
2. $m = 2$: left sequence is [1] : 0 pranayam, right sequence is [3, 4] : 3 pranayams : total pranayams $= 2 + 3 = 5$.
3. $m = 3$: left sequence is [1, 2] : 1 pranayam, right sequence is [4] : 0 pranayam : total pranayams $= 3+1 = 4$.
4. $m = 4$: left sequence is [1, 2, 3] : 2 pranayam, right sequence is empty [] : 0 pranayam : total pranayams $= 4 + 2 = 6$.

Hence the minimum number of pranayams needed in the worst case to guarantee the boon being granted = 4.

Therefore the optimal procedure is

$$f_n(l,\ r) = \underset{m \in [l,\ r]}{\mathrm{Min}} [m + \mathrm{Max}\{f_{n-1}(l,\ m-1),\ f_{n-1}(m+1,\ r)\}]$$

$$f_n(l,\ l) = 0 \quad \text{(the only kriya must be correct)}$$

Algorithm 29 Quantify Yogic Effect : Minimax Kriya Selection

```
function minmaxkriya(n)
    f[0..n][0..n] ← {0}

    for i ∈ [1, n] do
        for l ∈ [0, n − i] do
            r ← l + i
            f[l][r] ← ∞
            for m ∈ [l, r) do
                f[l][r] ← min[f[l][r], m + max(f[l][m − 1], f[m + 1][r])]
            end for
        end for
    end for

    return f[0][n]
end function
```

Time complexity is $\mathcal{O}(n^3)$. Space complexity is $\mathcal{O}(n^2)$.

```
int minmaxkriya(int n)
{
    std::vector<std::vector<int>> f(n+1, std::
        vector<int>(n+1, 0));

    for(int i = 1; i <= n; i++)
    {
        for(int l = 0; l <= n - i; l++)
        {
            int r = l + i ;

```

```
            f[l][r] = std::numeric_limits<int>::
                max();

            for(int m = l; m < r; m++)
            {
                f[l][r] = std::min(f[l][r], m +
                    std::max(f[l][m-1], f[m+1][r])
                    );
            }
        }
    }

    return f[0][n];
}
```

n	1	2	3	4	5	6	7	8	9	10	11	12	13	14	15
Pranayams	0	1	2	4	6	8	10	12	14	16	18	21	24	27	30

To re-iterate :

$$f_n(l,\ r) = \underset{m \in [l,\ r]}{\text{Min}} [m + \text{Max}\{f_{n-1}(l,\ m-1),\ f_{n-1}(m+1,\ r)\}]$$

Note that $f_n(l,\ r)$ is a monotonically increasing function in terms of the length of the interval $[l,\ r]$:

$$\therefore f_n(l_1,\ r) \le f_n(l_2,\ r) \quad \forall\, l_1 \le l_2, \text{ and}$$
$$f_n(l,\ r_1) \le f_n(l,\ r_2) \quad \forall\, r_1 \le r_2$$

With increasing m : length of the interval $[l,\ m-1]$ increases whereas length of the interval $[m+1,\ r]$ decreases.

In other words, $f_{n-1}(l,\ m-1)$ in a monotonically increasing function in m and $f_{n-1}(m+1,\ r)$ is a monotonically decreasing function in m.

Suppose $\exists\, m_\beta$:

$$f_{n-1}(l,\ m_\beta - 1) = f_{n-1}(m_\beta + 1,\ r)$$

$$\therefore \forall\, m < m_\beta,\ f_{n-1}(l,\ m-1) < f_{n-1}(l,\ m_\beta - 1) = f_{n-1}(m_\beta + 1,\ r) < f_{n-1}(m+1,\ r)$$

In other words :

$$m_\beta = \text{Max}\{m : f_{n-1}(l,\ m-1) \le f_{n-1}(m+1,\ r)\}, \text{ or}$$
$$m_\beta = \text{Min}\{m : f_{n-1}(l,\ m-1) > f_{n-1}(m+1,\ r)\}.$$

$$\therefore \text{Max}\{f_{n-1}(l,\ m-1),\ f_{n-1}(m+1,\ r)\} = \begin{cases} f_{n-1}(m+1,\ r) & \text{if } m \in [l,\ m_\beta] \\ f_{n-1}(l,\ m-1) & \text{if } m \in (m_\beta,\ r] \end{cases}$$

$$\therefore f_n(l,\ r) = \underset{m \in [l,\ r]}{\text{Min}} [f_L(l,\ r),\ f_R(l,\ r)]$$

where

$$f_L(l,\ r) = \underset{m \in [l,\ m_\beta]}{\text{Min}} \{m + f_{n-1}(m+1,\ r)\}, \text{ and}$$
$$f_R(l,\ r) = \underset{m \in (m_\beta,\ r]}{\text{Min}} \{m + f_{n-1}(l,\ m-1)\}$$
$$= 1 + m_\beta + f_{n-1}(l,\ m_\beta) \ \because \text{minimum value of } m = m_\beta + 1$$

Algorithm 30 Quantify Yogic Effect : Minimax Kriya Selection : Optimized Computation

```
function minmaxkriya(n)
    f[0..n][0..n] ← {0}

    for r ∈ [2, n] do
        m ← r − 1
        flmlist : deque<pair<fl, m> >                    ▷ m ∈ [l, m_β)

        for l ∈ [r − 1, 0) do
            while f[l][m − 1 > f[m + 1][r] do            ▷ Find m_β
                if flmlist is not empty and flmlist.front().second == m then
                    flmlist.pop_front();
                end if
                m ← m − 1
            end while

            fl ← l + f[l + 1][r]

            while flmlist is not empty and fl < flmlist.back().first do
                flmlist.pop_back()
            end while

            flmlist.push_back(fl, l)

            f[l][r] ← min[flmlist.front().first, 1 + m + f[l][m]]
        end for
    end for

    return f[1][n]
end function
```

Time complexity is $\mathcal{O}(n^2)$. Finding m_β is $\mathcal{O}(1)$ for a fixed $[l,\ r]$. Computation of f_L is also $\mathcal{O}(1)$ due to sliding window minimum logic for a fixed $[l,\ r]$.

Space complexity is $\mathcal{O}(n^2)$.

```cpp
int minmaxkriya(int n)
{
    std::vector<std::vector<int>> f(n + 1, std::
        vector<int>(n + 1, 0));

    for(int r = 2; r <= n; r++)
    {
        int m = r - 1;

        // stores <f_L, m>, where l <= m < m_beta
        std::deque<std::pair<int, int>> flmlist;

        // find f_L(l, r) : sliding window minimum
        for(int l = r - 1; l > 0; l--)
        {
            // find m_beta
```

```
            while(f[l][m-1] > f[m+1][r])
            {
                if(not flmlist.empty() and flmlist
                    .front().second == m)
                {
                    flmlist.pop_front();
                }
                --m;
            }

            int fl = l + f[l + 1][r];

            while(not flmlist.empty() and fl <
                flmlist.back().first)
            {
                flmlist.pop_back();
            }

            flmlist.emplace_back(fl, l);

            f[l][r] = std::min(flmlist.front().
                first, 1 + m + f[l][m]);
        }
    }

    return f[1][n];
}
```

■

§ Problem 36. *Trikaldarshi is a yogic state achieved by practicing the n kriyas as the vertices $v_i : i \in [1, n]$ of a convex polygon in a triangulated way where practicing the kriyas of a triangle with vertices $< v_i, v_j, v_k >$ requires $\phi(v_i, v_j, v_k)$ years and v_i represents the number of years required for the corresponding kriya. Determine the minimum possible years required to be a Trikaldarshi.* ◊

§§ Solution. Note that a triangulation of a convex polygon requires drawing all possible non-intersecting (except at a vertex) diagonals between non-adjacent vertices, thus forming $(n - 2)$ triangles for a n-sided convex polygon. It is required to find the minimum possible sum of respective ϕ years of its component triangles, i.e. we need to find an optimal triangulation.

Let $f_m(i, j)$ be the minimum possible years to triangulate a polygon $v_i \dots v_j$ in an optimal way with m steps.

If $j < i + 2$, then there are less than 3 points, hence no triangulation is possible. Otherwise, we enumerate all $v_k : k \in (i, j)$ to form a triangle with vertices $< v_i, v_j, v_k >$ which in turn results into left and right polygons to triangulate and so on.

Hence, the optimal procedure is

$$f_m(i, j) = \begin{cases} 0 & \text{If } j < i + 2 \\ \underset{i<k<j}{\text{Min}} \{f_{m-1}(i, k) + f_{m-1}(k, j) + \phi(v_i, v_j, v_k)\} & \text{otherwise} \end{cases}$$

Algorithm 31 Quantify Yogic Effect : Trikaldarshi

function trikal($v[0..n-1]$)
  $f[0..n-1][0..n-1] \leftarrow \{0\}$

  for $d \in [2,\ n)$ **do**
    for $i \in [0,\ n-d)$ **do**
      $j \leftarrow i + d$
      $f[i][j] \leftarrow \infty$
      for $k \in [i+1,\ j)$ **do**
        $f[i][j] \leftarrow \mathbf{min}[f[i][j],\ f[i][k] + f[k][j] + \phi(v_i, v_j, v_k)]$
      end for
    end for
  end for

  return $f[0][n-1]$
end function

Time complexity is $\mathcal{O}(n^3)$. Space complexity is $\mathcal{O}(n^2)$.

Assuming $\phi(v_i, v_j, v_k) = v[i] * v[j] * v[k]$:

```cpp
int trikal(std::vector<int> & v)
{
    int n = v.size(); // total number of kriya-vertices

    std::vector<std::vector<int>> f(n, std::vector<int>(n, 0));

    for(int d = 2; d < n; d++)
    {
        for(int i = 0; i < n - d; i++)
        {
            int j = i + d;

            f[i][j] = std::numeric_limits<int>::max();

            for(int k = i + 1; k < j; k++)
            {
                f[i][j] = std::min(f[i][j], f[i][k] + f[k][j] + v[i] * v[j] * v[k]);
            }
        }
    }

    return f[0][n-1];
}
```

Kriya Years Seq	Triangulation	Min Years
1, 2, 3	1*2*3	6
1, 2, 3, 4	min(1*2*3 + 1*4*3, 1*2*4 + 2*3*4)	18
1, 2, 3, 4, 5	optimal : 1*2*3 + 1*5*4 + 1*3*4	38

For determining the structure of the optimal solution, i.e. a list of the kriya-triangles participating in triangulation of the polygon can be printed after reconstruction from the optimal solution :

Algorithm 32 Quantify Yogic Effect : Trikaldarshi : Print Kriya-Triangles

```
function printtrikal(f<pair<mincost, mink> >[0..n − 1][0..n − 1], v[0..n − 1], i, j)
    if j ≥ i + 2 then
        print v[i], v[f[i][j].mink], v[j]

        printtrikal(f, v, i, f[i][j].mink)
        printtrikal(f, v, f[i][j].mink, j)
    end if
end function
function trikal(v[0..n − 1])
    f<pair<mincost, mink> >[0..n − 1][0..n − 1] ← {0}    ▷ 2D matrix of pair<mincost , mink>

    for d ∈ [2, n) do
        for i ∈ [0, n − d) do
            j ← i + d
            f[i][j].mincost ← ∞

            for k ∈ [i + 1, j) do
                localmin ← min[f[i][j].mincost, f[i][k] + f[k][j] + φ(v_i, v_j, v_k)]

                if localmin < f[i][j].mincost then
                    f[i][j].mincost ← localmin
                    f[i][j].mink = k
                end if
            end for
        end for
    end for

    printtrikal(f, v, 0, n − 1)

    return f[0][n − 1]
end function
```

Time complexity of *printtrikal* is $\mathcal{O}(n)$ because total number of kriya-triangles is $n-2$.

Hence total time complexity is $\mathcal{O}(n^3)$. Space complexity is $\mathcal{O}(n^2)$.

```
void print_trikal(std::vector<std::vector<std::
    pair<int, int>>> & f, std::vector<int> & v,
    int i, int j)
{
    if(j >= i+2)
```

```
    {
        std::cout << "<" << v[i] << "," <<  v[f[i][j].second] << "," << v[j] << ">";
        print_trikal(f, v, i, f[i][j].second);
        print_trikal(f, v, f[i][j].second, j);
    }
}

int trikal(std::vector<int> & v)
{
    int n = v.size(); // total number of kriya-vertices

    // 2-D matrix of pair<mincost, mink>
    std::vector<std::vector<std::pair<int, int>>> f(n, std::vector<std::pair<int, int>>(n));

    for(int d = 2; d < n; d++)
    {
        for(int i = 0; i < n - d; i++)
        {
            int j = i + d;

            f[i][j].first = std::numeric_limits<int>::max();

            for(int k = i + 1; k < j; k++)
            {
                int local_min = f[i][k].first + f[k][j].first + v[i] * v[j] * v[k];

                if(local_min < f[i][j].first)
                {
                    f[i][j].first = local_min;
                    f[i][j].second = k; // min k
                }
            }
        }
    }
    print_trikal(f, v, 0, n-1);

    return f[0][n-1].first;
}
```

Kriya-Polygon	Kriya-Triangles in Optimal Triangulation	Min Years
1, 2, 3	<1,2,3>	6
1, 2, 3, 4	<1,3,4> <1,2,3>	18
1, 2, 3, 4, 5	<1,4,5> <1,3,4> <1,2,3>	38
6, 2, 9, 8, 4, 12, 3, 5	<6,2,5> <2,3,5> <2,4,3> <2,8,4> <2,9,8> <4,12,3>	466

■

Chapter 13

Path to Heaven

13.1 Stairway

§ Problem 37. *Following the Kriya initiation of his disciple Ram to a specific monastic order, Guru shares the details of a stairway-like mystical yogic path of n-steps to reach the Heavenly abode. Ram is allowed to take at most $\delta \leq n$ steps at a given time. Determine the total number of distinct ways to reach Heaven.* ◊

§§ Solution. Let $f_m(k)$ be the number of distinct ways to reach the step-k, following an optimal policy of a m-stage process.

Note that Ram can reach the step-k in one of the δ ways : a single step from the $(n-1)^{th}$ step or a step of 2 from the $(n-2)^{th}$ step, $\cdots$, or a step of δ from the $(n-\delta)^{th}$ step.

$$\therefore f_m(k) = \begin{cases} \sum\limits_{i \in [1,\, \delta]} f_{m-1}(k-i) & \text{if } k > 1 \\ 1 & \text{if } k \leq 1 \end{cases}$$

Algorithm 33 Staircase to Heaven : Count Distinct Ways

```
function heaven(n, δ)
    if δ > n then
        return 0
```

```
    end if
    f[0..n] ← {0}
    f[0] ← 1
    f[1] ← 1

    for i ∈ [2, n] do
        s ← 0
        for j ∈ [1, δ], j ≤ i do
            s ← s + f[i − j]
        end for
        f[i] ← s
    end for

    return f[n]
end function
```

Time complexity is $\mathcal{O}(n\delta)$. Space complexity is $\mathcal{O}(n)$.

```cpp
int heaven(int n, int delta)
{
    if(delta > n) return 0;

    std::vector<int> f(n + 1, 0);

    f[0] = f[1] = 1;

    for(int i = 2; i <= n; i++)
    {
        int s = 0;

        for(int j = 1; j <= delta & j <= i; j++)
        {
            s += f[i-j];
        }

        f[i] = s;
    }

    return f[n];
}
```

n	δ	ways	no of ways
2	1	[1,1]	1
2	2	[1,1] [2]	2
3	2	[1,1,1] [1,2] [2,1]	3
3	3	[1,1,1] [1,2] [2,1] [3]	4
4	2	[1,1,1,1] [1,2,1] [2,1,1] [1,1,2] [2,2]	5

Suppose that Ram is allowed to take steps only from a given sequence, say $s_i : i \in [a,\ b]$, at a given time, then

$$\therefore f_m(k) = \begin{cases} \sum\limits_{i\in[a,\ b]} f_{m-1}(k - s_i) & \text{if } k > 1 \\ 1 & \text{if } k \leq 1 \end{cases}$$

Algorithm 34 Staircase to Heaven : Count Distinct Ways with step-list

```
function heaven(n, s[0..m − 1])
    f[0..n] ← {0}
    f[0] ← 1
    f[1] ← 1

    for i ∈ [2, n] do
        sum ← 0
        for e ∈ s[0..m − 1] do
            if e ≤ i then
                sum ← sum + f[i − e]
            end if
        end for
        f[i] ← sum
    end for

    return f[n]
end function
```

Time complexity is $\mathcal{O}(nm)$, m is the number of steps in the step-list. Space complexity is $\mathcal{O}(n)$.

```cpp
int heaven(int n, std::vector<int> & s)
{
    std::vector<int> f(n + 1, 0);

    f[0] = f[1] = 1;

    int ls = s.size();

    for(int i = 2; i <= n; i++)
    {
        int sum = 0;

        for(auto e : s)
        {
            if(e <= i)
            {
                sum += f[i-e];
            }
        }

        f[i] = sum;
    }

    return f[n];
}
```

n	step-list	ways	no of ways
2	1, 2	[1,1] [2]	2
4	2, 4	[2,2] [4]	2
6	2, 4, 6	[2,2,2] [2,4] [4,2] [6]	4

■

§ Problem 38. *In § Problem 37, each step* involves a specific number of pranayams, performing which Ram is allowed to take at most δ steps at a given time. Determine the minimum pranayams needed to reach Heaven, assuming that Ram can either start from the step-0 or step-1.* ◊

§§ Solution. Let $f_m(k)$ represent the minimum pranayams needed to reach step-k, following an optimal policy of a m-stage process.

Let p_i be the number of pranayams associated with step-i.

Note that Ram can reach the step-k in one of the δ ways : a single step from the $(n-1)^{th}$ step after performing p_{n-1} pranayams or a step of 2 from the $(n-2)^{th}$ step after performing p_{n-2} pranayams, $\cdots$, or a step of δ from the $(n-\delta)^{th}$ step after performing $p_{n-\delta}$ pranayams.

$$\therefore f_m(k) = \begin{cases} \underset{i\in[1,\ \delta]}{\text{Min}} \{f_{m-1}(k-i) + p_{k-i}\} & \text{if } k > 1 \\ 0 & \text{if } k \leq 1 \end{cases}$$

Algorithm 35 Staircase to Heaven : Optimal Pranayams

```
function heaven(p[0..n − 1], δ)
    f[0..n] ← {0}

    for i ∈ [2, n] do
        localmin ← ∞
        for j ∈ [1, δ], j ≤ i do
            localmin ← min(localmin, f[i − j] + p[i − j])
        end for
        f[i] ← localmin
    end for

    return f[n]
end function
```

Time complexity is $\mathcal{O}(n\delta)$. Space complexity is $\mathcal{O}(n)$.

```
int heaven(std::vector<int> & p, int delta)
{
    int n = p.size();

    std::vector<int> f(n + 1, 0);

    for(int i = 2; i <= n; i++)
    {

        int localmin = std::numeric_limits<int>::
            max();

```

*except the final one

```
        for(int j = 1; j <= delta and j <= i; j++)
        {
            localmin = std::min(localmin, f[i-j] +
                p[i-j]);
        }

        f[i] = localmin;
    }

    return f[n];
}
```

steplist-pranayams	δ	Optimal Steps-path Indices	Optimal Pranayams
2,3,4	2	1->final	3
2,3,4	3	0->final	2
1, 3, 1, 2, 1, 4, 1	2	0->2->4->6->final	4
1, 3, 1, 2, 1, 4, 1	3	0->2->4->final	3
1, 3, 1, 2, 1, 4, 1	7	0->final	2
1, 1, 1, 2, 1, 4, 1	3	1->4->final	2

■

13.2 Kriya Grid

§ **Problem 39.** *Guru shares the details of a secretive 2D $m \times n$ Kriya grid-path to Heaven with his disciple Ram. The very first and the last Kriya to practice are located at the top-left and bottom-right corners respectively. Starting from the first Kriya, Ram can select a Kriya only from the immediate right or down position in the grid at a given time. Determine the total number of distinct Kriya-paths to reach Heaven.* ◊

§§ **Solution**. Let $f_p(i,\ j)$ be the number of distinct kriya-paths to reach the grid-cell$(i,\ j)$, following an optimal sequence of p steps.

Note that, there is no grid-cell above the first row, hence contribution to $f_p(0,\ j)$ is only from the left cells:
$\therefore f_p(0,\ j) = f_{p-1}(0,\ j-1) = f_{p-2}(0,\ j-2) = \cdots = f_{p-j}(0,\ 0) = 1$
Similarly, there is no grid-cell to the left of the first column, hence contribution to $f_p(i,\ 0)$ is possible only from the cells above it:
$\therefore f_p(i,\ 0) = f_{p-1}(i-1,\ 0) = f_{p-2}(i-2,\ 0) = \cdots = f_{p-i}(0,\ 0) = 1$

$$\therefore f_p(i,\ j) = \begin{cases} 1 & \text{if } i = 0 \\ 1 & \text{if } j = 0 \\ f_{p-1}(i,\ j-1) + f_{p-1}(i-1,\ j) & \text{otherwise} \end{cases}$$

Algorithm 36 Distinct Kriya Grid Paths to Heaven

```
function kriyapaths(m, n)
    f[0..m − 1][0..n − 1] ← {1}

    for i ∈ [1, m] do
        for j ∈ [1, n] do
            f[i][j] ← f[i][j − 1] + f[i − 1][j]
        end for
    end for

    return f[m − 1][n − 1]
end function
```

Time complexity is $\mathcal{O}(mn)$. Space complexity is $\mathcal{O}(mn)$.

```
int kriyapaths(int m, int n)
{
    // m x n matrix : m rows, n columns
    std::vector<std::vector<int>> f(m, std::vector
        <int>(n, 1));

    for(int i = 1; i < m; i++)
    {
        for(int j = 1; j < n; j++)
        {
            f[i][j] = f[i][j-1] + f[i-1][j];
        }
    }

    return f[m-1][n-1];
}
```

Space optimization is possible by updating line-by-line because i depends only on $i - 1$.

Algorithm 37 Distinct Kriya Grid Paths to Heaven : Space Optimization

```
function kriyapaths(m, n)
    f[0..n − 1] ← {1}

    for i ∈ [1, m] do
        for j ∈ [1, n] do
            f[j] ← f[j] + f[j − 1]
        end for
    end for

    return f[m − 1]
end function
```

Time complexity is $\mathcal{O}(mn)$. Space complexity is $\mathcal{O}(n)$.

```
int kriyapaths(int m, int n)
{
```

```
    std::vector<int> f(n, 1);

    for(int i = 1; i < m; i++)
    {
        for(int j = 1; j < n; j++)
        {
            f[j] += f[j-1];
        }
    }

    return f[n-1];
}
```

d : down, r : right †

rows (m)	columns (n)	paths	path-count
3	2	ddr, rdd, drd	3
4	2	dddr, rddd, ddrd, drdd	4

■

§ Problem 40. *In § Problem 39, there are some special Kriyas in the grid, which are prohibited from practicing. Presence and absence of these Kriyas are represented as 1 and 0 respectively. Determine the total number of distinct Kriya-paths to reach Heaven.* ◊

§§ Solution. Let $g_p(i,\ j)$ be the number of distinct kriya-paths to reach the grid-cell$(i,\ j)$, following an optimal sequence of p steps.

Let $f_p(i,\ j)$ be the number of distinct kriya-paths to reach the grid-cell$(i,\ j)$, following an optimal sequence of p steps, assuming no prohibition.

$$\therefore g_p(i,\ j) = \begin{cases} 0 & \text{if grid-cell}(i,\ j) = 1 \\ f_p(i,\ j) & \text{otherwise} \end{cases}$$

where

$$f_p(i,\ j) = \begin{cases} 1 & \text{if } i = 0 \text{ and } j = 0 \\ f_{p-1}(0,\ j-1) & \text{if } i = 0 \\ f_{p-1}(i-1,\ 0) & \text{if } j = 0 \\ f_{p-1}(i,\ j-1) + f_{p-1}(i-1,\ j) & \text{otherwise} \end{cases}$$

Algorithm 38 Distinct Kriya Grid Paths to Heaven : With Prohibition

```
function kriyapaths(kriyagrid[0..m − 1][0..n − 1])
    if kriyagrid[0][0] ≡ 1 or kriyagrid[m − 1][n − 1] ≡ 1 then
        abort                                            ▷ No path
    end if
```

†Any kriya-path consists of m-1 down and n-1 right ones.

```
    f[0..m − 1][0..n − 1] ← {0}

    for i ∈ [0, m) do
        for j ∈ [0, n) do
            if kriyagrid[i][j] ≡ 1 then                ▷ Prohibited Kriya
                f[i][j] ← 0                                    ▷ No Path
            else if i ≡ 0 and j ≡ 0 then                  ▷ First Kriya
                f[i][j] ← 1                          ▷ kriyagrid[0][0] ≡ 0
            else if i ≡ 0 then                              ▷ First Row
                f[i][j] ← f[i][j − 1] ▷ Contribution from Kriyas in Left Cells
            else if j ≡ 0 then                           ▷ First Column
                f[i][j] ← f[i − 1][j] ▷ Contribution from Kriyas located Above
            else     ▷ Contribution from Kriyas located right and above
                f[i][j] ← f[i][j − 1] + f[i − 1][j]
            end if
        end for
    end for

    return f[m − 1][n − 1]
end function
```

Time complexity is $\mathcal{O}(mn)$. Space complexity is $\mathcal{O}(mn)$.

```
int kriyapaths(std::vector<std::vector<int>> & kriyagrid)
{
    // m x n matrix : m rows, n columns
    int m = kriyagrid.size();
    int n = kriyagrid[0].size();

    if(kriyagrid[0][0] == 1 or kriyagrid[m-1][n-1] == 1)
    {
        return 0;
    }

    std::vector<std::vector<int>> f(m, std::vector<int>(n, 0));

    for(int i = 0; i < m; i++)
    {
        for(int j = 0; j < n; j++)
        {
            if(kriyagrid[i][j] == 1) // prohibited kriya
            {
                f[i][j] = 0; // no contribution to path
            }
            else if(i == 0 and j == 0) // first
```

```
                        cell
                {
                    f[i][j] = 1; // kriyagrid[0][0] ==
                        0 => f[0][0] = 1
                }
                else if(i == 0) // first row
                {
                    f[i][j] = f[i][j-1]; //
                        contribution from left cells
                }
                else if(j == 0) // first column
                {
                    f[i][j] = f[i-1][j]; //
                        contribution from cells above
                        it
                }
                else // contribution from the cells
                    located left and above
                {
                    f[i][j] = f[i][j-1] + f[i-1][j];
                }
            }
        }

        return f[m-1][n-1];
}
```

Note that i depends on $i-1$, hence space can be optimized by row-wise updates :

Algorithm 39 Distinct Kriya Grid Paths to Heaven : With Prohibition : Space Optimization

```
function kriyapaths(kriyagrid[0..m − 1][0..n − 1])
    if kriyagrid[0][0] ≡ 1 or kriyagrid[m − 1][n − 1] ≡ 1 then
        abort                                              ▷ No path
    end if

    f[0..n − 1] ← {0}

    for i ∈ [0, m) do
        for j ∈ [0, n) do
            if kriyagrid[i][j] ≡ 1 then              ▷ Prohibited Kriya
                f[j] ← 0                                   ▷ No Path
            else if i ≡ 0 and j ≡ 0 then                ▷ First Kriya
                f[j] ← 1                        ▷ kriyagrid[0][0] ≡ 0
            else if i ≡ 0 then                           ▷ First Row
                f[j] ← f[j − 1]   ▷ Contribution from Kriyas in Left Cells
            else                     ▷ Accumulate Kriyas line-by-line
```

```
                $f[j] \leftarrow f[j] + f[j-1]$
            end if
        end for
    end for

    return $f[n-1]$
end function
```

Time complexity is $\mathcal{O}(mn)$. Space complexity is $\mathcal{O}(n)$.

```cpp
int kriyapaths(std::vector<std::vector<int>> &
    kriyagrid)
{
    // m x n matrix : m rows, n columns
    int m = kriyagrid.size();
    int n = kriyagrid[0].size();

    if(kriyagrid[0][0] == 1 or kriyagrid[m-1][n-1]
        == 1)
    {
        return 0;
    }

    std::vector<int> f(n, 0);

    for(int i = 0; i < m; i++)
    {
        for(int j = 0; j < n; j++)
        {
            if(kriyagrid[i][j] == 1)
            {
                f[j] = 0;
            }
            else if(i == 0 and j == 0)
            {
                f[j] = 1;
            }
            else if(i == 0)
            {
                f[j] = f[j-1];
            }
            else
            {
                f[j] += f[j-1];
            }
        }
    }

    return f[n-1];
}
```

Kriya Grid itself can be used to record the paths to bring space complexity to $\mathcal{O}(1)$:

Algorithm 40 Distinct Kriya Grid Paths to Heaven : With Prohibition : Space Optimization : Alternative

```
function kriyapaths(kriyagrid[0..m − 1][0..n − 1])
    if kriyagrid[0][0] ≡ 1 or kriyagrid[m − 1][n − 1] ≡ 1 then
        abort                                              ▷ No path
    end if

    for i ∈ [0, m) do
        for j ∈ [0, n) do
            if kriyagrid[i][j] ≡ 1 then                    ▷ Prohibited Kriya
                kriyagrid[i][j] ← 0                        ▷ No Path
            else if i ≡ 0 and j ≡ 0 then                   ▷ First Kriya
                kriyagrid[i][j] ← 1                        ▷ kriyagrid[0][0] ≡ 0
            else if i ≡ 0 then                             ▷ First Row
                kriyagrid[i][j] ← kriyagrid[i][j − 1]      ▷ Contribution from Kriyas in Left Cells
            else if j ≡ 0 then                             ▷ First Column
                kriyagrid[i][j] ← kriyagrid[i − 1][j]      ▷ Contribution from Kriyas located Above
            else            ▷ Contribution from Kriyas located left and above
                kriyagrid[i][j] ← kriyagrid[i][j−1]+kriyagrid[i−1][j]
            end if
        end for
    end for

    return f[m − 1][n − 1]
end function
```

Time complexity is $\mathcal{O}(mn)$. Space complexity is $\mathcal{O}(1)$.

```cpp
int kriyapaths(std::vector<std::vector<int>> & kriyagrid)
{
    // m x n matrix : m rows, n columns
    int m = kriyagrid.size();
    int n = kriyagrid[0].size();

    if(kriyagrid[0][0] == 1 or kriyagrid[m-1][n-1] == 1)
    {
        return 0;
    }

    for(int i = 0; i < m; i++)
    {
        for(int j = 0; j < n; j++)
        {
            if(kriyagrid[i][j] == 1)
            {
```

```
                kriyagrid[i][j] = 0;
            }
            else if(i == 0 and j == 0)
            {
                kriyagrid[i][j] = 1;
            }
            else if(i == 0)
            {
                kriyagrid[i][j] = kriyagrid[i][j-1];
            }
            else if(j == 0)
            {
                kriyagrid[i][j] = kriyagrid[i-1][j];
            }
            else
            {
                kriyagrid[i][j] = kriyagrid[i][j-1] + kriyagrid[i-1][j];
            }
        }
    }

    return kriyagrid[m-1][n-1];
}
```

kriya grid	paths	path-count
0 0 0 0 1 0	rdd, drd	2
0 0 1 0 0 0 0 0	rddd	1

■

§ Problem 41. *In § Problem 39, each Kriya bears a specific number of Pranayams to accomplish it. Determine the minimum possible number of Pranayams to reach Heaven.* ◊

§§ Solution. Let $f_p(i,\ j)$ be the minimum number of Pranayams to reach the grid-cell$(i,\ j)$, following an optimal sequence of p steps.

Ram can reach the grid-cell$(i,\ j)$ either from the left grid-cell$(i,\ j-1)$ or the above grid-cell$(i-1,\ j)$ except in the first row (i.e. $i=0$, which could be reached only from the left grid-cell$(0,\ j-1)$) and in the first column (i.e. $j=0$, which can be reached only from the above grid-cell$(i-1,\ 0)$).

$$\therefore f_p(i,\ j) = \begin{cases} \text{grid-cell}(i,\ j) & \text{if } i = 0 \text{ and } j = 0 \\ f_{p-1}(0,\ j-1) + \text{grid-cell}(0,\ j) & \text{if } i = 0\text{, i.e. first row} \\ f_{p-1}(i-1,\ 0) + \text{grid-cell}(i,\ 0) & \text{if } j = 0\text{, i.e. first col} \\ \text{Min}[f_{p-1}(i,\ j-1),\ f_{p-1}(i-1,\ j)] + \text{grid-cell}(i,\ j) & \text{otherwise} \end{cases}$$

Algorithm 41 Kriya Grid Paths to Heaven : Optimal Pranayams

```
function kriyapaths(kriyagrid[0..m − 1][0..n − 1])
    f[0..m − 1][0..n − 1] ← {0}
    for i ∈ [0, m) do
        for j ∈ [0, n) do
            if i ≡ 0 and j ≡ 0 then
                f[i][j] ← kriyagrid[i][j]
            else if i ≡ 0 then                                  ▷ First Row
                f[i][j] ← f[i][j − 1] + kriyagrid[i][j]
            else if j ≡ 0 then                                  ▷ First Column
                f[i][j] ← f[i − 1][j] + kriyagrid[i][j]
            else
                f[i][j] ← min(f[i][j − 1], f[i − 1][j]) + kriyagrid[i][j]
            end if
        end for
    end for

    return f[m − 1][n − 1]
end function
```

Time complexity is $\mathcal{O}(mn)$. Space complexity is $\mathcal{O}(mn)$.

```cpp
int heaven(std::vector<std::vector<int>> &
    kriyagrid)
{
    if(kriyagrid.empty() or kriyagrid[0].empty())
        return 0;

    int m = kriyagrid.size(); // number of rows
    int n = kriyagrid[0].size(); // number of
        columns

    std::vector<std::vector<int>> f(m, std::vector
        <int>(n, 0));
    for(int i = 0; i < m; i++)
    {
        for(int j = 0; j < n; j++)
        {
            if(i == 0 and j == 0)
            {
                f[i][j] = kriyagrid[i][j];
            }
            else if(i == 0) // first row
            {
```

```
                f[i][j] = f[i][j-1] + kriyagrid[i][j];
            }
            else if(j == 0) // first column
            {
                f[i][j] = f[i-1][j] + kriyagrid[i][j];
            }
            else
            {
                f[i][j] = std::min(f[i][j-1], f[i-1][j]) + kriyagrid[i][j];
            }
        }
    }
    return f[m-1][n-1];
}
```

kriya grid	Optimal Path	Optimal Pranayams
1 5 6 1 9 8	1->5->1->8	15
1 5 6 4 1 8 3 6	1->6->1->3->6	17

■

§ Problem 42. *Guru shares the details of a secretive 2D $m \times n$ Kriya grid-path to Heaven with his disciple Ram. Ram is allowed to select only one Kriya from each row such that selected Kriyas in the adjacent rows can differ by at-most one column position. Each Kriya bears a specific number of Pranayams to accomplish it. Starting from the first row to the last row, practicing all the selected (m) Kriyas opens the gateway to Heaven. Determine the minimum possible number of Pranayams to reach Heaven.* ◊

§§ Solution. Let $f_p(i, j)$ be the minimum possible number of Pranayams to reach the grid-cell(i, j), following an optimal sequence of p steps.

Note that, any Kriya can be selected in the first row (i.e. i = 0).

For the first column (i.e. $j = 0$), hence there are only two choices of grid-cells in the previous row to reach the grid-cell(i, j) :

1. grid-cell$(i - 1, j)$, or
2. grid-cell$(i - 1, j + 1)$.

For the last column (i.e. $j = n - 1$), the only two choices are

1. grid-cell($i-1$, $j-1$), or
2. grid-cell($i-1$, j).

Whereas, for any other columns other than the first or last one, there are three possible choices:

1. grid-cell($i-1$, $j-1$), or
2. grid-cell($i-1$, j), or
3. grid-cell($i-1$, $j+1$).

$$\therefore f_p(i,\ j) = \begin{cases} \text{grid-cell}(i,j) & \text{if } i = 0\text{, else} \\ \text{grid-cell}(i,j) + \begin{cases} \text{Min}[f_{p-1}(i-1,\ j),\ f_{p-1}(i-1,\ j+1)] & \text{if } j = 0 \\ \text{Min}[f_{p-1}(i-1,\ j-1),\ f_{p-1}(i-1,\ j)] & \text{if } j = n-1 \\ \text{Min}[f_{p-1}(i-1,\ j-1),\ f_{p-1}(i-1,\ j),\ f_{p-1}(i-1,\ j+1)] & \text{otherwise} \end{cases} \end{cases}$$

Note that, the last row of f-matrix contains the minimum possible Pranayams for the respective grid-cells. Minimal entry in the last row is the required answer we are looking for.

Algorithm 42 Constrained Kriya Grid Paths to Heaven : Optimal Pranayams

function kriyapaths($kriyagrid[0..m-1][0..n-1]$)
  $f[0..m-1][0..n-1] \leftarrow \{0\}$
  for $i \in [0,\ m)$ **do**
    for $j \in [0,\ n)$ **do**
      if $i \equiv 0$ **then** ▷ First Row
        $f[i][j] \leftarrow kriyagrid[i][j]$
      else if $j \equiv 0$ **then** ▷ First Column
        $f[i][j] \leftarrow kriyagrid[i][j] + \textbf{min}(f[i-1][j], f[i-1][j+1])$
      else if $j \equiv n-1$ **then** ▷ Last Column
        $f[i][j] \leftarrow kriyagrid[i][j] + \textbf{min}(f[i-1][j-1], f[i-1][j])$
      else
        $f[i][j] \leftarrow kriyagrid[i][j] + \textbf{min}(f[i-1][j-1],\ f[i-1][j],\ f[i-1][j+1])$
      end if
    end for
  end for

  return min $(f[m-1])$ ▷ Minimum entry of Last Row
end function

Time complexity is $\mathcal{O}(mn)$. Space complexity is $\mathcal{O}(mn)$. Space complexity is $\mathcal{O}1$ with usage of Kriya Grid as f-matrix.

```
int heaven(std::vector<std::vector<int>> &
    kriyagrid)
{
    if(kriyagrid.empty() or kriyagrid[0].empty())
        return 0;
```

```
    int m = kriyagrid.size(); // number of rows
    int n = kriyagrid[0].size(); // number of columns

    std::vector<std::vector<int>> f(m, std::vector<int>(n, 0));

    for(int j = 0; j < n; j++) // i = 0, i.e. first row
    {
        f[0][j] = kriyagrid[0][j];
    }

    for(int i = 1; i < m; i++)
    {
        for(int j = 0; j < n; j++)
        {
            int pranayams = f[i-1][j];

            if(j > 0)
            {
                pranayams = std::min(pranayams, f[i-1][j-1]);
            }

            if(j < n-1)
            {
                pranayams = std::min(pranayams, f[i-1][j+1]);
            }

            f[i][j] = kriyagrid[i][j] + pranayams;
        }
    }

    // last row of f-matrix contains the minimum possible pranayams
    // the minimum entry in the last row is the required answer
    int minpranayams = std::numeric_limits<int>::max();

    for(auto e : f[m-1])
    {
        minpranayams = std::min(minpranayams, e);
    }

    return minpranayams;
}
```

kriya grid	Optimal Path	Optimal Pranayams
1 5 6 1 9 8	1->1->8	10
1 5 6 4 1 8 3 6	1->4->1->3	9
4 5 2 6 6 4 3 1 7 2 9 8 3 6 1 7	2->3->2->1	8

■

§ Problem 43. *Determine the minimum possible number of Pranayams to reach Heaven if selected Kriyas in the adjacent rows of § Problem 42 belong to different column-positions.* ◊

§§ Solution.

$$\therefore f_p(i,\ j) = \begin{cases} \text{grid-cell}(i, j) & \text{if } i = 0 \\ \text{grid-cell}(i, j)\ +\ \underset{k \neq j}{\overset{k \in [0,n)}{\text{Min}}}\ [f_{p-1}(i-1,\ k)] & \text{otherwise} \end{cases}$$

Algorithm 43 Constrained Kriya Grid Paths to Heaven : Optimal Pranayams : Diff Cols

```
function kriyapaths(kriyagrid[0..m − 1][0..n − 1])
    f[0..m − 1][0..n − 1] ← {0}
    for i ∈ [0, m) do
        for j ∈ [0, n) do
            if i ≡ 0 then                                   ▷ First Row
                f[i][j] ← kriyagrid[i][j]
            else
                f[i][j] ← kriyagrid[i][j] + Min_{k∈[0,m), k≠j} (f[i − 1][k])
            end if
        end for
    end for

    return min (f[m − 1])   ▷ Minimum entry of Last Row
end function
```

Time complexity is $\mathcal{O}(m^2 n)$. Space complexity is $\mathcal{O}(mn)$.

```
int heaven(std::vector<std::vector<int>> &
    kriyagrid)
{
    if(kriyagrid.empty() or kriyagrid[0].empty())
        return 0;
```

```

    int m = kriyagrid.size(); // number of rows
    int n = kriyagrid[0].size(); // number of columns

    std::vector<std::vector<int>> f(m, std::vector<int>(n, 0));

    for(int i = 0; i < m; i++)
    {
        for(int j = 0; j < n; j++)
        {
            if(i == 0) // first row
            {
                f[i][j] = kriyagrid[i][j];
            }
            else
            {
                int pranayams = std::numeric_limits<int>::max();

                for(int k = 0; k < n; k++)
                {
                    if(k != j)
                    {
                        pranayams = std::min(pranayams, f[i-1][k]);
                    }
                }

                f[i][j] = kriyagrid[i][j] + pranayams;
            }
        }
    }

    // last row of f-matrix contains the minimum possible pranayams
    // the minimum entry in the last row is the required answer
    int minpranayams = std::numeric_limits<int>::max();

    for(auto e : f[m-1])
    {
        minpranayams = std::min(minpranayams, e);
    }

    return minpranayams;
}
```

Computation of finding the minimum can be improved by resolving to finding the first and second minimum of the row $f[i-1]$ to do the needful. Kriya Grid can be used as f-matrix.

Algorithm 44 Constrained Kriya Grid Paths to Heaven : Optimal Pranayams : Diff Cols : Optimized

function firstsecondmins($v[0..n-1]$)
  $firstmin \leftarrow \infty$
  $secondmin \leftarrow \infty$
  $firstminindex \leftarrow 0$
  $secondminindex \leftarrow 0$

  for $i \in [0,\ n)$ **do**
    if $v[i] < firstmin$ **then**
      $secondmin \leftarrow firstmin$
      $firstmin \leftarrow v[i]$
      $secondminindex \leftarrow firstminindex$
      $firstminindex \leftarrow i$
    else if $v[i] < secondmin$ and $i \neq firstminindex$ **then**
      $secondmin \leftarrow v[i]$
      $secondminindex \leftarrow i$
    end if
  end for

  return $\{firstminindex,\ secondminindex\}$
end function

function kriyapaths($kriyagrid[0..m-1][0..n-1]$)
  for $i \in [1,\ m)$ **do**
    <firstmin, secondmin> $\leftarrow firstsecondmins(kriyagrid[i-1]$
    for $j \in [0,\ n)$ **do**
      if $j \equiv firstmin$ **then**
        $kriyagrid[i][j] \leftarrow kriyagrid[i][j] + kriyagrid[i-1][secondmin]$
      else
        $kriyagrid[i][j] \leftarrow kriyagrid[i][j] + kriyagrid[i-1][firstmin]$
      end if
    end for
  end for

  return min $(kriyagrid[m-1])$ ▷ Minimum element of Last Row
end function

Time complexity is $\mathcal{O}(mn)$. Space complexity is $\mathcal{O}(1)$.

```
// <firstmin_index, secondmin_index>
std::pair<int, int> first_secondmins(std::vector<
    int> & v)
{
```

```
    int firstmin = std::numeric_limits<int>::max();
    int secondmin = std::numeric_limits<int>::max();
    int firstmin_index = 0, secondmin_index = 0;

    int n = v.size();

    for(int i = 0; i < n; i++)
    {
        if(v[i] < firstmin)
        {
            secondmin = firstmin;
            firstmin = v[i];
            secondmin_index = firstmin_index;
            firstmin_index = i;
        }
        else if(v[i] < secondmin and i != firstmin_index)
        {
            secondmin = v[i];
            secondmin_index = i;
        }
    }
    return {firstmin_index, secondmin_index};
}

int heaven(std::vector<std::vector<int>> & kriyagrid)
{
    if(kriyagrid.empty() or kriyagrid[0].empty()) return 0;

    int m = kriyagrid.size(); // number of rows
    int n = kriyagrid[0].size(); // number of columns

    for(int i = 1; i < m; i++)
    {
        std::pair<int, int> p = first_secondmins(kriyagrid[i-1]);

        for(int j = 0; j < n; j++)
        {
            if(j == p.first)
            {
                kriyagrid[i][j] += kriyagrid[i-1][p.second];
            }
            else
            {
                kriyagrid[i][j] += kriyagrid[i-1][p.first];
            }
```

```
            }
        }

        // last row of f-matrix (Kriya Grid) contains
            the minimum possible pranayams
        // the minimum entry in the last row is the
            required answer
        int minpranayams = std::numeric_limits<int>::
            max();

        for(auto e : kriyagrid[m-1])
        {
            minpranayams = std::min(minpranayams, e);
        }

        return minpranayams;
}
```

kriya grid	Optimal Path	Optimal Pranayams
1 5 6 1 9 8	1->1->9	11
1 5 6 4 1 8 3 6	1->4->1->6	12
4 5 2 6 6 4 3 1 7 2 9 8 3 6 1 7	2->1->2->1	6
1 2 3 4 5 6 7 8 9	1->5->7	13

■

§ **Problem 44.** *Guru instructs his disciple Ram to practice all the Kriyas as per the given schedule of starting years to reach Heaven. Given a pranayam-list to practice Kriyas for 1, 5 or 10 consecutive years, determine the minimum possible pranayams needed to reach Heaven.* ◊

§§ **Solution**. Let $f_n(i)$ be the minimum possible pranayams to practice the Kriyas till i^{th} year, following an optimal sequence of n-steps.

If there is no Kriya scheduled to practice in the current year, then no pranayam is needed for the current year, i.e. required pranayams are the same as was earlier (i.e. till previous year).

If the current year is scheduled for Kriya practice, then there are three choices (1, 5 or 10) for selecting the pranayams from the given list, say $py[0..2]$.

$$\therefore f_n(i) = \begin{cases} f_{n-1}(i-1) & \text{if no Kriya for year } i \\ \text{Min}\{f_{n-1}(i-1) + py[0],\ f_{n-1}(i-5) + py[1],\ f_{n-1}(i-10) + py[2]\} & \text{otherwise} \end{cases}$$

Algorithm 45 Optimal Pranayams to reach Heaven

function minpranayams($kriyayears[], prans[0..2]$)
  $n \leftarrow kriyayears[kriyayears.size() - 1]$
  $f[0..n] \leftarrow \{0\}$

  for $year \in kriyayears$ **do** ▷ Scheduled Ones
    $f[year] \leftarrow 1$
  end for
  $f[0] \leftarrow 0$

  for $i \in [1,\ n]$ **do**
    if $f[i] \neq 1$ **then** ▷ No Kriya to practice for the year i
      $f[i] \leftarrow f[i-1]$
    else
      $minp \leftarrow$ **min** $(f[i-1] + prans[0], f[i-5] + prans[1], f[i-10] + prans[2])$
    end if
  end for

  return f.back()
end function

Time complexity is $\mathcal{O}(n)$. Space complexity is $\mathcal{O}(n)$, where n is the maximum numbered year (i.e. the last one) in the scheduled kriya years' list.

```
int minpranayams(std::vector<int> & kriyayears,
    std::vector<int> & pranayams)
{
    int n = kriyayears.back();

    std::vector<int> f(n+1, 0);

    for(int year : kriyayears)
    {
        f[year] = 1; // marking the years
            scheduled to practice
    }

    f[0] = 0;

    for(int i = 1; i <= n; ++i)
    {
        if(not f[i]) // not in list of years
            scheduled
        {
            f[i] = f[i-1]; // same as previous
                year
```

```
        }

        else
        {
            int minp = f[i-1] + pranayams[0];
            minp = std::min(minp, f[std::max(0, i - 5)] + pranayams[1]);
            minp = std::min(minp, f[std::max(0, i - 10)] + pranayams[2]);
            f[i] = minp;
        }
    }

    return f.back();
}
```

kriya years	pranayams for 1, 5, 10 years	Optimal Plan	Optimal Pranayams
1, 3, 5, 6, 7, 15	2, 5, 7	7 + 2	9

■

§ **Problem 45.** *Given a sequential list of α Kriyas, Ram starts to practice with the first Kriya onwards such that with each of β Pranayams, Ram can select the Kriya to his left or right, or continue practicing the same Kriya. Determine total number of ways such that Ram ends up practicing the first Kriya (index 0) after β Pranayams.* ◊

§§ **Solution**. Assuming 0-indexed based list, let $f_n(p,\ k)$ be the total number of ways such that Ram ends up practicing Kriya k after p Pranayams with an optimal policy of n-stage process.

There are three possibilities to reach the state $(p,\ k)$:

1. From left : $f_{n-1}(p-1,\ k-1)$
2. From right : $f_{n-1}(p-1,\ k+1)$, and
3. Stay at k : $f_{n-1}(p-1,\ k)$.

Note that $f_n(0,\ 0) \equiv 1$: Ram ends up practicing first Kriya (index 0) only with no Pranayam.

$$\therefore f_n(p,\ k) = \begin{cases} 1 & \text{if } p \equiv 0 \text{ and } k \equiv 0 \\ f_{n-1}(p-1,\ k-1) + f_{n-1}(p-1,\ k) + f_{n-1}(p-1,\ k+1) & \text{otherwise} \end{cases}$$

Note that with β Pranayams, Ram can practice up to the Kriya with index β.

Algorithm 46 Count ways : First Kriya

function firstkriya(β, α)
  $n \leftarrow$ **min**(β, α)
  $f[0..\beta][0..n-1] \leftarrow \{0\}$

for $p \in [1, \beta]$ **do**
  for $k \in [0, n)$ **do**
    $f[p][k] \leftarrow f[p-1][k]$ ▷ Continue to practice the same Kriya
    if $k > 0$ **then**
      $f[p][k] \leftarrow f[p][k] + f[p-1][k-1]$ ▷ Left to right
    end if

    if $k < n - 1$ **then**
      $f[p][k] \leftarrow f[p][k] + f[p-1][k+1]$ ▷ Right to left
    end if

  end for
end for

return $f[\beta][0]$
end function

Time complexity is $\mathcal{O}(\beta^2)$. Space complexity is $\mathcal{O}(\beta^2)$.

```cpp
// beta Pranayams, alpha Kriyas
int firstkriya(int beta, int alpha)
{
    int n = std::min(beta, alpha); // max no of
        Kriyas with beta Pranayams

    std::vector<std::vector<int>> f(beta + 1, std
        ::vector<int>(n, 0));

    f[0][0] = 1;

    for(int p = 1; p <= beta; p++)
    {
        for(int k = 0; k < n; k++)
        {
            f[p][k] = f[p-1][k];

            if(k - 1 >= 0)
            {
                f[p][k] += f[p-1][k-1];
            }

            if(k + 1 < n)
            {
                f[p][k] += f[p-1][k+1];
            }
        }
    }

    return f[beta][0];
}
```

Algorithm 47 Count ways : First Kriya : Space Optimization

```
function firstkriya(β, α)
    n ← min(β, α)
    f[0..n − 1] ← {0}

    for p ∈ [1, β] do
        prev ← 0
        cur ← 0
        for k ∈ [0, n) do
            cur ← f[k]
            f[k] ← f[k] + prev + (k + 1 < n ? f[k + 1] : 0)
            prev ← cur
        end for
    end for

    return f[0]
end function
```

Time complexity is $\mathcal{O}(\beta^2)$. Space complexity is $\mathcal{O}(\beta)$.

```
int firstkriya(int beta, int alpha)
{
    int n = std::min(beta, alpha); // max no of Kriyas with beta Pranayams

    std::vector<int> f(n, 0);

    f[0] = 1;

    for(int p = 1; p <= beta; p++)
    {
        int prev = 0, cur = 0;

        for(int k = 0; k < n; k++)
        {
            cur = f[k];
            f[k] += prev + (k+1 < n ? f[k+1] : 0);
            prev = cur;
        }
    }

    return f[0];
}
```

l : left, r : right, c : stays same

Kriyas (α)	Pranayams(β)	Ways	Count Ways
3	2	rl, cc	2
4	3	rlc, crl, rcl, ccc	4

■

§ Problem 46. *Ram starts practicing Kriyas as in $m \times n$ Kriya Grid by selecting Kriyas one at a time from the adjacent grid-cells located to his left, right, up and down. During the selection process, which is restricted to at most β in number, Ram may inadvertently move out of the grid. Once he is out, he can never reach Heaven. Determine total number of ways to not reach Heaven, starting from a grid-cell$(r,\ c)$.* ◊

§§ Solution. Let $f_p(s,\ r,\ c)$ be the total number of ways to move out of the grid (i.e. loose all hopes to reach Heaven) after s selections, starting from a grid-cell$(r,\ c)$.

Note that there are four adjacent cells to the grid-cell$(r,\ c)$, namely:

1. Left : $(r,\ c-1)$
2. Right : $(r,\ c+1)$
3. Up : $(r-1,\ c)$
4. Down : $(r+1,\ c)$

Hence starting from any of these four adjacent grid-cells, Ram is out of the grid after $s-1$ selections in the following number of ways respectively:

1. $f_{p-1}^{L} = f_{p-1}(s-1,\ r,\ c-1)$
2. $f_{p-1}^{R} = f_{p-1}(s-1,\ r,\ c+1)$
3. $f_{p-1}^{U} = f_{p-1}(s-1,\ r-1,\ c)$
4. $f_{p-1}^{D} = f_{p-1}(s-1,\ r+1,\ c)$

$$\therefore f_p(s,\ r,\ c) = \begin{cases} 1 & \text{if } (r,\ c) \text{ is out of the grid} \\ f_{p-1}^{L} + f_{p-1}^{R} + f_{p-1}^{U} + f_{p-1}^{D} & \text{otherwise} \end{cases}$$

Algorithm 48 Out of Kriya Grid : Count ways

```
function outofkgrid(m, n, β, r, c)
    f[0..β][0..m − 1][0..n − 1] ← {0}

    for s ∈ [1, β] do
        for i ∈ [0, m) do
            for j ∈ [0, n) do
                fl ← (j ≡ 0 ? 1 : f[s − 1][i][j − 1]          ▷ Left
                fr ← (j ≡ n − 1 ? 1 : f[s − 1][i][j + 1]      ▷ Right
                fu ← (i ≡ 0 ? 1 : f[s − 1][i − 1][j]          ▷ Up
                fd ← (i ≡ m − 1 ? 1 : f[s − 1][i + 1][j]      ▷ Down

                f[s][i][j] ← fl + fr + fu + fd
            end for
        end for
    end for

    return f[β][r][c]
end function
```

Time complexity is $\mathcal{O}(mn\beta)$. Space complexity is $\mathcal{O}(mn\beta)$.

§ Problem 47. *Guru shares a secretive triangular Kriya grid with his disciple Ram. Starting from the top row, Ram is allowed to select only one Kriya in each row, which is adjacent to the previous Kriya. Each Kriya bears a specific number of Pranayams associated with it. After practicing one Kriya per row, practicing of any Kriya of the bottom row opens a gateway to Heaven. Determine the minimum possible number of Pranayams to reach Heaven.* ◊

§§ Solution. Let $f_p(r,\ c)$ be the minimum possible number of Pranayams to reach the grid-cell$(r,\ c)$ from top, following an optimal policy and p-steps.

Note that adjacent grid-cells in the previous row are grid-cell$(r-1,\ c)$ and grid-cell$(r-1,\ c-1)$.

$$\therefore f_p(r,\ c) = \text{Min}\{f_{p-1}(r-1,\ c),\ f_{p-1}(r-1,\ c-1)\} + kriyagrid(r,\ c)$$

Algorithm 50 Triangular Kriya Grid : Optimal Pranayams

```
function triheaven(kriyagrid[0..n − 1][])
    for r ∈ [1, n) do
        for c ∈ [0, r] do
            if c ≡ 0 then
                kriyagrid[r][c] ← kriyagrid[r][c] + kriyagrid[r − 1][c]
            else if c ≡ r then
                kriyagrid[r][c] ← kriyagrid[r][c] + kriyagrid[r − 1][c − 1]
            else
                kriyagrid[r][c] ← kriyagrid[r][c]+
              min{kriyagrid[r − 1][c], kriyagrid[r − 1][c − 1]}
            end if
        end for
    end for

    return min[kriyagrid[n − 1]]
end function
```

Time complexity is $\mathcal{O}(n^2)$, where n is the number of rows in the given triangular grid. Space complexity is $\mathcal{O}(1)$.

```
int triheaven(std::vector<std::vector<int>> &
    kriyagrid)
{
    int n = kriyagrid.size(); // number of rows

    for(int r = 1; r < n; r++)
    {
        for(int c = 0; c <= r; c++)
        {
            if(c == 0)
            {
```

```
                kriyagrid[r][c] += kriyagrid[r-1][c];
            }
            else if(c == r)
            {
                kriyagrid[r][c] += kriyagrid[r-1][c-1];
            }
            else
            {
                kriyagrid[r][c] += std::min(kriyagrid[r-1][c], kriyagrid[r-1][c-1]);
            }
        }
    }

    return *std::min_element(std::begin(kriyagrid.back()), std::end(kriyagrid.back()));
}
```

Triangular Kriya Grid	Optimal Path	Optimal Pranayam
1 2 3 5 4 6 9 8 7 10	1->2->4->7	14
7 2 1 3 5 8 6 5 4 9	7->1->5->4, 7->2->3->5	17

Note that the optimal path 1->2->4->7 is same as 7->4->2->1. Hence Ram can start from the bottom row as well and move to the top row from a computational perspective. Starting from the bottom row, minimum possible Pranayams for these grid-cells are the Pranayams associated with the grid-cells themselves.

$$\therefore f_p(r,\ c) = \text{Min}\{f_{p-1}(r+1,\ c),\ f_{p-1}(r+1,\ c+1)\} + kriyagrid(r,\ c)$$

Algorithm 51 Triangular Kriya Grid : Optimal Pranayams : Alternative

function triheaven($kriyagrid[0..n-1][]$)
    for $r \in [n-2,\ 0]$ **do**
        for $c \in [0,\ r]$ **do**
            $kriyagrid[r][c] \leftarrow kriyagrid[r][c] +$
                $\textbf{min}\{kriyagrid[r+1][c],\ kriyagrid[r+1][c+1]\}$
        end for
    end for

return *kriyagrid*[0][0]
end function

Time complexity is $\mathcal{O}(n^2)$, where n is the number of rows in the given triangular grid. Space complexity is $\mathcal{O}(1)$.

```cpp
int triheaven(std::vector<std::vector<int>> & kriyagrid)
{
    int n = kriyagrid.size();

    for(int r = n-2; r >=0; r--)
    {
        for(int c = 0; c <= r; c++)
        {
            kriyagrid[r][c] += std::min(kriyagrid[r+1][c], kriyagrid[r+1][c+1]);
        }
    }

    return kriyagrid[0][0];
}
```

■

§ Problem 48. *Given a square Kriya Grid, each grid-cell bearing a specific number of Pranayams respectively, find the maximal square Kriya sub-grid such that each grid-cell bears equal Pranayams.* ◊

§§ Solution. Let $f_p(r,\ c)$ be the length of the maximal square Kriya sub-grid with grid-cell$(r,\ c)$ being the bottom-right most one.

Note that there are only three candidates adjacent to the grid-cell$(r,\ c)$, namely:

1. left : $(r,\ c-1)$
2. up : $(r-1,\ c)$
3. upper-left : $(r-1,\ c-1)$

And the corresponding lengths are:

1. $f^{l}_{p-1} \equiv f_{p-1}(r,\ c-1)$
2. $f^{u}_{p-1} \equiv f_{p-1}(r-1,\ c)$
3. $f^{ul}_{p-1} \equiv f_{p-1}(r-1,\ c-1)$

$$g \equiv grid$$

$$\therefore f_p(r,\ c) = \begin{cases} 1 & \text{if } r \equiv 0 : \text{first row or } c \equiv 0 : \text{first column} \\ \text{Min}\left[f^{l}_{p-1},\ f^{u}_{p-1},\ f^{ul}_{p-1}\right] + 1 & \text{if } g(r,c) \equiv g(r,c-1) \equiv g(r-1,c) \equiv g(r-1,c-1) \\ 1 & \text{otherwise} \end{cases}$$

$\underset{\substack{r\in[0,\ m) \\ c\in[0,\ n)}}{\text{Max}} \{f_p(r,\ c)\}$ yields the length of the maximal Kriya sub-grid with equal Pranayams in each grid-cell.

Algorithm 52 Maximal Square Kriya Grid

function maxsquare($g[0..m-1][0..n-1]$)
  $f[0..m-1][0..n-1] \leftarrow \{0\}$
  $maxlen \leftarrow 0$

  for $r \in [0,\ m)$ **do**
    for $c \in [0,\ n)$ **do**
      if $r \equiv 0$ or $c \equiv 0$ **then** ▷ First row or first column
        $f[r][c] \leftarrow 1$ ▷ Unit square
      else
        if $g[r][c] \equiv g[r][c-1] \equiv g[r-1][c] \equiv g[r-1][c-1]$ **then**
          $f[r][c] \leftarrow \textbf{min}\{f[r][c-1],\ f[r-1][c],\ f[r-1][c-1]\} + 1$
        else
          $f[r][c] \leftarrow 1$ ▷ Unit square
        end if
      end if
      $maxlen \leftarrow \textbf{max}\{maxlen,\ f[r][c]\}$
    end for
  end for

  return $maxlen$
end function

Time complexity is $\mathcal{O}(mn)$. Space complexity is $\mathcal{O}(mn)$.

```cpp
int maxsquare(std::vector<std::vector<int>> & g)
{
    int m = g.size(); // rows
    int n = g[0].size(); // columns

    std::vector<std::vector<int>> f(m, std::vector
        <int>(n, 0));

    int maxlen = 0;

    for(int r = 0; r < m; r++)
    {
        for(int c = 0; c < n; c++)
        {
            if(r == 0 or c == 0) // first row or
                first column
            {
                f[r][c] = 1; // unit square
            }
            else
            {
                if(g[r][c] == g[r][c-1] and
                   g[r][c] == g[r-1][c] and
                   g[r][c] == g[r-1][c-1])
                {
                    f[r][c] = std::min(std::min(f[
                        r][c-1], f[r-1][c]), f[r
```

```
                            -1][c-1]) + 1;
                    }
                    else
                    {
                        f[r][c] = 1; // unit square
                    }
                }

                maxlen = std::max(maxlen, f[r][c]);
            }
        }

    return maxlen;
}
```

Square Kriya Grid	Max-Square Kriya Sub-Grid	Side Length
3 3 4 4 2 2 1 1 4 4 4 3 5 5 4 4 4 1 6 6 4 4 4 4 3 2 1 2 3 4	4 4 4 4 4 4 4 4 4	3
3 3 4 4 2 2 1 1 1 1 3 3 1 1 1 1 4 1 1 1 1 1 4 4 1 1 1 1 3 4	1 1 1 1 1 1 1 1 1 1 1 1 1 1 1 1	4

■

§ **Problem 49.** *Labeling a prohibited Kriya as* 0 *in contrast to a normal one as* 1*, Ram is armed with* m *zeroes and* n *ones to practice as many Kriya-sequences as possible from a given list of Kriya-sequences. Determine the maximum number of Kriya-sequences, Ram can practice.* ◊

§§ **Solution**. Let $f_p(z, o)$ be the maximum number of Kriya-sequences possible with z zeroes and o ones, following an optimal policy with p-steps.

Assuming the current Kriya-sequence has z_c zeroes and o_c ones, there are two choices : either to practice the current one or not.

$$\therefore f_p(z, o) = \text{Max}\{f_{p-1}(z, o), f_{p-1}(z - z_c, o - o_c) + 1\}$$

Algorithm 53 Max Zerones Kriya Sequences

function zerones($ks[]$, m, n)
    $f[0..m][0..n] \leftarrow \{0\}$
    return $f[m][n]$

```
    for s ∈ ks do
        zc ← 0
        oc ← 0

        for c ∈ s do
            if c ≡ 0 then
                zc ← zc + 1
            else
                oc ← oc + 1
            end if
        end for

        for z ← m; z ≥ zc; z ← z − 1 do
            for o ← n; o ≥ oc; o ← o − 1 do
                f[z][o] ← max(f[z][o], f[z − zc][o − oc] + 1)
            end for
        end for

    end for

    return f[m][n]
end function
```

Time complexity is $\mathcal{O}(qs + qmn)$, where q is the number of Kriya-sequences, s is the average length of a Kriya-sequence. Space complexity is $\mathcal{O}(mn)$.

```cpp
int zerones(std::vector<std::string> & ks, int m,
    int n)
{
    std::vector<std::vector<int>> f(m+1, std::
        vector<int>(n+1, 0));

    for(auto s : ks)
    {
        int zc = 0, oc = 0;

        for(auto c : s)
        {
            c == '0' ? ++zc : ++oc;
        }

        for(int z = m; z >= zc; --z)
        {
            for(int o = n; o >= oc; --o)
            {
                f[z][o] = std::max(f[z][o], f[z -
                    zc][o - oc] + 1);
            }
        }
    }

    return f[m][n];
}
```

Kriya Sequence List = {"00110", "0", "1", "1010111", "110"}

m(zeroes)	n(ones)	**Kriya Sequences**	**Max Count of Kriya Sequences**
2	3	0, 1, 110	3
3	2	0, 1 or 0, 110	2
6	5	0, 1, 110, 00110	4
8	11	0, 1, 110, 00110, 1010111	5
1	1	0, 1	2
2	5	0, 1, 110	3

■

§ Problem 50. *Given a Kriya, represented by a positive integer α, determine the minimum possible number of Pranayams with sum as α, where each Pranayam is a perfect square number.* ◊

§§ Solution. Let $f_p(\beta)$ be the minimum possible number of Pranayams with sum as β, following an optimal policy with p-steps.

$$\therefore f_p(\beta) = \begin{cases} 0 & \text{if } \beta \equiv 0 \\ \text{Min}\big[f_{p-1}(\beta - \gamma^2) + 1\big] & \text{otherwise, } \forall\, \gamma : 1 \leq \gamma^2 \leq \beta \end{cases}$$

Algorithm 54 Perfect Kriya

```
function perfectkriya(α)
    f[0..α] ← {∞}
    f[0] ← 0

    for β ∈ [1, α] do
        for γ ∈ [1, √β] do
            f[β] ← min(f[β], f[β − γ²] + 1)
        end for
    end for

    return f[α]
end function
```

Time complexity is $\mathcal{O}(\alpha\sqrt{\alpha})$. Space complexity is $\mathcal{O}(\alpha)$.

```
int perfectkriya(int alpha)
{
    std::vector<int> f(alpha + 1, std::
        numeric_limits<int>::max());

    f[0] = 0;

    for(int beta = 1; beta <= alpha; beta++)
    {
```

```
        for(int gamma = 1; gamma * gamma <= beta;
            gamma++)
        {
            f[beta] = std::min(f[beta], f[beta -
                gamma * gamma] + 1);
        }
    }

    return f[alpha];
}
```

Kriya (α)	Pranayams	Min Count
29	$2^2 + 5^2$	2
35	$1^2 + 3^2 + 5^2$	3

■

§ Problem 51. *Ram has a special divine power γ as a result of previous practice of Kriyas. After many years of Kriya practice subsequently, Ram is granted two boons namely α and β respectively which can be used as many times he wish. Ram can use α to select all of the special divine powers he has at that point of time and use β to double their numbers after selection. Determine the minimum possible number of usage to end up with n γ.* ♢

§§ Solution. Note that Ram has just one divine power γ to start with.

After using α followed by β (i.e. no of usage = 2 : $\alpha\beta$), there are 2 γ. Another usage of β (i.e. no of usage = 3 : $\alpha\beta\beta$) leads to 3 γ.

Now, using α, Ram can select all of 3 γ. Using β again (i.e. no of usage = 5 : $\alpha\beta\beta\alpha\beta$) results into 6 γ.

There is another way to generate 6 γ : use α to select the only γ to start with and use β to lead to 2 γ. Now use α to select all of γ (i.e. 2) followed by using β to result into 4 γ. Another usage of β leads to 6 γ in total. Total no of usage is again 5 : $\alpha\beta\alpha\beta\beta$.

Let $f_p(\delta)$ be the minimum possible number of usage to end up with δ γ, following an optimal policy with p-steps.

$$\therefore f_p(\delta) = \underset{\phi \in (1,\ \delta)}{\text{Min}} \{f_{p-1}(\phi) + \delta \div \phi\} : \delta \textbf{ mod } \phi \equiv 0$$

Algorithm 55 Generate Kriya

function genkriya(n)
  $f[0..n] \leftarrow \{0\}$

  for $\delta \in [2,\ n]$ **do**

    $f[\delta] \leftarrow \delta$
    for $\phi \leftarrow \delta - 1;\ \phi > 1;\ \phi \leftarrow \phi - 1$ **do**
        $f[\delta] \leftarrow \mathbf{min}\left(f[\delta],\ f[\phi] + \dfrac{\delta}{\phi}\right)$
    end for
end for

return $f[n]$
end function

Time complexity is $\mathcal{O}(n^2)$. Space complexity is $\mathcal{O}(n)$.

```cpp
int genkriya(int n)
{
    std::vector<int> f(n + 1, 0);

    for(int delta = 2; delta <= n; delta++)
    {
        f[delta] = delta;

        for(int phi = delta - 1; phi > 1; phi--)
        {
            if(delta % phi == 0)
            {
                f[delta] = std::min(f[delta], f[
                    phi] + delta / phi);
            }
        }
    }

    return f[n];
}
```

n : no of γ	Usage	Optimal Usage
6	$\alpha\beta\alpha\beta\beta$ or $\alpha\beta\beta\alpha\beta$	5
8	$\alpha\beta\alpha\beta\beta\beta$ or $\alpha\beta\alpha\beta\alpha\beta$ or $\alpha\beta\beta\beta\alpha\beta$	6

■

§ Problem 52. *Guru shares a sequence of Kriyas with his disciple Ram, where each Kriya bears a specific number of Pranayams. At a given point of time, Ram is allowed to select any two Kriyas having Pranayams as α and β (say) respectively. After selection process is over, these two Kriyas get transformed into a new Kriya bearing $|\alpha - \beta|$ Pranayams. As a result, two Kriyas bearing equal Pranayams vanish altogether after selection. At the end of the process, there is at most one Kriya left. Determine the minimum possible Pranayam of the last Kriya if any.* ◊

§§ Solution. Note that Pranayam is 0 if there is no Kriya left at the end and this problem is equivalent to partitioning the entire sequence S into two sets having closest sum of Pranayams so that the minimum possible difference of the sums can be computed subsequently.

Let the two sets be S_α and S_β. Note that $S_\alpha - S_\beta = 2S_\alpha - (S_\alpha + S_\beta) = 2S_\alpha - S$.

Let $f_p(\gamma)$ stand for whether it is possible to build a set with sum γ, following an optimal policy with p-steps.

$$\therefore f_p(\gamma) = \begin{cases} 1 & \text{if } \gamma \equiv 0 \\ f_{p-1}(\gamma) \vee f_{p-1}(\gamma - \delta) & \text{otherwise, } \forall\, \delta \in S \end{cases}$$

Algorithm 56 Vanish Kriya

```
function vanishkriya(kriyaseq[0..n − 1])
    sumpranayams ← ∑ kriyaseq[0..n − 1]
    minpranayam ← sumpranayams
    f[0..sumpranayams/2] ← {false}
    f[0] ← true

    for pranayam ∈ kriyaseq[0..n − 1] do
        for γ ← sumpranayams/2; γ ≥ pranayam; γ ← γ − 1 do
            f[γ] ← f[γ] or f[γ − pranayam]
            if f[γ] then
                minpranayam ←
   min[minpranayam, |sumpranayams − 2 × γ|]
            end if
        end for
    end for

    return minpranayam
end function
```

Time complexity is $\mathcal{O}(ns)$, where s represents the sum. Space complexity is $\mathcal{O}(s)$.

```cpp
int vanishkriya(std::vector<int> & kriyaseq)
{
    int sumpranayams = 0;

    for(auto pranayam : kriyaseq)
    {
        sumpranayams += pranayam;
    }

    int minpranayam = sumpranayams;

    std::vector<bool> f(sumpranayams/2 + 1, false)
        ;

    f[0] = true;
```

```

    for(auto pranayam : kriyaseq)
    {
        for(auto gamma = sumpranayams/2; gamma >=
            pranayam; gamma--)
        {
            f[gamma] = f[gamma] || f[gamma -
                pranayam];

            if(f[gamma])
            {
                minpranayam = std::min(minpranayam
                    , std::abs(sumpranayams - 2 *
                    gamma));
            }
        }
    }

    return minpranayam;
}
```

Kriya Sequence	Optimal Process	Optimal Pranayam
4	4	4
4, 2	<4,2>=>2 => ks : 2	2
4, 2, 6	<2,6>=>4 => ks : 4, 4 <4,4>=>0 => ks : {}	0
4, 2, 6, 10	<6,10>=>4 => ks : 4, 2, 4 <4,4>=>0 => ks : 2	2
4, 2, 6, 9	<6,9>=>3 => ks : 4, 2, 3 <4,2>=>2 => ks : 2, 3 <2,3>=>1 => ks : 1	1
4, 2, 6, 8	<6,8>=>2 => ks : 4, 2, 2 <4,2>=>2 => ks : 2, 2 <2,2>=>0 => ks : {}	0

■

§ Problem 53. *Given a $m \times n$ rectangular Kriya Grid where each grid-cell is an unit square, Ram splits it into square Kriya Grids. Determine the minimum possible number of the square Kriya Grids while maintaining each grid-cell of these Grids as an unit square.* ◊

§§ Solution. Let $f_p(r,\ c)$ be the minimum possible number of the square Kriya Grids after splitting a $r \times c$ rectangle, using an optimal policy with p-steps.

$$\therefore f_p(r,\ c) = \begin{cases} 1 & \text{if } r \equiv c \\ \underset{\substack{row \in [1, \frac{r}{2}] \\ col \in [1, \frac{c}{2}]}}{\text{Min}} [f_{p-1}(row,\ c) + f_{p-1}(r - row,\ c),\ f_{p-1}(r,\ col) + f_{p-1}(r,\ c - col)] & \text{otherwise} \end{cases}$$

Algorithm 57 Split Kriya

```
function splitkriya(m, n)
    f[0..m − 1][0..n − 1] ← {∞}

    for r ∈ [1, m] do
        for c ∈ [1, n] do
            if r ≡ c then                                ▷ Square Kriya Grid
                f[r][c] ← 1
            else
                for row ∈ [1, ⌊r/2⌋] do
                    f[r][c] ← min(f[r][c], f[row][c] + f[r − row][c])
                end for
                for col ∈ [1, ⌊c/2⌋] do
                    f[r][c] ← min(f[r][c], f[r][col] + f[r][c − col])
                end for
            end if
        end for
    end for

    return f[m][n]
end function
```

Time complexity is $\mathcal{O}(mn\ \mathbf{max}(m,\ n))$. Space complexity is $\mathcal{O}(mn)$.

```cpp
int splitkriya(int m, int n)
{
    std::vector<std::vector<int>> f(m + 1, std::vector<int>(n + 1, std::numeric_limits<int>::max()));

    for(int r = 1; r <= m; r++)
    {
        for(int c = 1; c <= n; c++)
        {
            if(r == c)
            {
                f[r][c] = 1;
            }
            else
            {
                for(int row = 1; row <= r/2; row++)
                {
                    f[r][c] = std::min(f[r][c], f[row][c] + f[r-row][c]);
                }

                for(int col = 1; col <= c/2; col++)
                {
                    f[r][c] = std::min(f[r][c], f[r][col] + f[r][c-col]);
```

```
                }
            }
        }
    }

    return f[m][n];
}
```

m : row	n : col	Optimal Split	Optimal Squares
12	13	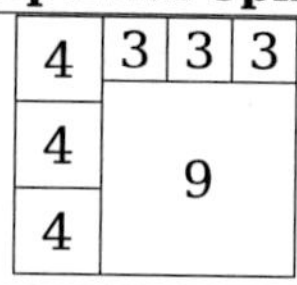	7
4	5	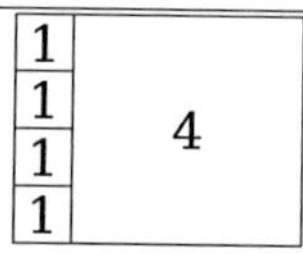	5
2	5	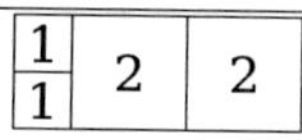	4

■

§ Problem 54. *Guru shares a $m \times n$ Kriya grid with his disciple Ram. Each grid-cell bears a energy-level, positive/zero/negative, represented by a specific number of Pranayams. Starting from the top-left grid-cell, Ram needs to reach the bottom-right grid-cell in order to enter the Heaven while maintaining the minimum threshold of γ Pranayams throughout. He is allowed to move only to his right or down at a given point of time. Determine the minimum possible number of Pranayams, Ram should have before starting the Kriya journey, in order to enter the Heaven.* ◊

§§ Solution. Let $f_p(r,\ c)$ be the minimum possible number of Pranayams to enter the grid-cell$(r,\ c)$, in order to enter the Heaven, using an optimal policy with p-steps.

$$\therefore f_p(r,\ c) = \text{Max}[\gamma,\ \text{Min}\{f_{p-1}(r+1,\ c),\ f_{p-1}(r,\ c+1)\} - grid(r,\ c)]$$

Algorithm 58 Threshold Kriya

```
function thresholdkriya(kg[0..m − 1][0..n − 1], γ)
    f[0..m][0..n] ← {∞}
    f[m][n − 1] ← γ
    f[m − 1][n] ← γ

    for r ∈ [m − 1, 0] do
        for c ∈ [n − 1, 0] do
```

```
7:            f[r][c] ←
8:        max{γ, Min(f[r + 1][c], f[r][c + 1]) − kg[r][c]}
9:        end for
10:    end for

11:    return f[0][0]
12: end function
```

Time complexity is $\mathcal{O}(mn)$. Space complexity is $\mathcal{O}(mn)$.

```cpp
int thresholdkriya(std::vector<std::vector<int>> &
    kg, int gamma)
{
    int m = kg.size(); // rows
    int n = kg[0].size(); // columns

    std::vector<std::vector<int>> f(m + 1, std::
        vector<int>(n + 1, std::numeric_limits<int
        >::max()));

    f[m][n-1] = f[m-1][n] = gamma; //

    for(int r = m - 1; r >= 0; r--)
    {
        for(int c = n - 1; c >= 0; c--)
        {
            f[r][c] = std::max(gamma, std::min(f[r
                +1][c], f[r][c+1]) - kg[r][c]);
        }
    }

    return f[0][0];
}
```

Algorithm 59 Threshold Kriya : Space Optimization

```
1: function thresholdkriya(kg[0..m − 1][0..n − 1], γ)
2:     f[0..n] ← {∞}
3:     f[n − 1] ← γ

4:     for r ∈ [m − 1, 0] do
5:         for c ∈ [n − 1, 0] do
6:             f[c] ← max{γ, Min(f[c], f[c + 1]) − kg[r][c]}
7:         end for
8:     end for

9:     return f[0]
10: end function
```

Time complexity is $\mathcal{O}(mn)$. Space complexity is $\mathcal{O}(n)$.

```cpp
int thresholdkriya(std::vector<std::vector<int>> &
    kg, int gamma)
```

```
{
    int m = kg.size(); // rows
    int n = kg[0].size(); // columns

    std::vector<int> f(n + 1, std::numeric_limits<
        int>::max());

    f[n-1] = gamma; //

    for(int r = m - 1; r >= 0; r--)
    {
        for(int c = n - 1; c >= 0; c--)
        {
            f[c] = std::max(gamma, std::min(f[c],
                f[c+1]) - kg[r][c]);
        }
    }

    return f[0];
}
```

Kriya Grid	γ : Min Threshold	Optimal Path	Optimal Pranayam
$\begin{matrix} -1 & -2 & 4 \\ -6 & -8 & 1 \\ 7 & 9 & -6 \end{matrix}$	3	-1->-2->4->1->-6	7 (7-1-2+4+1-6 = 3)

■

§ Problem 55. *Guru shares a secretive ordered contiguous sequence of Kriyas with his disciple Ram. Each Kriya in this sequence has two types of Pranayams :*

1. *θ : One has to practice θ Pranayams from the beginning before one can start with this Kriya. This signifies the absolute position of the Kriya in the sequence.*
2. *ϕ : One can select to practice at most ϕ Pranayams to advance to higher Kriyas. This signifies the rejuvenation step associated with the Kriya.*

It takes β Pranayams to reach Heaven. Starting with $\alpha \geq \beta$ Pranayams, determine the minimum number of rejuvenation steps needed to enter Heaven. ◊

§§ Solution. Let $f_p(l,\ k)$ be the maximum number of Pranayams one can get by using $k \leq l$ rejuvenation steps out of first l rejuvenation centers, using an optimal policy of Ram needs the minimum k such that $f_p(l,\ k) \geq \beta$ to enter Heaven.

$$\therefore f_p(l,\ k) = \begin{cases} \alpha & \text{if } k \equiv 0 \\ \underset{k \in [1,\ l]}{\text{Max}} \{f_{p-1}(l-1,\ k-1) + ks[l-1].\phi\} & \text{if } f_{p-1}(l-1,\ k-1) \geq ks[l-1].\theta \end{cases}$$

Algorithm 60 Rejuvenate Kriya

$kriya \equiv <\theta, \phi>$

function rejuvenatekriya($kriyaseq[0..n-1],\ \alpha,\ \beta$)
    $f[0..n][0..n] \leftarrow \{\alpha\}$

    for $l \in [0,\ n)$ **do**
        for $k \in [l,\ 0]$ **do**
            if $f[l][k] \geq kriyaseq[l].\theta$ **then**
                $f[l+1][k+1] \leftarrow$
                    $\mathbf{max}\{f[l+1][k+1],\ f[l][k] + kriyaseq[l].\phi\}$
            end if
        end for
    end for

    for $l \in [0,\ n]$ **do**
        for $k \in [0,\ n]$ **do**
            if $f[l][k] \geq \beta$ **then**
                return k
            end if
        end for
    end for

    return -1
end function

Time complexity is $\mathcal{O}(n^2)$. Space complexity is $\mathcal{O}(n^2)$.

```cpp
struct kriya
{
    int theta;
    int phi;
};

int rejuvenate(std::vector<kriya> & ks, int alpha,
     int beta)
{
    int n = ks.size();

    std::vector<std::vector<int>> f(n + 1, std::
        vector<int>(n + 1, alpha));

    for(int l = 0; l < n; l++)
    {
        for(int k = l; k >= 0; k--)
        {
            if(f[l][k] >= ks[l].theta)
            {
                f[l+1][k+1] = std::max(f[l+1][k
                    +1], f[l][k] + ks[l].phi);
            }
        }
    }

    for(int l = 0; l <= n; l++)
    {
        for(int k = 0; k <= n; k++)
```

```
            {
                if(f[l][k] >= beta)
                {
                    return k;
                }
            }
        }

        return -1;
}
```

Algorithm 61 Rejuvenate Kriya : Space Optimization

$kriya \equiv < \theta, \phi >$
function rejuvenatekriya($kriyaseq[0..n-1]$, α, β)
  $f[0..n] \leftarrow \{\alpha\}$

  for $l \in [0,\ n)$ **do**
    for $k \in [l,\ 0]$ **do**
      if $f[k] \geq kriyaseq[l].\theta$ **then**
        $f[k+1] \leftarrow \mathbf{max}\{f[k+1],\ f[k] + kriyaseq[l].\phi\}$
      end if
    end for
  end for

  for $l \in [0,\ n]$ **do**
    if $f[k] \geq \beta$ **then**
      return k
    end if
  end for

  return -1
end function

Time complexity is $\mathcal{O}(n^2)$. Space complexity is $\mathcal{O}(n)$.

```
int rejuvenate(std::vector<kriya> & ks, int alpha,
      int beta)
{
    int n = ks.size();

    std::vector<int> f(n + 1, alpha);

    for(int l = 0; l < n; l++)
    {
        for(int k = l; k >= 0; k--)
        {
            if(f[k] >= ks[l].theta )
            {
                f[k+1] = std::max(f[k+1], f[k] +
                    ks[l].phi);
```

```
            }
        }
    }

    for(int l = 0; l <= n; l++)
    {
        if(f[l] >= beta)
        {
            return l;
        }
    }

    return -1;
}
```

Kriya Sequence	α	β	Optimal Path	Stops
{{5, 8}, {10, 17}, {11, 6}, {15, 28}}	10	40	Start with 10 Stop at 10, Rejuvenate with 15 Stop at 15, Rejuvenate with 25 Reach at 40	2
{{20, 200}}	25	100	Start with 25 Stop at 20, Rejuvenate with 95 Reach 100	1
{{20, 200}}	30	29	Start with 30 No Stop Reach 29	0

■

§ Problem 56. *Guru shares a secretive list of α Kriyas with his disciple Ram, where each Kriya is β-dimensional, bearing $1, 2, 3, \cdots, \beta$ Pranayams. Ram is allowed to select any one out of β dimensions per Kriya at a given point of time. Practicing one-dimensional aspect of all of α Kriyas, such that total number of Pranayams is γ, opens a gateway to Heaven. Determine the total number of possible ways to enter Heaven.* ◊

§§ Solution. Let $f_n(k, p)$ be the total number of possible ways to get a sum total as p Pranayams with k Kriyas, following an optimal policy with n-steps.

$$\therefore f_n(k, p) = \begin{cases} 1 & \text{if } k \equiv 0 \text{ and } p \equiv 0 \\ \sum\limits_{\delta \in [1, \beta]} \{f_{n-1}(k-1, p-\delta)\} & \text{otherwise} \end{cases}$$

Algorithm 62 β-Dimensional Kriya

function ways2heaven(α, β, γ)
  $f[0..\alpha][0..\gamma] \leftarrow \{0\}$
  $f[0][0] \leftarrow 1$

  for $k \in [1, \alpha)$ **do**

for $\delta \in [1,\ \beta]$ **do**
    for $p \in [\delta,\ \gamma]$ **do**
        $f[k][p] \leftarrow f[k][p] + f[k-1][p-\delta]$
    end for
end for
end for

return $f[\alpha][\gamma]$
end function

Time complexity is $\mathcal{O}(\alpha\beta\gamma)$. Space complexity is $\mathcal{O}(\alpha\gamma)$.

```
int ways2heaven(int alpha, int beta, int gamma)
{
    std::vector<std::vector<int>> f(alpha + 1, std
        ::vector<int>(gamma + 1, 0));

    f[0][0] = 1;

    for(int k = 1; k <= alpha; k++)
    {
        for(int delta = 1; delta <= beta; delta++)
        {
            for(int p = delta; p <= gamma; p++)
            {
                f[k][p] += f[k-1][p - delta];
            }
        }
    }

    return f[alpha][gamma];
}
```

Algorithm 63 β-Dimensional Kriya : Space Optimization

function ways2heaven(α, β, γ)
    $f[0..\gamma] \leftarrow \{0\}$
    $f[0] \leftarrow 1$

    for $k \in [1,\ \alpha)$ **do**
        for $p \in [\gamma,\ 0]$ **do**
            $f[p] \leftarrow 0$
            for $\delta \in [1,\ \beta\ and\ p]$ **do**
                $f[p] \leftarrow f[p] + f[p-\delta]$
            end for
        end for
    end for

    return $f[\gamma]$
end function

Time complexity is $\mathcal{O}(\alpha\beta\gamma)$. Space complexity is $\mathcal{O}(\gamma)$.

```
int ways2heaven(int alpha, int beta, int gamma)
{
    std::vector<int> f(gamma + 1, 0);

    f[0] = 1;

    for(int k = 1; k <= alpha; k++)
    {
        for(int p = gamma; p >= 0; p--)
        {
            f[p] = 0;

            for(int delta = 1; delta <= beta and
                delta <= p; delta++)
            {
                f[p] += f[p - delta];
            }
        }
    }

    return f[gamma];
}
```

α	β	γ	Ways	Count
1	6	4	<4>	1
2	6	4	<1,3><3,1><2,2>	3
3	4	5	<1,1,3><1,3,1><3,1,1><2,2,1><2,1,2><1,2,2>	6
4	3	4	<1,1,1,1>	1

■

§ Problem 57. *Guru shares a secretive square Kriya n-grid with his disciple Ram. Starting from a given grid-cell*$(r,\ c)$*, Ram can move to any one out of eight possible grid-cells (up : u, down : d, left : l, right : r) at a given point of time : uul, uur, ddl, ddr, lld, llu, rrd, rru. Determine total number of possible ways of making* λ *moves.* ◊

§§ Solution. Let $f_p(x,\ y,\ m)$ be the total number of ways to reach the grid-cell$(x,\ y)$ after m moves, following an optimal policy with p-steps.

Note that the directions of the eight possible grid-cells can be represented as

$$D : (-2,-1), (-2,1), (2,-1), (2,1), (1,-2), (-1,-2), (1,2), (-1,2)$$

$$\therefore f_p(x,\ y,\ m) = \begin{cases} 1 & \text{if } m \equiv 0 \\ \sum\limits_{(dx,\ dy) \in D} \{f_{p-1}(x+dx,\ y+dy,\ m-1)\} & \text{otherwise} \end{cases}$$

Algorithm 64 Kriya Moves

function kriyamoves($n,\ \lambda,\ r,\ c$)
  if $\lambda \equiv 0$ **then**

```
        return 1
    end if
    f[0..n − 1][0..n − 1] ← {1}
    ds : <-2,-1> <-2,1> <2,-1> <2,1> <1,-2> <-1,-2> <1,2> <-1,2>    ▷ Directions

    for m ∈ [0, λ) do
        g[0..n − 1][0..n − 1] ← 0
        for i ∈ [0, n) do
            for j ∈ [0, n) do
                for d ∈ ds do
                    x ← i + d[0]
                    y ← j + d[1]
                    if x < 0 ∨ x ≥ n ∨ y < 0 ∨ y ≥ n then    ▷ Outside Kriya Grid
                        skip
                    end if
                    g[i][j] ← g[i][j] + f[x][y]
                end for
            end for
        end for
        f ← g
    end for

    return f[r][c]
end function
```

Time complexity is $\mathcal{O}(n^2\lambda)$. Space complexity is $\mathcal{O}(n^2)$.

```
int kriyamoves(int n, int lambda, int r, int c)
{
    if(lambda == 0) return 1;

    std::vector<std::vector<int>> f(n, std::vector
        <int>(n, 1));

    std::vector<std::vector<int>> ds{{-2, -1},
        {-2, 1}, {2, -1}, {2, 1}, {1, -2}, {-1,
        -2}, {1, 2}, {-1, 2}};

    for(int m = 0; m < lambda; m++)
    {
        std::vector<std::vector<int>> g(n, std::
            vector<int>(n, 0));

        for(int i = 0; i < n; i++)
        {
            for(int j = 0; j < n; j++)
            {
                for(auto d : ds)
                {
                    int x = i + d[0];
                    int y = j + d[1];
```

```
                    if(x < 0 or x >= n or y < 0 or
                        y >= n) continue;

                    g[i][j] += f[x][y];
                }
            }
        }

        f = g;
    }

    return f[r][c];
}
```

Square Grid : n	λ : Moves	<r, c>	Ways	Count
3	1	<1, 0>	<rrd> <rru >	2
3	2	<1, 0>	<rrd, llu> <rrd, uul> <rru, lld> <rru, ddl>	4
4	1	<1, 1>	<ddl> <ddr> <rru> <rrd>	4

■

§ Problem 58. *Given a sequential ordered list α of Kriyas, Ram can mark a given Kriya as positive or negative. Each Kriya bears a specific number of Pranayams. Determine total possible ways of marking the Kriyas so that total sum of Pranayams is γ.* ◊

§§ Solution. Let $f_p(k,\ s)$ be the number the ways for the first k Kriyas to reach a sum of Pranayams as s, using an optimal policy of p-steps.

$$\therefore f_p(k,\ s) = \begin{cases} 1 & \text{if } k \equiv 0 \text{ and } s \equiv 0 \\ \sum\limits_{k \in [0,\alpha)} \{f_{p-1}(k-1,\ s + kriyaseq[k]) + f_{p-1}(k-1,\ s - kriyaseq[k])\} & \text{otherwise} \end{cases}$$

Algorithm 65 Marking Kriya

function markriya($kriyaseq[0..\alpha-1],\ \gamma$)
  $f[0..\alpha][< sum, count > ....]$ ▷ pair : <sum of pranayams, count>
  $f[0][0] \leftarrow 1$

  for $k \in [0,\ \alpha)$ **do**
    for $e \in f[k]$ **do**
      $sump \leftarrow e.sump$
      $count \leftarrow e.count$

      $f[k+1][sump + kriyaseq[k]] \leftarrow f[k+1][sump + kriyaseq[k]] + count$
      $f[k+1][sump - kriyaseq[k]] \leftarrow f[k+1][sump - kriyaseq[k]] + count$
    end for
  end for

  return $f[\alpha][\gamma]$

end function

Time complexity is $\mathcal{O}(\alpha\gamma)$. Space complexity is $\mathcal{O}(\alpha\gamma)$.

```cpp
int markriya(std::vector<int> & ks, int gamma)
{
    int alpha = ks.size();

    // pair : <sum of pranayams, count>
    std::vector<std::unordered_map<int, int>> f(
        alpha + 1);

    f[0][0] = 1;

    for(int k = 0; k < alpha; k++)
    {
        for(auto & e : f[k])
        {
            int sump = e.first;
            int count = e.second;

            f[k+1][sump + ks[k]] += count;
            f[k+1][sump - ks[k]] += count;
        }
    }

    return f[alpha][gamma];
}
```

Algorithm 66 Marking Kriya : Space Optimization

function markriya($kriyaseq[0..\alpha - 1]$, γ)
  $f[< sump, count > ....]$ ▷ pair : <sum of pranayams, count>
  $f[0] \leftarrow 1$

  for $kriya \in kriyaseq$ **do**
    $g[< sump, count > ..]$
    for $e \in f$ **do**
      $sump \leftarrow e.sump$
      $count \leftarrow e.count$

      $f[sump + kriya] \leftarrow f[sump + kriya] + count$
      $f[sump - kriya] \leftarrow f[sump - kriya] + count$
    end for

    $f \leftarrow g$
  end for

  return $f[\gamma]$
end function

Time complexity is $\mathcal{O}(\alpha\gamma)$. Space complexity is $\mathcal{O}(\gamma)$.

```
int markriya(std::vector<int> & ks, int gamma)
{
    int alpha = ks.size();

    // pair : <sum of pranayams, count>
    std::unordered_map<int, int> f;

    f[0] = 1;

    for(auto kriya : ks)
    {
        std::unordered_map<int, int> g;

        for(auto e : f)
        {
            int sump = e.first;
            int count = e.second;

            g[sump + kriya] += count;
            g[sump - kriya] += count;
        }

        f = g;
    }

    return f[gamma];
}
```

Kriya Sequence	γ : Target Sum	Ways	Count
1, 2, 3, 4, 5	3	<+1-2+3-4+5> <-1+2+3+4-5> <-1-2-3+4+5>	3

■

§ Problem 59. *Given a sequence of Kriyas, where each Kriya bears a distinct number of Pranayams specific to that Kriya, determine the total possible ways to select Kriyas such that the total sum of Pranayams is λ.* ◊

§§ Solution. Let $f_n(s)$ be the number of ways to select Kriyas with sum total of Pranayams as s, following an optimal sequence with n-steps.

$$\therefore f_n(s) = \begin{cases} 1 & \text{if } s \equiv 0 \\ \sum\limits_{p \in KriyaSeq} f_{n-1}(s-p) & \text{otherwise, if } s \geq p \end{cases}$$

Algorithm 67 Kriya Selection

function kriyaways($kriyaseq[0..n-1]$, λ)
    $f[0..\lambda] \leftarrow \{0\}$
    $f[0] \leftarrow 1$

```
    for s ∈ [1, λ] do
        for p ∈ kriyaseq do
            if s ≥ p then
                f[s] ← f[s] + f[s − p]
            end if
        end for
    end for

    return f[λ]
end function
```

Time complexity is $\mathcal{O}(n\lambda)$. Space complexity is $\mathcal{O}(\lambda)$.

```cpp
int kriyaways(std::vector<int> & ks, int lambda)
{
    std::vector<int> f(lambda + 1, 0);

    f[0] = 1;

    for(int s = 1; s <= lambda; s++)
    {
        for(auto p : ks)
        {
            if(s >= p)
            {
                f[s] += f[s-p];
            }
        }
    }

    return f[lambda];
}
```

■

§ Problem 60. *Guru shares a secretive Kriya grid as shown ahead with his disciple Ram :*

1	*2*	*3*
4	*5*	*6*
7	*8*	*9*
	0	

Numbered grid-cells represent number of Pranayams associated with that Kriya.

Starting from any numbered grid-cell, Ram can move to any one out of eight possible numbered grid-cells only (up : u, down : d, left : l, right : r) at a given point of time : uul, uur, ddl, ddr, lld, llu, rrd, rru. Determine total number of possible sets of Kriyas using up to λ *moves (counting the start as a move).* ◊

§§ Solution. Possible (to and fro) paths : $paths$:

Starting Position	Possible Destinations
0	<4> <6>
1	<6> <8>
2	<7> <9>
3	<4> <8>
4	<3> <9> <0>
5	<>
6	<1> <7> <0>
7	<2> <6>
8	<1> <3>
9	<2> <4>

Let $f_n(m,\ p)$ be the number of sets of Kriyas such that the last Kriya bears p Pranayams after m moves, using an optimal sequence of n-steps.

$$\therefore f_n(m,\ p) = \begin{cases} 1 & \text{if } m \equiv 0 \\ \sum\limits_{path \in paths(p)} f_{n-1}(m-1,\ path) & \text{otherwise} \end{cases}$$

Algorithm 68 Kriya Sets : Possible Moves

```
function kriyasets(λ)
    paths : <4,6> <6,8> <7,9> <4,8> <3,9,0> <> <1,7,0> <2,6> <1,3> <2,4>
    f[0..λ − 1][0..9] ← {0}
    for p ∈ [0, 10) do
        f[0][p] ← 1                                   ▷ First Kriya
    end for

    for m ∈ [1, λ) do
        for p ∈ [0, 9] do
            for path ∈ paths[p] do
                f[m][p] ← f[m][p] + f[m − 1][path]
            end for
        end for
    end for

    nsets ← 0
    for p ∈ [0, 10) do
        nsets ← nsets + f[λ − 1][p]
    end for
    return nsets
end function
```

Time complexity is $\mathcal{O}(\lambda\times 10\times 10) \equiv \mathcal{O}(\lambda)$. Space complexity is $\mathcal{O}(\lambda \times 10) \equiv \mathcal{O}(\lambda)$.

```
int kriyasets(int lambda)
{
```

```
    std::vector<std::vector<int>> paths{{4,6},
        {6,8}, {7,9}, {4,8}, {3,9,0}, {}, {1,7,0},
         {2,6}, {1,3}, {2,4}};

    std::vector<std::vector<int>> f(lambda, std::
        vector<int>(10, 0));

    for(int p = 0; p < 10; p++)
    {
        f[0][p] = 1; // starting Kriya
    }

    for(int m = 1; m < lambda; m++)
    {
        for(int p = 0; p <= 9; p++)
        {
            for(auto path : paths[p])
            {
                f[m][p] += f[m-1][path];
            }
        }
    }

    int nsets = 0;

    for(int p = 0; p < 10; p++)
    {
        nsets += f[lambda-1][p];
    }

    return nsets;
}
```

Algorithm 69 Kriya Sets : Space Optimization

function kriyasets(λ)
  paths : <4,6> <6,8> <7,9> <4,8> <3,9,0> <> <1,7,0> <2,6> <1,3> <2,4>
  $f[0..9] \leftarrow \{1\}$

  for $m \in [1,\ \lambda)$ **do**
    $g[0..10) \leftarrow \{0\}$
    for $p \in [0,\ 9]$ **do**
      for $path \in paths[p]$ **do**
        $g[path] \leftarrow g[path] + f[p]$
      end for
    end for
    $f \leftarrow g$
  end for

  $nsets \leftarrow 0$
  for $p \in [0,\ 10)$ **do**

```
            nsets ← nsets + f[p]
        end for
        return nsets
    end function
```

Time complexity is $\mathcal{O}(\lambda)$. Space complexity is $\mathcal{O}(1)$.

```cpp
int kriyasets(int lambda)
{
    std::vector<std::vector<int>> paths{{4,6},
        {6,8}, {7,9}, {4,8}, {3,9,0}, {}, {1,7,0},
         {2,6}, {1,3}, {2,4}};

    std::vector<int> f(10, 1);

    for(int m = 1; m < lambda; m++)
    {
        std::vector<int> g(10, 0);

        for(int p = 0; p <= 9; p++)
        {
            for(auto path : paths[p])
            {
                g[path] += f[p];
            }
        }
        f = g;
    }

    int nsets = 0;

    for(int p = 0; p < 10; p++)
    {
        nsets += f[p];
    }

    return nsets;
}
```

λ : **Moves**	**No of Distinct KriyaSets**
1	10
2	20
3	46
4	104
5	240

■

§ Problem 61. *Given n Kriyas, Ram is allowed to associate any number of Pranayams from 1 to 6 at random with equal probability with any Kriya. Guru imposes a constraint that a particular Pranayam $i : \forall i \in [1,\ 6]$ can be associated at most p_i times. Determine the total possible number of distinct Pranayam-sets with n Kriyas.* ♢

§§ Solution. Let $f_p(\alpha,\ \beta,\ \gamma)$ be the number of distinct sets of Pranayam ending with γ consecutive β Pranayams with α Kriyas using an optimal sequence of p-steps.

$$\therefore f_p(\alpha,\ \beta,\ \gamma) = \begin{cases} \sum\limits_{\phi \in [1,\ p_i]} f_p(\alpha - 1,\ \lambda,\ \phi) & \text{if } \gamma \equiv 1,\ \lambda \neq \beta \\ f_p(\alpha - 1,\ \beta,\ \gamma - 1) & \text{otherwise, if } p_\beta > \gamma \end{cases}$$

Algorithm 70 Count Distinct Pranayams Sets

```
function countpranayams(n, plist[0..5])
    f[0..n][0..6][0..15] ← {0}                    ▷ Assume p_i ∈ [1, 15]
    for β ∈ [1, 6] do
        f[1][β][1] ← 1                 ▷ 1 Kriya, 1 occurrence : 1 set
    end for
    for α ∈ [2, n] do
        for β ∈ [1, 6] do
            for λ ∈ [1, 6] do
                for γ ∈ [1, plist[λ − 1] + 1] do
                    if λ ≠ β then                    ▷ Different Kriya
                        f[α][β][1] ← f[α][β][1] + f[α − 1][λ][γ]
                    else if γ < plist[λ − 1] + 1 then              ▷ Consecutive Kriya
                        f[α][β][γ] ← f[α][β][γ] + f[α − 1][β][γ − 1]
                    end if
                end for
            end for
        end for
    end for

    npsets ← 0
    for β ∈ [1, 6] do
        for γ ∈ [1, plist[β − 1]] do
            npsets ← npsets + f[n][β][γ]
        end for
    end for
    return npsets
end function
```

Time complexity is $\mathcal{O}(n)$. Space complexity is $\mathcal{O}(n)$.

```
int countpranayams(int n, std::vector<int> & plist
    )
{
    std::vector<std::vector<std::vector<int>>> f(n
        + 1, std::vector<std::vector<int>>(7, std
        ::vector<int>(16, 0)));

    for(int beta = 1; beta < 7; beta++)
    {
```

```
        f[1][beta][1] = 1; // 1 Kriya, 1 occurrence => 1 Pranayam-set
    }

    for(int alpha = 2; alpha <= n; alpha++)
    {
        for(int beta = 1; beta <= 6; beta++)
        {
            for(int lambda = 1; lambda <= 6; lambda++)
            {
                for(int gamma = 1; gamma <= plist[lambda - 1] + 1; gamma++)
                {
                    if(lambda != beta) // different Kriya
                    {
                        f[alpha][beta][1] += f[alpha - 1][lambda][gamma];
                    }
                    else if(gamma < plist[lambda - 1] + 1)
                    {
                        f[alpha][beta][gamma] += f[alpha - 1][beta][gamma - 1];
                    }
                }
            }
        }
    }

    int npsets = 0;

    for(int beta = 1; beta <= 6; beta++)
    {
        for(int gamma = 1; gamma <= plist[beta - 1]; gamma++)
        {
            npsets += f[n][beta][gamma];
        }
    }

    return npsets;
}
```

```
int countpranayams(int n, std::vector<int> & plist)
{
    // f[alpha][beta] : count of Pranayam-sets ending with beta after alpha Kriya
    std::vector<std::vector<int>> f(n + 1, std::vector<int>(7, 0));
```

```
    std::vector<int> g(n + 1); // g[alpha] = Sum(f[alpha])

    for(int beta = 0; beta < 6; beta++)
    {
        g[1] += f[1][beta] = 1; // 1 Kriya, 1 Pranayam : 1 Pranayam-set
    }

    for(int alpha = 2; alpha <= n; alpha++)
    {
        for(int beta = 0; beta < 6; beta++)
        {
            int gamma = alpha - plist[beta];
            int prune = gamma <= 1 ? std::max(gamma, 0) : g[gamma - 1] - f[gamma - 1][beta];

            f[alpha][beta] = g[alpha - 1] - prune;
            g[alpha] += f[alpha][beta];
        }
    }

    return g[n];
}
```

No of Kriyas	plist	Count of Pranayam Sets
2	<1,1,2,5,4,3>	34 (6 * 6 - 2)
2	<1,1,2,5,4,1>	33 (6 * 6 - 3)
3	<1,1,2,5,4,1>	182

■

§ **Problem 62.** *Guru shares a secretive list of Kriyas with his disciple Ram, where each Kriya bears a specific number of Pranayams. Ram is allowed to practice these Kriyas after dividing the list into two sub-sets such that total number of Pranayams in both sub-sets is equal. Determine if Ram will be able to partition the list as required.* ◊

§§ **Solution**. Let $f_p(\alpha,\ \beta)$ represents the possibility of getting the number of Pranayams as β with first α Kriyas, using an optimal policy with p-steps.

There are two possibilities :

1. the present Kriya α (which bears $list[\alpha]$ Pranayams) is not considered for summing the Pranayams to β, i.e. the first $\alpha - 1$ Kriyas adds up to β Pranayams :
$$\therefore f_p^{nc}(\alpha,\ \beta) = f_{p-1}(\alpha - 1,\ \beta)$$
2. the present Kriya α contributes to β Pranayams, i.e. the first $\alpha - 1$ Kriyas adds up to $\beta - list[\alpha]$ Pranayams and

the next Kriya contributes $list[\alpha]$ Pranayams to make the total Pranayams as β :

$$\therefore f_p^c(\alpha,\ \beta) = f_{p-1}(\alpha - 1,\ \beta - list[\alpha])$$

$$\therefore f_p(\alpha,\ \beta) = f_p^{nc}(\alpha,\ \beta) \textbf{ or } f_p^c(\alpha,\ \beta) = f_{p-1}(\alpha - 1,\ \beta) \textbf{ or } f_{p-1}(\alpha - 1,\ \beta - list[\alpha])$$

Algorithm 71 Partition Kriya : Iso-Pranayams Sets

function partitionkriya($list[0..n-1]$)
  $sump \leftarrow$ **sum**($list[0..n-1]$)
  if $sump$ is not even **then** ▷ Not possible to partition into two equal sum sets
    return $false$
  end if
  $targetp \leftarrow \frac{sump}{2}$
  $f[0..n][0..targetp] \leftarrow \{false\}$
  $f[0][0] \leftarrow true$
  for $\alpha \in [1,\ n]$ **do**
    $f[\alpha][0] \leftarrow true$
  end for
  for $\beta \in [1,\ targetp]$ **do**
    $f[0][\beta] \leftarrow false$ ▷ No Kriya : No sum to β
  end for
  for $\alpha \in [1,\ n]$ **do**
    for $\beta \in [1,\ targetp]$ **do**
      $f[\alpha][\beta] \leftarrow f[\alpha - 1]\beta]$
      if $\beta \geq list[\alpha - 1]$ **then**
        $f[\alpha][\beta] \leftarrow f[\alpha][\beta]$ **or** $f[\alpha - 1][\beta - list[\alpha - 1]]$
      end if
    end for
  end for
  return $f[n][targetp]$
end function

Time complexity is $\mathcal{O}(n \times sum)$. Space complexity is $\mathcal{O}(n \times sum)$.

```cpp
bool partitionkriya(std::vector<int> & list)
{
    int sump = 0;

    for(auto p : list)
    {
        sump += p;
    }

    if(sump % 2 != 0) // odd : (sump & 1) == 1
    {
        return false;
    }

    int targetp = sump / 2;
```

```cpp

    int n = list.size();

    std::vector<std::vector<int>> f(n + 1, std::vector<int>(targetp + 1, false));

    f[0][0] = true;

    for(int alpha = 1; alpha < n + 1; alpha++)
    {
        f[alpha][0] = true;
    }

    for(int beta = 1; beta < targetp + 1; beta++)
    {
        f[0][beta] = false; // No Kriya => not possible to sum to beta
    }

    for(int alpha = 1; alpha < n + 1; alpha++)
    {
        for(int beta = 1; beta < targetp + 1; beta++)
        {
            f[alpha][beta] = f[alpha - 1][beta];

            if(beta >= list[alpha - 1])
            {
                f[alpha][beta] = f[alpha][beta] or f[alpha - 1][beta - list[alpha - 1]];
            }
        }
    }

    return f[n][targetp];
}
```

Algorithm 72 Partition Kriya : Iso-Pranayams Sets : Space Optimization

function partitionkriya($list[0..n-1]$)
  $sump \leftarrow$ **sum**($list[0..n-1]$)
  if $sump$ is not even **then** ▷ Not possible to partition into two equal sum sets
    return $false$
  end if
  $targetp \leftarrow \dfrac{sump}{2}$
  $f[0..targetp] \leftarrow \{false\}$
  $f[0] \leftarrow true$
  for $p \in list[0..n-1]$ **do**
    for $\beta \in [targetp, 1]$ **do**

if $\beta \geq p$ **then**
$f[\beta] \leftarrow f[\beta]$ **or** $f[\beta - p]$
end if
end for
end for
return $f[targetp]$
end function

Time complexity is $\mathcal{O}(n \times sum)$. Space complexity is $\mathcal{O}(sum)$.

```
bool partitionkriya(std::vector<int> & list)
{
    int sump = 0;

    for(auto p : list)
    {
        sump += p;
    }

    if(sump & 1 == true) // odd
    {
        return false;
    }

    int targetp = sump / 2;

    int n = list.size();

    std::vector<int> f(targetp + 1, false);

    f[0] = true;

    for(auto p : list)
    {
        for(int beta = targetp; beta > 0; beta--)
        {
            if(beta >= p)
            {
                f[beta] = f[beta] or f[beta - p];
            }
        }
    }

    return f[targetp];
}
```

Kriya List	Partition ?
<3, 8, 13, 2>	Yes (<3, 8, 2> <13>)
<4, 8, 13, 2>	No

■

§ Problem 63. *Guru shares two Kriyas : K_α and K_β with his disciple Ram, where each Kriya bears γ Pranayams. Allowed practice sessions consist of the following four equal-probable operations :*

1. *Practice 100 Pranayams of K_α and 0 Pranayams of K_β*
2. *Practice 75 Pranayams of K_α and 25 Pranayams of K_β*
3. *Practice 50 Pranayams of K_α and 50 Pranayams of K_β*
4. *Practice 25 Pranayams of K_α and 75 Pranayams of K_β*

Ram can practice the remaining Pranayams in case if it is less than the required one for the operation. Determine the probability that Ram will be able to finish practice of the Kriya K_α first, plus half the probability of finishing practice of both Kriyas simultaneously. ◊

§§ Solution. Let $f_p(\alpha,\ \beta)$ be the required probability with α units of Pranayams of Kriya K_α and β units of Pranayams of Kriya K_β, using an optimal policy with p-steps.

Treating 25 Pranayams as one unit, these four operations with the respective probabilities are:

1. 4 of K_α and 0 of K_β : $f_{p-1}(\alpha-4,\ \beta) \equiv f^a_{p-1}$
2. 3 of K_α and 1 of K_β : $f_{p-1}(\alpha-3,\ \beta-1) \equiv f^b_{p-1}$
3. 2 of K_α and 2 of K_β : $f_{p-1}(\alpha-2,\ \beta-2) \equiv f^c_{p-1}$
4. 1 of K_α and 3 of K_β : $f_{p-1}(\alpha-1,\ \beta-3) \equiv f^d_{p-1}$

$$\therefore f_p(\alpha,\ \beta) = \begin{cases} 0.5 & \text{if } \alpha \le 0 \wedge \beta \le 0 \\ 1.0 & \text{if } \alpha \le 0 \\ 0.0 & \text{if } \beta \le 0 \\ \frac{1}{4}\{f^a_{p-1} + f^b_{p-1} + f^c_{p-1} + f^d_{p-1}\} & \text{otherwise} \end{cases}$$

Algorithm 73 Kriya Probability

```
function pkriya(α, β, g[0..γ][0..γ])
    if α ≤ 0 and β ≤ 0 then
        return 0.5
    end if
    if α ≤ 0 then
        return 1.0
    end if
    if β ≤ 0 then
        return 0.0
    end if
    if g[α][β] > 0 then
        return g[α][β]
    end if
    a ← pkriya(α − 4, β, g)
    b ← pkriya(α − 3, β − 1, g)
    c ← pkriya(α − 2, β − 2, g)
    d ← pkriya(α − 1, β − 3, g)
    g[α][β] ← 0.25[a + b + c + d]
    return g[α][β]
end function
```

function probkriya(γ)
  $f[0..\gamma][0..\gamma] \leftarrow \{0\}$
  return $pkriya\left(\frac{\gamma}{4}, \frac{\gamma}{4}, f\right)$
end function

Time complexity is $\mathcal{O}(n^2)$. Space complexity is $\mathcal{O}(n^2)$.

```
double pkriya(int alpha, int beta, std::vector<std
    ::vector<double>> & g)
{
    if(alpha <= 0 and beta <= 0) return 0.5;

    if(alpha <= 0) return 1.0;

    if(beta <= 0) return 0.0;

    if(g[alpha][beta] > 0) return g[alpha][beta];

    g[alpha][beta] = 0.25 *(pkriya(alpha - 4, beta
        , g) + pkriya(alpha - 3, beta - 1, g) +
        pkriya(alpha - 2, beta - 2, g) + pkriya(
        alpha - 1, beta - 3, g));

    return g[alpha][beta];
}


double probkriya(int gamma)
{
    std::vector<std::vector<double>> f(gamma + 1,
        std::vector<double>(gamma + 1, 0.0));

    return pkriya(gamma/25, gamma/25, f);
}
```

γ	**Probability**
50	0.625 $[0.25 \times (1 + 1 + 0.5 + 0)]$
100	0.71875
150	0.757812

■

§ Problem 64. *Guru shares a secretive* $2 \times n$ *Kriya grid with his disciple Ram. Ram is allowed to practice Kriyas in only in a set of 2 adjacent grid-cells like* 2×1 *or* 1×2 *:*

1. 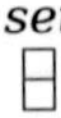
2. 

or 3 grid-cells of **L***-shape which can be rotated like*

1. 
2. 
3. 
4. 

Determine total number of ways to practice the entire Kriya grid by using any combinations of the six sets enlisted before. ◊

§§ **Solution**. Let $f_p(n)$ be the required number of ways following an optimal sequence of p-steps. There are three possibilities to move forward grid-by-grid:

1. Start with one  to cover one grid-cell, i.e. $2 \times 1 : f_{p-1}(n-1)$
2. Start with two  like  to cover two grid-cells, i.e. $2 \times 2 : f_{p-1}(n-2)$
3. Start with any combination of two **L**-shaped ones to cover three grid-cells, i.e. 2×3 and $n-3$ of  or  to cover the rest of $n-3$ grid-cells, i.e. $2 \times (n-3) : 2\sum_{k=0}^{n-3} f_{p-1}(k)$

$$
\begin{aligned}
\therefore f_p(n) &= f_{p-1}(n-1) + f_{p-1}(n-2) + 2\sum_{k=0}^{n-3} f_{p-1}(k) \\
&= f_{p-1}(n-1) + f_{p-1}(n-3) + \left[f_{p-1}(n-2) + f_{p-1}(n-3) + 2\sum_{k=0}^{n-4} f_{p-1}(k) \right] \\
&= f_{p-1}(n-1) + f_{p-1}(n-3) + f_{p-1}(n-1) \\
\therefore f_p(n) &= 2f_{p-1}(n-1) + f_{p-1}(n-3) : n > 3
\end{aligned}
$$

Note that (p-subscript is omitted for simplicity), for a given n, $f(n-1)$ and $f(n-2)$ contribute to $f(n)$ in one way, whereas $f(n-3) \cdots f(0)$ contribute to $f(n)$ in two ways:

$f(0) = 1$

$f(1) = 1 \equiv$ 

$f(2) = 2 \equiv$ 

$f(3) = 5 \equiv$  $\equiv f2 +$ , $f(1) +$ 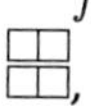, $f(0) +$ 

$f(4) = 11 \equiv f(3) +$ , $f(2)+$ , $f(1) +$ , $f(0) +$ 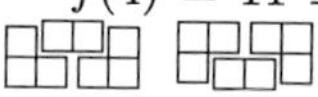

$$
\begin{aligned}
\therefore f(n) &= f(n-1) + f(n-2) + 2[f(n-3) + \cdots + f(0)] \\
&= 2f(n-1) + f(n-3)
\end{aligned}
$$

$$
\therefore f_p(n) = \begin{cases} 1 & \text{if } 0 \le n \le 2 \\ 2f_{p-1}(n-1) + f_{p-1}(n-3) & \text{if } n \ge 3 \end{cases}
$$

Algorithm 74 Combine Kriya

```
function combinekriya(n)
```

```
2:     f[0..n] ← {1}
3:     f[2] ← 2
4:     for i ∈ [3, n] do
5:         f[i] ← 2f[i − 1] + f[i − 3]
6:     end for
7:     return f[n]
8: end function
```

Time complexity is $\mathcal{O}(n)$. Space complexity is $\mathcal{O}(n)$.

```cpp
int combinekriya(int n)
{
    std::vector<int> f(n + 1, 1);

    f[2] = 2;

    for(int i = 3; i <= n; i++)
    {
        f[i] = 2 * f[i - 1] + f[i - 3];
    }

    return f[n];
}
```

Grid	Ways to cover grid
2×3	5
2×4	11
2×5	24

■

Chapter 14

Kriya Sequence

§ Problem 65. *Guru shares two secretive Kriya contiguous sequences, K_α and K_β with his disciple Ram, having the same number n of Kriyas in each sequence. Each Kriya bears a certain number of Pranayams specific to that Kriya. Ram is allowed to interchange the Kriya K_α^i with K_β^i, where $i \in [0,\ n-1]$. Determine the minimum possible interchanges required to sort both the sequences in strictly non-decreasing order.* ◇

§§ Solution. Let $f_p(i)$ be the minimum interchanges required to sort up to K_α^i and K_β^i, using an optimal policy with p-steps.

$$\therefore f_p(i) = \text{Min}\Big[f_p^{ic}(i),\ f_p^{noic}(i)\Big]$$

where $f_p^{ic}(i)$ and $f_p^{noic}(i)$ stand for the minimum interchanges required to sort up to K_α^i and K_β^i with and without interchanging K_α^i with K_β^i respectively.

$$\therefore f_p^{ic}(i) = \begin{cases} f_{p-1}^{ic}(i-1)+1 & \text{if } K_\alpha^{i-1} < K_\alpha^i \text{ and } K_\beta^{i-1} < K_\beta^i \\ f_{p-1}^{noic}(i-1)+1 & \text{if } K_\alpha^{i-1} < K_\beta^i \text{ and } K_\beta^{i-1} < K_\alpha^i \end{cases}$$

$$\therefore f_p^{noic}(i) = \begin{cases} f_{p-1}^{noic}(i-1) & \text{if } K_\alpha^{i-1} < K_\alpha^i \text{ and } K_\beta^{i-1} < K_\beta^i \\ f_{p-1}^{ic}(i-1) & \text{if } K_\alpha^{i-1} < K_\beta^i \text{ and } K_\beta^{i-1} < K_\alpha^i \end{cases}$$

Algorithm 75 Sort Kriya : Optimal Interchanges

```
function sortkriya(ka[0..n − 1], kb[0..n − 1])
```

$fic[0..n-1] \leftarrow \{\infty\}$
$fnoic[0..n-1] \leftarrow \{\infty\}$
$fic[0] \leftarrow 1$
$fnoic[0] \leftarrow 0$

for $i \in [1, n-1]$ **do**
  if $ka[i-1] < ka[i]$ and $kb[i-1] < kb[i]$ **then**
    $fic[i] \leftarrow fic[i-1]+1$ ▷ interchange ka[i-1] with kb[i-1] and ka[i] with kb[i]
    $fnoic[i] \leftarrow fnoic[i-1]$
  end if
  if $ka[i-1] < kb[i]$ and $kb[i-1] < ka[i]$ **then**
    $fic[i] \leftarrow$ **min**$(fic[i],\ fnoic[i-1]+1)$ ▷ no interchange of ka[i-1] with kb[i-1]
    $fnoic[i] \leftarrow$ **min**$(fnoic[i],\ fic[i-1])$ ▷ interchange of ka[i-1] with kb[i-1]
  end if
end for
return min$(fic[n-1],\ fnoic[n-1])$
end function

Time complexity is $\mathcal{O}(n)$. Space complexity is $\mathcal{O}(n)$.

```
int sortkriya(std::vector<int> & ka, std::vector<int> & kb)
{
    int n = ka.size();

    std::vector<int> fic(n, std::numeric_limits<int>::max());
    std::vector<int> fnoic(n, std::numeric_limits<int>::max());

    fic[0] = 1;
    fnoic[0] = 0;

    for(int i = 1; i < n; i++)
    {
        if(ka[i-1] < ka[i] and kb[i-1] < kb[i])
        {
            fic[i] = fic[i-1] + 1; // interchange ka[i-1] with kb[i-1] and ka[i] with kb[i]
            fnoic[i] = fnoic[i-1]; // no interchange required
        }

        if(ka[i-1] < kb[i] and kb[i-1] < ka[i])
        {
            fic[i] = std::min(fic[i], fnoic[i-1] + 1); // no interchange of ka[i-1] with kb[i-1], interchange of ka[i] with kb[i]
            fnoic[i] = std::min(fnoic[i], fic[i
```

```
                    -1]); // interchange of ka[i-1]
                    with kb[i-1], no interchange
                    required for ka[i] with kb[i]
        }
    }

    return std::min(fic[n-1], fnoic[n-1]);
}
```

Algorithm 76 Sort Kriya : Space Optimization

function sortkriya($ka[0..n-1]$, $kb[0..n-1]$)
    $ic \leftarrow 1$
    $noic \leftarrow 0$

    for $i \in [1,\ n-1]$ **do**
        $icnxt \leftarrow \infty$
        $noicnxt \leftarrow \infty$
        if $ka[i-1] < ka[i]$ and $kb[i-1] < kb[i]$ **then**
            $icnxt \leftarrow$ **min**$(icnxt,\ ic+1)$ ▷ interchange ka[i-1] with kb[i-1] and ka[i] with kb[i]
            $noicnxt \leftarrow$ **min**$(noicnxt,\ noic)$ ▷ no interchange required
        end if
        if $ka[i-1] < kb[i]$ and $kb[i-1] < ka[i]$ **then**
            $icnxt \leftarrow$ **min**$(icnxt,\ noic+1)$ ▷ no interchange of ka[i-1] with kb[i-1]
            $noicnxt \leftarrow$ **min**$(noicnxt,\ ic)$ ▷ interchange of ka[i-1] with kb[i-1]
        end if
        $ic \leftarrow icnxt$
        $noic \leftarrow noicnxt$
    end for
    return min$(ic,\ noic)$
end function

Time complexity is $\mathcal{O}(n)$. Space complexity is $\mathcal{O}(1)$.

```
int sortkriya(std::vector<int> & ka, std::vector<
    int> & kb)
{
    int n = ka.size();

    int ic = 1;
    int noic = 0;

    for(int i = 1; i < n; i++)
    {
        int icnxt = std::numeric_limits<int>::max
            ();
        int noicnxt = std::numeric_limits<int>::
            max();
```

```
        if(ka[i-1] < ka[i] and kb[i-1] < kb[i])
        {
            icnxt = std::min(icnxt, ic + 1); // interchange ka[i-1] with kb[i-1] and ka[i] with kb[i]
            noicnxt = std::min(noicnxt, noic); // no interchange required
        }

        if(ka[i-1] < kb[i] and kb[i-1] < ka[i])
        {
            icnxt = std::min(icnxt, noic + 1); // no interchange of ka[i-1] with kb[i-1], interchange of ka[i] with kb[i]
            noicnxt = std::min(noicnxt, ic); // interchange of ka[i-1] with kb[i-1], no interchange required for ka[i] with kb[i]
        }

        ic = icnxt;
        noic = noicnxt;
    }

    return std::min(ic, noic);
}
```

K_α	K_β	**Optimal Interchanges**
<1, 6, 9, 8>	<2, 5, 7, 10>	1 : interchange the last elements
<7, 6, 9, 8>	<2, 8, 7, 10>	2 : interchange the first and third elements

■

§ Problem 66. *Guru shares a secretive contiguous sequence of Kriyas with his disciple Ram, where each Kriya has its own distinct number of Pranayams. Determine the number of longest increasing subsequences of Kriyas.* ◊

§§ Solution. Let $f_p(k)$ be the number of longest increasing subsequences ending with the Kriya s_k and $g_p(k)$ be the corresponding length, following an optimal sequence of p-steps.

$$\therefore g_p(k) = \left\{ \text{ Max}[g_{p-1}(l) + 1] \quad \forall\, l \in [0,\ k) \text{ if } s_k > s_l \right.$$

$$\therefore f_p(k) = \left\{ \sum_{l \in [0,\ k)} f_{p-1}(l) \quad \text{if } s_k \equiv s_l + 1 \right.$$

Algorithm 77 Longest Increasing Subsequence (LIS) of Kriyas

```
function liskriya(s[0..n − 1])
    maxl ← 0                                   ▷ length of lis
    nlis ← 0                                   ▷ number of lis
    f[0..n − 1] ← {1}                          ▷ number of lis ending with s[k] : 0 ≤ k < n
    g[0..n − 1] ← {1}                          ▷ length of lis ending with s[k] : 0 ≤ k < n

    for k ∈ [0, n) do
        for l ∈ [0, k) do
            if s[k] > s[l] then
                if g[l] + 1 > g[k] then
                    g[k] ← g[l] + 1
                    f[k] ← f[l]
                else if g[l] + 1 ≡ g[k] then
                    f[k] ← f[k] + f[l]
                end if
            end if
        end for
        maxl ← max(maxl, g[k])
    end for
    for k ∈ [0, n) do
        if g[k] ≡ maxl then
            nlis ← nlis + f[k]
        end if
    end for
    return nlis
end function
```

Time complexity is $\mathcal{O}(n^2)$. Space complexity is $\mathcal{O}(n)$.

```cpp
//lis : longest increasing subsequence

int liskriya(std::vector<int> & s)
{
    int n = s.size(); // number of Kriyas

    int maxl = 0; // length of lis
    int nlis = 0; // number of lis

    std::vector<int> f(n, 1); // number of lis
        ending with s[k] : 0 <= k < n
    std::vector<int> g(n, 1); // length of lis
        ending with s[k] : 0 <= k < n

    for(int k = 0; k < n; k++)
    {
        for(int l = 0; l < k; l++)
        {
            if(s[k] > s[l])
            {
                if(g[l] + 1 > g[k])
                {
```

```
                g[k] = g[l] + 1;
                f[k] = f[l];
            }
            else if(g[l] + 1 == g[k])
            {
                f[k] += f[l];
            }
        }
    }

    maxl = std::max(maxl, g[k]);
}

for(int k = 0; k < n; k++)
{
    if(g[k] == maxl)
    {
        nlis += f[k];
    }
}

return nlis;
}
```

Kriya Sequence	LIS Kriyas	Count of LIS
<1, 2, 4, 3, 6>	<1, 2, 4, 6> <1, 2, 3, 6>	2
<1, 2, 4, 3, 6, 5>	<1, 2, 4, 6> <1, 2, 4, 5> <1, 2, 3, 6> <1, 2, 3, 5>	4

■

§ Problem 67. *Determine total number of possible ways of forming Kriya sequences of length n using five Kriyas : α, β, γ, δ and θ : obeying the following constraints:*

- $\alpha \implies \beta$, *i.e. α may only be followed by β.*
- $\beta \implies \alpha$ *or* γ.
- $\gamma \not\Rightarrow \gamma$, *i.e. γ may not be followed by γ.*
- $\delta \implies \gamma$ *or* θ.
- $\theta \implies \alpha$.

◊

§§ Solution. Let the Kriyas be indexed as :

Kriya	α	β	γ	δ	θ
Index	0	1	2	3	4

Let $f_p(m,\ k)$ be the number of ways of forming Kriya sequences with $m \in [0,\ 5]$ Kriyas ending with k^{th} index Kriya : $k \in [0,\ 4]$.

$$\therefore f_p(m,\ k) = \begin{cases} 1 & \forall k \in [0,\ 4],\ \text{if } m \equiv 0 \\ f_{p-1}(m-1,\ 1) & \text{if } k \equiv 0 \\ f_{p-1}(m-1,\ 0) + f_{p-1}(m-1,\ 2) & \text{if } k \equiv 1 \\ f_{p-1}(m-1,\ 0) + f_{p-1}(m-1,\ 1) + f_{p-1}(m-1,\ 3) + f_{p-1}(m-1,\ 4) & \text{if } k \equiv 2 \\ f_{p-1}(m-1,\ 2) + f_{p-1}(m-1,\ 4) & \text{if } k \equiv 3 \\ f_{p-1}(m-1,\ 0) & \text{if } k \equiv 4 \end{cases}$$

Algorithm 78 Permute Kriyas

```
function permutekriya(n)
    f[0..n − 1][0..4] ← {0}
    f[0] ← {1, 1, 1, 1, 1}
    for m ∈ [1, n) do
        f[m][0] ← f[m − 1][1]                                  ▷ α ⟹ β
        f[m][1] ← f[m − 1][0] + f[m − 1][2]                    ▷ β ⟹ α, γ
        f[m][2] ← f[m−1][0] + f[m−1][1] + f[m−1][3] + f[m−1][4]  ▷ γ ⟹ α, β, δ, θ
        f[m][3] ← f[m − 1][2] + f[m − 1][4]                    ▷ δ ⟹ γ, θ
        f[m][4] ← f[m − 1][0]                                  ▷ θ ⟹ α
    end for
    return f[n − 1][0] + f[n − 1][1] + f[n − 1][2] + f[n − 1][3] + f[n − 1][4]
end function
```

Time complexity is $\mathcal{O}(n)$. Space complexity is $\mathcal{O}(n)$.

```cpp
int permutekriya(int n)
{
    std::vector<std::vector<int>> f(n, std::vector<int>(5, 0));

    f[0] = {1, 1, 1, 1, 1};

    for(int m = 1; m < n; m++)
    {
        // 0 => 1 : alpha => beta
        f[m][0] = f[m - 1][1];

        // 1 => 0, 2 : beta => alpha, gamma
        f[m][1] = f[m - 1][0] + f[m - 1][2];

        // 2 => 0, 1, 3, 4 : gamma => alpha, beta, delta, theta
        f[m][2] = f[m - 1][0] + f[m - 1][1] + f[m - 1][3] + f[m - 1][4];

        // 3 => 2, 4 : delta => gamma, theta
        f[m][3] = f[m - 1][2] + f[m - 1][4];

        // 4 => 0 : theta => alpha
        f[m][4] = f[m - 1][0];
    }

    return f[n-1][0] + f[n-1][1] + f[n-1][2] + f[n-1][3] + f[n-1][4];
}
```

n	Count
1	5 : α, β, γ, δ and θ
2	10 : $\alpha\beta$, $\beta\alpha$, $\beta\gamma$, $\gamma\alpha$, $\gamma\beta$, $\gamma\delta$, $\gamma\theta$, $\delta\gamma$, $\delta\theta$ and $\theta\alpha$
3	19
4	35
5	68

■

§ Problem 68. *Guru shares two sequences of Kriyas with his disciple Ram. Determine the maximum possible number of Kriyas in their common subsequence.* ◊

§§ Solution. $<\delta_1, \delta_2, \cdots, \delta_p>$ is a subsequence of $<\alpha_1, \alpha_2, \cdots, \alpha_m>$ if $\alpha_{i_j} \equiv \delta_j \; \forall j \in [1, p] : i_1 < i_2 < \cdots < i_p$.

If $<\delta_1, \delta_2, \cdots, \delta_p>$ is the common subsequence of $<\alpha_1, \alpha_2, \cdots, \alpha_m>$ and $<\beta_1, \beta_2, \cdots, \beta_n>$ having maximum possible number of Kriyas (say LCS : Longest Common Subsequence), then

1. if $\alpha_m \equiv \beta_n$, then $\delta_p \equiv \alpha_m \equiv \beta_n$ and $<\delta_1, \delta_2, \cdots, \delta_{p-1}>$ is an LCS of $<\alpha_1, \alpha_2, \cdots, \alpha_{m-1}>$ and $<\beta_1, \beta_2, \cdots, \beta_{n-1}>$.
2. if $\alpha_m \neq \beta_n$, then $\delta_p \neq \alpha_m \implies : <\delta_1, \delta_2, \cdots, \delta_p>$ is an LCS of $<\alpha_1, \alpha_2, \cdots, \alpha_{m-1}>$ and $<\beta_1, \beta_2, \cdots, \beta_n>$.
3. if $\alpha_m \neq \beta_n$, then $\delta_p \neq \beta_n \implies : <\delta_1, \delta_2, \cdots, \delta_p>$ is an LCS of $<\alpha_1, \alpha_2, \cdots, \alpha_m>$ and $<\beta_1, \beta_2, \cdots, \beta_{n-1}>$.

Let $f_q(i, j)$ be the length of the LCS of $<\alpha_1, \alpha_2, \cdots, \alpha_i>$ and $<\beta_1, \beta_2, \cdots, \beta_j>$, using an optimal policy of q-steps.

$$\therefore f_q(i, j) = \begin{cases} 0 & \text{if } i \equiv 0 \text{ or } j \equiv 0 \\ f_{q-1}(i-1, j-1) + 1 & \text{if } i, j > 0 \text{ and } \alpha_i \equiv \beta_j \\ \text{Max}[f_{q-1}(i, j-1) + f_{q-1}(i-1, j)] & \text{if } i, j > 0 \text{ and } \alpha_i \neq \beta_j \end{cases}$$

Algorithm 79 Length of LCS Kriya

```
function lcskriya(α[0..m − 1], β[0..n − 1])
    f[0..m][0..n] ← {0}
    for i ∈ [1, m] do
        for j ∈ [1, n] do
            if α[i − 1] ≡ β[j − 1] then
                f[i][j] ← f[i − 1][j − 1] + 1
            else
                f[i][j] ← max(f[i][j − 1], f[i − 1][j])
            end if
        end for
    end for
    return f[m][n]
end function
```

Time complexity is $\mathcal{O}(mn)$. Space complexity is $\mathcal{O}(mn)$.

```cpp
int lcskriya(std::vector<int> & alpha, std::vector
    <int> & beta)
{
    int m = alpha.size();
    int n = beta.size();


    std::vector<std::vector<int>> f(m + 1, std::
        vector<int>(n + 1, 0));

    for(int i = 1; i <= m; i++)
    {
        for(int j = 1; j <= n; j++)
        {
            if(alpha[i-1] == beta[j-1])
            {
                f[i][j] = f[i-1][j-1] + 1;
            }
            else
            {
                f[i][j] = std::max(f[i][j-1], f[i
                    -1][j]);
            }
        }
    }

    return f[m][n];
}
```

Reconstruction from the optimal solution to find the LCS itself :

Algorithm 80 LCS Kriya

function lcskriya($\alpha[0..m-1]$, $\beta[0..n-1]$)
  $f[0..m-1][0..n-1] \leftarrow \{0\}$
  for $i \in [1,\ m]$ **do**
    for $j \in [1,\ n]$ **do**
      if $\alpha[i-1] \equiv \beta[j-1]$ **then**
        $f[i][j] \leftarrow f[i-1][j-1] + 1$
      else
        $f[i][j] \leftarrow$ **max**$(f[i][j-1],\ f[i-1][j])$
      end if
    end for
  end for
  $len \leftarrow f[m][n]$ ▷ length of LCS
  $lcs[0..len-1] \leftarrow \{0\}$
  $i \leftarrow m$
  $j \leftarrow n$
  while $i > 0$ and $j > 0$ **do**
    if $\alpha[i-1] \equiv \beta[j-1]$ **then**
      $lcs[len-1] \leftarrow \alpha[i-1]$

```
            i ← i − 1
            j ← j − 1
            len ← len − 1
        else if f[i − 1][j] > f[i][j − 1] then
            i ← i − 1
        else
            j ← j − 1
        end if
    end while
    return lcs
end function
```

Time complexity is $\mathcal{O}(mn)$. Space complexity is $\mathcal{O}(mn)$. Time complexity of the reconstruction part (i.e. while loop) is $\mathcal{O}(m+n)$.

```cpp
std::vector<int> lcskriya(std::vector<int> & alpha
    , std::vector<int> & beta)
{
    int m = alpha.size();
    int n = beta.size();


    std::vector<std::vector<int>> f(m + 1, std::::
        vector<int>(n + 1, 0));

    for(int i = 1; i <= m; i++)
    {
        for(int j = 1; j <= n; j++)
        {
            if(alpha[i-1] == beta[j-1])
            {
                f[i][j] = f[i-1][j-1] + 1;
            }
            else
            {
                f[i][j] = std::max(f[i][j-1], f[i
                    -1][j]);
            }
        }
    }

    int len = f[m][n]; // length of LCS

    std::vector<int> lcs(len, 0);

    int i = m, j = n;

    while(i > 0 and j > 0)
    {
        if(alpha[i-1] == beta[j-1])
        {
            lcs[len-1] = alpha[i-1];
            --i;
            --j;
```

```
            --len;
        }
        else if(f[i-1][j] > f[i][j-1])
        {
            --i;
        }
        else
        {
            --j;
        }
    }

    return lcs;
}
```

First Kriya Seq	Second Kriya Seq	LCS	Count
<1, 2, 3, 2, 4, 1, 2>	<2, 4, 3, 1, 2, 1>	2412 2312 2321	4
<1, 2, 3, 4, 5>	<1, 3, 5>	<1, 3, 5>	3
<1, 4, 3, 5>	<4, 5, 6>	<4, 5>	2
<1, 2, 3, 4>	<4, 5, 6>	<4>	1
<1, 2, 3>	<4, 5, 6>	<>	0
<1, 2, 3>	<1, 2, 3>	<1, 2, 3>	3

Recursive approach to print LCS :

Algorithm 81 Compute and Print LCS Kriya

function printlcs($f[0..m][0..n]$, $\alpha[0..m-1]$, $\beta[0..n-1]$, i, j)
    if $i \equiv 0$ or $j \equiv 0$ **then**
        return
    end if
    if $\alpha[i-1] \equiv \beta[j-1]$ **then**
        printlcs(f, α, β, $i-1$, $j-1$)
        print $\alpha[i-1]$
    else if $f[i][j-1] > f[i-1][j]$ **then**
        printlcs(f, α, β, i, $j-1$)
    else
        printlcs(f, α, β, $i-1$, j)
    end if
end function

function lcskriya($\alpha[0..m-1]$, $\beta[0..n-1]$)
    $f[0..m-1][0..n-1] \leftarrow \{0\}$
    for $i \in [1, m]$ **do**
        for $j \in [1, n]$ **do**
            if $\alpha[i-1] \equiv \beta[j-1]$ **then**
                $f[i][j] \leftarrow f[i-1][j-1] + 1$
            else

```
                $f[i][j] \leftarrow$ max($f[i][j-1]$, $f[i-1][j]$)
            end if
        end for
    end for

    printlcs($f$, $\alpha$, $\beta$, $m$, $n$)
end function
```

Time complexity of the function **printlcs** is $\mathcal{O}(m+n)$.

```cpp
void printlcs(std::vector<std::vector<int>> & f,
    std::vector<int> & alpha, std::vector<int> &
    beta, int i, int j)
{
    if(i == 0 or j == 0) return;

    if(alpha[i-1] == beta[j-1])
    {
        printlcs(f, alpha, beta, i-1, j-1);
        std::cout << alpha[i-1];
    }
    else if(f[i][j-1] > f[i-1][j])
    {
        printlcs(f, alpha, beta, i, j-1);
    }
    else
    {
        printlcs(f, alpha, beta, i-1, j);
    }
}

void lcskriya(std::vector<int> & alpha, std::
    vector<int> & beta)
{
    int m = alpha.size();
    int n = beta.size();


    std::vector<std::vector<int>> f(m + 1, std::
        vector<int>(n + 1, 0));

    for(int i = 1; i <= m; i++)
    {
        for(int j = 1; j <= n; j++)
        {
            if(alpha[i-1] == beta[j-1])
            {
                f[i][j] = f[i-1][j-1] + 1;
            }
            else
            {
                f[i][j] = std::max(f[i][j-1], f[i
                    -1][j]);
            }
        }
```

```
    }

    printlcs(f, alpha, beta, m, n);
}
```

Alternatively :

Algorithm 82 Compute and Print LCS Kriya : Alternative

function printlcs($g[0..m][0..n],\ \alpha[0..m-1],\ i,\ j$)
    $Directions : None = 0,\ Up = 1,\ Left = 2,\ UpLeft = 3$
    if $i \equiv 0$ or $j \equiv 0$ **then**
        return
    end if
    if $g[i][j] \equiv UpLeft$ **then**
        printlcs($f,\ \alpha,\ i-1,\ j-1$)
        print $\alpha[i-1]$
    else if $g[i][j] \equiv Up$ **then**
        printlcs($g,\ \alpha,\ i-1,\ j$)
    else
        printlcs($g,\ \alpha,\ i,\ j-1$)
    end if
end function

function lcskriya($\alpha[0..m-1],\ \beta[0..n-1]$)
    $f[0..m][0..n] \leftarrow \{0\}$
    $g[0..m][0..n] \leftarrow \{0\}$
    for $i \in [0,\ m]$ **do**
        $g[i][0] \leftarrow Up$
    end for
    for $j \in [0,\ n]$ **do**
        $g[0][j] \leftarrow Left$
    end for
    for $i \in [1,\ m]$ **do**
        for $j \in [1,\ n]$ **do**
            if $\alpha[i-1] \equiv \beta[j-1]$ **then**
                $f[i][j] \leftarrow f[i-1][j-1] + 1$
                $g[i][j] \leftarrow UpLeft$
            else if $f[i-1][j] \geq f[i][j-1]$ **then**
                $f[i][j] \leftarrow f[i-1][j]$
                $g[i][j] \leftarrow Up$
            else
                $f[i][j] \leftarrow f[i][j-1]$
                $g[i][j] \leftarrow Left$
            end if
        end for
    end for

    printlcs($g,\ \alpha,\ m,\ n$)

    return $f[m][n]$
end function

```
enum class Dir : int
{
    None, Up, Left, UpLeft
}; // None = 0, Up = 1, Left = 2, UpLeft = 3

void printlcs(std::vector<std::vector<int>> & g,
    std::vector<int> & alpha, int i, int j)
{
    if(i == 0 or j == 0) return;

    if(g[i][j] == static_cast<int>(Dir::UpLeft))
    {
        printlcs(g, alpha, i-1, j-1);
        std::cout << alpha[i-1];
    }
    else if(g[i][j] == static_cast<int>(Dir::Up))
    {
        printlcs(g, alpha, i-1, j);
    }
    else
    {
        printlcs(g, alpha, i, j-1);
    }
}

int lcskriya(std::vector<int> & alpha, std::vector
    <int> & beta)
{
    int m = alpha.size();
    int n = beta.size();


    std::vector<std::vector<int>> f(m + 1, std::
        vector<int>(n + 1, 0));
    std::vector<std::vector<int>> g(m + 1, std::
        vector<int>(n + 1, 0));

    for(int i = 0; i <= m; i++)
    {
        g[i][0] = static_cast<int>(Dir::Up);
    }

    for(int j = 0; j <= n; j++)
    {
        g[0][j] = static_cast<int>(Dir::Left);
    }

    for(int i = 1; i <= m; i++)
    {
        for(int j = 1; j <= n; j++)
        {
            if(alpha[i-1] == beta[j-1])
```

```
                {
                    f[i][j] = f[i-1][j-1] + 1;
                    g[i][j] = static_cast<int>(Dir::UpLeft);
                }
                else if(f[i-1][j] >= f[i][j-1])
                {
                    f[i][j] = f[i-1][j];
                    g[i][j] = static_cast<int>(Dir::Up);
                }
                else
                {
                    f[i][j] = f[i][j-1];
                    g[i][j] = static_cast<int>(Dir::Left);
                }
            }
        }

        printlcs(g, alpha, m, n);

        return f[m][n];
}
```

Computing all the LCS :

Algorithm 83 Compute All The LCS Kriya

```
function lcsall(f[0..m][0..n], α[0..m − 1], β[0..n − 1], i, j)
    if i ≡ 0 or j ≡ 0 then
        vv[][]
        vv.add([])
        return vv
    end if
    if α[i − 1] ≡ β[j − 1] then
        vv[][] ← lcsall(f, α, β, i − 1, j − 1)
        Add α[i − 1] to each v ∈ vv[][]
        return vv
    else
        if f[i][j − 1] ≥ f[i − 1][j] then
            left[][] ← lcsall(f, α, β, i, j − 1)
        end if
        if f[i − 1][j] ≥ f[i][j − 1] then
            up[][] ← lcsall(f, α, β, i − 1, j)
        end if
        return(up + left)                         ▷ Merge
    end if
end function
```

function lcskriya($\alpha[0..m-1]$, $\beta[0..n-1]$)
    $f[0..m][0..n] \leftarrow \{0\}$
    for $i \in [1,\ m]$ **do**
        for $j \in [1,\ n]$ **do**
            if $\alpha[i-1] \equiv \beta[j-1]$ **then**
                $f[i][j] \leftarrow f[i-1][j-1] + 1$
            else
                $f[i][j] \leftarrow$ **max**($f[i][j-1],\ f[i-1][j]$
            end if
        end for
    end for

    $lv[][] \leftarrow$ **lcsall**($f,\ \alpha,\ \beta,\ m,\ n$)
    return lv ▷ After removing duplicates
end function

```cpp
std::vector<std::vector<int>> lcsall(std::vector<
    std::vector<int>> & f, std::vector<int> &
    alpha, std::vector<int> & beta, int i, int j)
{
    if(i == 0 or j == 0)
    {
        return std::vector<std::vector<int>>(1,
            std::vector<int>());
    }

    if(alpha[i-1] == beta[j-1])
    {
        std::vector<std::vector<int>> vv = lcsall(
            f, alpha, beta, i-1, j-1);

        for(auto & v : vv)
        {
            v.push_back(alpha[i-1]);
        }
        return vv;
    }

    else
    {
        std::vector<std::vector<int>> up, left;

        if(f[i][j-1] >= f[i-1][j])
        {
            left = lcsall(f, alpha, beta, i, j-1);
        }

        if(f[i-1][j] >= f[i][j-1])
        {
            up = lcsall(f, alpha, beta, i-1, j);
        }

        for(auto & v : left)
        {
```

```
                up.push_back(v);
            }
            return up;
        }
}

std::set<std::vector<int>> lcskriya(std::vector<
    int> & alpha, std::vector<int> & beta)
{
    int m = alpha.size();
    int n = beta.size();

    std::vector<std::vector<int>> f(m + 1, std::
        vector<int>(n + 1, 0));

    for(int i = 1; i <= m; i++)
    {
        for(int j = 1; j <= n; j++)
        {
            if(alpha[i-1] == beta[j-1])
            {
                f[i][j] = f[i-1][j-1] + 1;
            }
            else
            {
                f[i][j] = std::max(f[i][j-1], f[i
                    -1][j]);
            }
        }
    }

    std::vector<std::vector<int>> lv = lcsall(f,
        alpha, beta, m, n);

    std::set<std::vector<int>> ls(lv.begin(), lv.
        end());

    return ls;
}
```

First Kriya Seq	Second Kriya Seq	LCS	Count
<1, 2, 3, 2, 4, 1, 2>	<2, 4, 3, 1, 2, 1>	2312 2321 2412	4
<1, 2, 3, 1, 2, 3, 1, 1>	<1, 3, 2, 1, 3, 2, 1>	12121 12131 12321 13121 13131 13211 13231	7

Algorithm 84 Length of LCS Kriya : Space Optimization

```
function lcskriya(α[0..m − 1], β[0..n − 1])
    f[0..min(m, n)] ← {0}
    for i ∈ [1, m] do
        prev ← 0                                        ▷ f[i − 1, j − 1]
        for j ∈ [1, n] do
            cur ← f[j]                                  ▷ f[i − 1][j]
            if α[i − 1] ≡ β[j − 1] then
                f[j] ← prev + 1          ▷ f[i][j] ← f[i − 1][j − 1] + 1
            else
                f[j] ← max(f[j − 1], cur)        ▷ f[i][j] ← max(f[i][j − 1], f[i − 1][j])
            end if
            prev ← cur
        end for
    end for
    return f.back()                                     ▷ f[m][n]
end function
```

Time complexity is $\mathcal{O}(mn)$. Space complexity is $\mathcal{O}(\mathbf{min}(m,\ n) + 1)$.

```cpp
int lcskriya(std::vector<int> & alpha, std::vector<int> & beta)
{
    int m = alpha.size();
    int n = beta.size();


    std::vector<int> f(std::min(m, n) + 1, 0);

    for(int i = 1; i <= m; i++)
    {
        int prev = 0; // f[i-1, j-1]

        for(int j = 1; j <= n; j++)
        {
            int cur = f[j]; // f[i-1][j]

            if(alpha[i-1] == beta[j-1])
            {
                // f[i][j] = f[i-1][j-1] + 1;
                f[j] = prev + 1;
            }
            else
            {
                // f[i][j] = std::max(f[i][j-1], f[i-1][j]);
                f[j] = std::max(f[j-1], cur);
            }

            prev = cur;
        }
    }

    return f.back(); //f[m][n];
```

```
}
```

■

§ Problem 69. *Guru shares two sequences of Kriyas with his disciple Ram. Determine the minimum possible number of Kriyas in their common supersequence.* ◊

§§ Solution. $<\delta_1, \delta_2, \cdots, \delta_p>$ is a supersequence of $<\alpha_1, \alpha_2, \cdots, \alpha_m>$ if $\delta_{i_j} \equiv \alpha_j \; \forall j \in [1, m] : i_1 < i_2 < \cdots < i_m$, i.e. $<\alpha_1, \alpha_2, \cdots, \alpha_m>$ is a subsequence of $<\delta_1, \delta_2, \cdots, \delta_p>$.

If $<\delta_1, \delta_2, \cdots, \delta_p>$ is the common supersequence of $<\alpha_1, \alpha_2, \cdots, \alpha_m>$ and $<\beta_1, \beta_2, \cdots, \beta_n>$ having minimum possible number of Kriyas (say SCS : Shortest Common Supersequence), then all the Kriyas of both the Kriya sequences occur in the SCS in the original order.

1. if $\alpha_m \equiv \beta_n$, then $\delta_p \equiv \alpha_m \equiv \beta_n$ and $<\delta_1, \delta_2, \cdots, \delta_{p-1}>$ is an SCS of $<\alpha_1, \alpha_2, \cdots, \alpha_{m-1}>$ and $<\beta_1, \beta_2, \cdots, \beta_{n-1}>$.
2. if $\alpha_m \neq \beta_n$, then
   a) $\delta_p \equiv \alpha_m \implies <\delta_1, \delta_2, \cdots, \delta_{p-1}>$ is an SCS of $<\alpha_1, \alpha_2, \cdots, \alpha_{m-1}>$ and $<\beta_1, \beta_2, \cdots, \beta_n>$.
   b) $\delta_p \equiv \beta_n \implies <\delta_1, \delta_2, \cdots, \delta_{p-1}>$ is an SCS of $<\alpha_1, \alpha_2, \cdots, \alpha_m>$ and $<\beta_1, \beta_2, \cdots, \beta_{n-1}>$.

Let $f_q(i, j)$ be the length of the SCS of $<\alpha_1, \alpha_2, \cdots, \alpha_i>$ and $<\beta_1, \beta_2, \cdots, \beta_j>$, using an optimal policy of q-steps.

$$\therefore f_q(i, j) = \begin{cases} j & \text{if } i \equiv 0 \\ i & \text{if } j \equiv 0 \\ f_{q-1}(i-1, j-1) + 1 & \text{if } i, j > 0 \text{ and } \alpha_i \equiv \beta_j \\ \text{Min}[f_{q-1}(i, j-1), f_{q-1}(i-1, j)] + 1 & \text{if } i, j > 0 \text{ and } \alpha_i \neq \beta_j \end{cases}$$

Algorithm 85 Length of SCS Kriya

```
function scskriya(α[0..m − 1], β[0..n − 1])
    f[0..m][0..n] ← {0}
    for i ∈ [0, m] do
        f[i][0] ← i
    end for
    for j ∈ [0, n] do
        f[0][j] ← j
    end for
    for i ∈ [1, m] do
        for j ∈ [1, n] do
            if α[i − 1] ≡ β[j − 1] then
                f[i][j] ← f[i − 1][j − 1] + 1
            else
                f[i][j] ← min(f[i][j − 1], f[i − 1][j]) + 1
            end if
        end for
    end for
    return f[m][n]
end function
```

Time complexity is $\mathcal{O}(mn)$. Space complexity is $\mathcal{O}(mn)$.

```cpp
int scskriya(std::vector<int> & alpha, std::vector<int> & beta)
{
    int m = alpha.size();
    int n = beta.size();

    std::vector<std::vector<int>> f(m + 1, std::vector<int>(n + 1, 0));

    for(int i = 0; i <= m; i++)
    {
        f[i][0] = i;
    }

    for(int j = 0; j <= n; j++)
    {
        f[0][j] = j;
    }

    for(int i = 1; i <= m; i++)
    {
        for(int j = 1; j <= n; j++)
        {
            if(alpha[i-1] == beta[j-1])
            {
                f[i][j] = f[i-1][j-1] + 1;
            }
            else
            {
                f[i][j] = std::min(f[i][j-1], f[i-1][j]) + 1;
            }
        }
    }

    return f[m][n];
}
```

Reconstruction of SCS from the optimal solution :

Algorithm 86 Reconstruction of SCS Kriya from Optimal Solution

1: **function** scskriya($\alpha[0..m-1]$, $\beta[0..n-1]$)
2: $\quad f[0..m][0..n] \leftarrow \{0\}$
3: $\quad$ **for** $i \in [0, m]$ **do**
4: $\quad\quad f[i][0] \leftarrow i$
5: $\quad$ **end for**
6: $\quad$ **for** $j \in [0, n]$ **do**
7: $\quad\quad f[0][j] \leftarrow j$
8: $\quad$ **end for**

```
    for i ∈ [1, m] do
        for j ∈ [1, n] do
            if α[i − 1] ≡ β[j − 1] then
                f[i][j] ← f[i − 1][j − 1] + 1
            else
                f[i][j] ← min(f[i][j − 1], f[i − 1][j]) + 1
            end if
        end for
    end for

    len ← f[m][n]                                  ▷ Length of SCS
    scs[0..len − 1] ← {0}
    i ← m
    j ← n
    while i > 0 and j > 0 do
        if α[i − 1] ≡ β[j − 1] then
            scs[len − 1] ← α[i − 1]
            i ← i − 1
            j ← j − 1
            len ← len − 1
        else if f[i − 1][j] > f[i][j − 1] then
            scs[len − 1] ← β[j − 1]
            j ← j − 1
            len ← len − 1
        else
            scs[len − 1] ← α[i − 1]
            i ← i − 1
            len ← len − 1
        end if
    end while
    while i > 0 do
        scs[len − 1] ← α[i − 1]
        i ← i − 1
        len ← len − 1
    end while
    while j > 0 do
        scs[len − 1] ← β[j − 1]
        j ← j − 1
        len ← len − 1
    end while
    return scs
end function
```

Time complexity of the reconstruction part (starting from while loop) is $\mathcal{O}(m + n)$.

```cpp
std::vector<int> scskriya(std::vector<int> & alpha
    , std::vector<int> & beta)
{
    int m = alpha.size();
    int n = beta.size();
```

```cpp


    std::vector<std::vector<int>> f(m + 1, std::vector<int>(n + 1, 0));

    for(int i = 0; i <= m; i++)
    {
        f[i][0] = i;
    }

    for(int j = 0; j <= n; j++)
    {
        f[0][j] = j;
    }

    for(int i = 1; i <= m; i++)
    {
        for(int j = 1; j <= n; j++)
        {
            if(alpha[i-1] == beta[j-1])
            {
                f[i][j] = f[i-1][j-1] + 1;
            }
            else
            {
                f[i][j] = std::min(f[i][j-1], f[i-1][j]) + 1;
            }
        }
    }

    int len = f[m][n]; // length of SCS

    std::vector<int> scs(len, 0);

    int i = m, j = n;

    while(i > 0 and j > 0)
    {
        if(alpha[i-1] == beta[j-1])
        {
            scs[len - 1] = alpha[i-1];
            --i; --j; --len;
        }
        else if(f[i-1][j] > f[i][j-1])
        {
            scs[len - 1] = beta[j-1];
            --j; --len;
        }
        else
        {
            scs[len - 1] = alpha[i-1];
            --i; --len;
        }
    }
```

```
    while(i > 0)
    {
        scs[len - 1] = alpha[i-1];
        --i; --len;
    }

    while(j > 0)
    {
        scs[len - 1] = beta[j-1];
        --j; --len;
    }

    return scs;
}
```

First Kriya Seq	Second Kriya Seq	SCS	Count
<1, 2, 3, 2, 4, 1, 2>	<2, 4, 3, 1, 2, 1>	<1, 2, 3, 2, 4, 3, 1, 2, 1> <1, 2, 4, 3, 1, 2, 4, 1, 2> <1, 2, 4, 3, 2, 4, 1, 2, 1>	9
<1, 2, 1, 3>	<3, 1, 2>	<3, 1, 2, 1, 3>	4

Note that since LCS computes the common Kriyas of longest length in the given two Kriya sequences, hence the length of SCS can be computed by subtracting the length of LCS from the sum of the lengths of both Kriya sequences :

$$scs = m + n - lcs$$

```
int scskriya(std::vector<int> & alpha, std::vector
    <int> & beta)
{
    int m = alpha.size();
    int n = beta.size();

    int lcs = lcskriya(alpha, beta);

    return m + n - lcs;
}
```

Recursive approach to print SCS :

Algorithm 87 Print SCS : Recursive Approach

```
function printscs(f[0..m][0..n], α[0..m−1], β[0..n−1], i, j)
    if i ≡ 0 then
        for k ∈ [0, j) do
            print β[k]
            return
        end for
    end if
    if j ≡ 0 then
```

```
        for k ∈ [0, i) do
            print α[k]
            return
        end for
    end if
    if α[i − 1] ≡ β[j − 1] then
        printscs(f, α, β, i − 1, j − 1)
        print β[j − 1]
    else if f[i − 1][j] > f[i][j − 1] then
        printscs(f, α, β, i, j − 1)
        print β[j − 1]
    else
        printscs(f, α, β, i − 1, j)
        print α[i − 1]
    end if
end function
```

Time complexity is $\mathcal{O}(m+n)$. Space complexity is $\mathcal{O}(1)$.

```cpp
void printscs(std::vector<std::vector<int>> & f,
    std::vector<int> & alpha, std::vector<int> &
    beta, int i, int j)
{
    if(i == 0)
    {
        for(int k = 0; k < j; k++)
        {
            std::cout << beta[k];
        }
        return;
    }

    if(j == 0)
    {
        for(int k = 0; k < i; k++)
        {
            std::cout << alpha[k];
        }
        return;
    }

    if(alpha[i-1] == beta[j-1])
    {
        printscs(f, alpha, beta, i-1, j-1);
        std::cout << alpha[i-1];
    }
    else if(f[i-1][j] > f[i][j-1])
    {
        printscs(f, alpha, beta, i, j-1);
        std::cout << beta[j-1];
    }
    else
    {
```

```
        printscs(f, alpha, beta, i-1, j);
        std::cout << alpha[i-1];
    }
}

void scskriya(std::vector<int> & alpha, std::
    vector<int> & beta)
{
    int m = alpha.size();
    int n = beta.size();


    std::vector<std::vector<int>> f(m + 1, std::
        vector<int>(n + 1, 0));

    for(int i = 0; i <= m; i++)
    {
        f[i][0] = i;
    }

    for(int j = 0; j <= n; j++)
    {
        f[0][j] = j;
    }

    for(int i = 1; i <= m; i++)
    {
        for(int j = 1; j <= n; j++)
        {
            if(alpha[i-1] == beta[j-1])
            {
                f[i][j] = f[i-1][j-1] + 1;
            }
            else
            {
                f[i][j] = std::min(f[i][j-1], f[i
                    -1][j]) + 1;
            }
        }
    }

    printscs(f, alpha, beta, m, n);
}
```

Computation of all SCS Kriya sequences :

Algorithm 88 Compute All The SCS Kriya

```
1: function scsall(f[0..m][0..n], α[0..m − 1], β[0..n − 1], i, j)
2:     if i ≡ 0 then
3:         vv[][]
4:         v[].add(β[0..j))
5:         vv.insert(v)
```

```
        return vv
    end if
    if j ≡ 0 then
        vv[][]
        v[].add(α[0..i))
        vv.insert(v)
        return vv
    end if
    if α[i − 1] ≡ β[j − 1] then
        vv[][] ← scsall(f, α, β, i − 1, j − 1)
        Add α[i − 1] to each v ∈ vv[][]
        return vv
    else
        up[][], left[][]
        if f[i][j − 1] ≥ f[i − 1][j] then
            left[][] ← scsall(f, α, β, i − 1, j)
            for v ∈ left do        ▷ v is reference here, not copy
                v.add(α[i − 1])
            end for
        end if
        if f[i − 1][j] ≥ f[i][j − 1] then
            up[][] ← scsall(f, α, β, i, j − 1)
            for v ∈ up do                  ▷ v is reference here
                v.add(β[j − 1])
            end for
        end if
        return(up + left)                          ▷ Merge
    end if
end function

function scskriya(α[0..m − 1], β[0..n − 1])
    f[0..m][0..n] ← {0}
    for i ∈ [0, m] do
        f[i][0] ← i
    end for
    for j ∈ [0, n] do
        f[0][j] ← j
    end for
    for i ∈ [1, m] do
        for j ∈ [1, n] do
            if α[i − 1] ≡ β[j − 1] then
                f[i][j] ← f[i − 1][j − 1] + 1
            else
                f[i][j] ← min(f[i][j − 1], f[i − 1][j] + 1
            end if
        end for
    end for

    lv[][] ← scsall(f, α, β, m, n)
    return lv                  ▷ After removing duplicates
```

end function

```
std::vector<std::vector<int>> scsall(std::vector<
    std::vector<int>> & f, std::vector<int> &
    alpha, std::vector<int> & beta, int i, int j)
{
    if(i == 0)
    {
        std::vector<std::vector<int>> vv;

        std::vector<int> v(beta.begin(), beta.
            begin() + j);

        vv.push_back(v);

        return vv;
    }

    if(j == 0)
    {
        std::vector<std::vector<int>> vv;

        std::vector<int> v(alpha.begin(), alpha.
            begin() + i);

        vv.push_back(v);

        return vv;
    }

    if(alpha[i-1] == beta[j-1])
    {
        std::vector<std::vector<int>> vv = scsall(
            f, alpha, beta, i-1, j-1);

        for(auto & v : vv) // & is important here
        {
            v.push_back(alpha[i-1]);
        }
        return vv;
    }
    else
    {
        std::vector<std::vector<int>> up, left;

        if(f[i][j-1] >= f[i-1][j])
        {
            left = scsall(f, alpha, beta, i-1, j);

            for(auto & v : left)
            {
                v.push_back(alpha[i-1]);
            }
        }

        if(f[i-1][j] >= f[i][j-1])
        {
```

```
            up = scsall(f, alpha, beta, i, j-1);

            for(auto & v : up)
            {
                v.push_back(beta[j -1]);
            }
        }

        for(auto & v : left)
        {
            up.push_back(v);
        }

        return up;
    }
}


std::set<std::vector<int>> scskriya(std::vector<int> & alpha, std::vector<int> & beta)
{
    int m = alpha.size();
    int n = beta.size();


    std::vector<std::vector<int>> f(m + 1, std::vector<int>(n + 1, 0));

    for(int i = 0; i <= m; i++)
    {
        f[i][0] = i;
    }

    for(int j = 0; j <= n; j++)
    {
        f[0][j] = j;
    }

    for(int i = 1; i <= m; i++)
    {
        for(int j = 1; j <= n; j++)
        {
            if(alpha[i-1] == beta[j -1])
            {
                f[i][j] = f[i-1][j-1] + 1;
            }
            else
            {
                f[i][j] = std::min(f[i][j-1], f[i-1][j]) + 1;
            }
        }
    }

    std::vector<std::vector<int>> lv = scsall(f, alpha, beta, m, n);
```

```cpp

    std::set<std::vector<int>> ls(lv.begin(), lv.end());

    return ls;
}
```

SCS can also be computed from LCS by inserting the unmatched Kriyas from the two Kriya sequences in the LCS in the same order.

Algorithm 89 Computation SCS from LCS Kriya

function scskriya($\alpha[0..m-1]$, $\beta[0..n-1]$)
    $f[0..m][0..n] \leftarrow \{0\}$
    for $i \in [1,\ m]$ **do**
        for $j \in [1,\ n]$ **do**
            if $\alpha[i-1] \equiv \beta[j-1]$ **then**
                $f[i][j] \leftarrow f[i-1][j-1] + 1$
            else
                $f[i][j] \leftarrow$ **max**$(f[i][j-1],\ f[i-1][j])$
            end if
        end for
    end for

    $queue : scs$
    while $m > 0$ and $n > 0$ **do**
        $kriya \leftarrow 0$
        if $m \equiv 0$ **then**
            $kriya \leftarrow \beta[--n]$
        else if $n \equiv 0$ **then**
            $kriya \leftarrow \alpha[--m]$
        else if $\alpha[m-1] \equiv \beta[n-1]$ **then**
            $kriya \leftarrow \alpha[--m] \leftarrow \beta[--n]$
        else if $f[m-1][n] \equiv f[m][n]$ **then**
            $kriya \leftarrow \alpha[--m]$
        else if $f[m][n-1] \equiv f[m][n]$ **then**
            $kriya \leftarrow \beta[--n]$
        end if

        $scs.addAtFront(kriya)$
    end while
    return scs
end function

Time complexity is $\mathcal{O}(mn)$. Space complexity is $\mathcal{O}(mn)$. Time complexity of computing SCS after computing LCS (i.e. while loop) is $\mathcal{O}(m+n)$.

```cpp
std::deque<int> scskriya(std::vector<int> & alpha, std::vector<int> & beta)
```

```
{
    int m = alpha.size();
    int n = beta.size();


    std::vector<std::vector<int>> f(m + 1, std::
        vector<int>(n + 1, 0));

    for(int i = 1; i <= m; i++)
    {
        for(int j = 1; j <= n; j++)
        {
            if(alpha[i-1] == beta[j-1])
            {
                f[i][j] = f[i-1][j-1] + 1;
            }
            else
            {
                f[i][j] = std::max(f[i][j-1], f[i
                    -1][j]);
            }
        }
    }

    std::deque<int> scs;

    while(m > 0 or n > 0)
    {
        int kriya = 0;

        if(m == 0)
        {
            kriya = beta[--n];
        }
        else if(n == 0)
        {
            kriya = alpha[--m];
        }
        else if(alpha[m-1] == beta[n-1])
        {
            kriya = alpha[--m] = beta[--n];
        }
        else if(f[m-1][n] == f[m][n])
        {
            kriya = alpha[--m];
        }
        else if(f[m][n-1] == f[m][n])
        {
            kriya = beta[--n];
        }

        scs.push_front(kriya);
    }

    return scs;
```

```
}
```

Alternatively :

Algorithm 90 SCS Kriya : Alternative Solution from LCS

```
function scskriya(α[0..m − 1], β[0..n − 1])
    f[0..m − 1][0..n − 1] ← {0}
    for i ∈ [1, m] do
        for j ∈ [1, n] do
            if α[i − 1] ≡ β[j − 1] then
                f[i][j] ← f[i − 1][j − 1] + 1
            else
                f[i][j] ← max(f[i][j − 1], f[i − 1][j])
            end if
        end for
    end for
    len ← f[m][n]                                  ▷ length of LCS
    lcs[0..len − 1] ← {0}
    i ← m
    j ← n
    while i > 0 and j > 0 do
        if α[i − 1] ≡ β[j − 1] then
            lcs[len − 1] ← α[i − 1]
            i ← i − 1
            j ← j − 1
            len ← len − 1
        else if f[i − 1][j] > f[i][j − 1] then
            i ← i − 1
        else
            j ← j − 1
        end if
    end while

    scs[]
    i ← j ← 0
    for kriya ∈ lcs do
        while α[i] ≠ kriya do
            scs.add(α[i])
            i ← i + 1
        end while
        while β[j] ≠ kriya do
            scs.add(β[j])
            j ← j + 1
        end while

        scs.add(kriya)
        i ← i + 1
        j ← j + 1
```

```
        end for

        for k ∈ [i, m) do
            scs.add(α[k])
        end for
        for k ∈ [j, n) do
            scs.add(β[k])
        end for
        return scs
    end function
```

Time complexity is $\mathcal{O}(mn)$. Space complexity is $\mathcal{O}(mn)$.

```cpp
std::vector<int> scskriya(std::vector<int> & alpha
    , std::vector<int> & beta)
{
    int m = alpha.size();
    int n = beta.size();


    std::vector<std::vector<int>> f(m + 1, std::
        vector<int>(n + 1, 0));

    for(int i = 1; i <= m; i++)
    {
        for(int j = 1; j <= n; j++)
        {
            if(alpha[i-1] == beta[j-1])
            {
                f[i][j] = f[i-1][j-1] + 1;
            }
            else
            {
                f[i][j] = std::max(f[i][j-1], f[i
                    -1][j]);
            }
        }
    }

    int len = f[m][n]; // length of LCS

    std::vector<int> lcs(len, 0);

    int i = m, j = n;

    while(i > 0 and j > 0)
    {
        if(alpha[i-1] == beta[j-1])
        {
            lcs[len-1] = alpha[i-1];
            --i;
            --j;
            --len;
        }
        else if(f[i-1][j] > f[i][j-1])
```

```
            {
                --i;
            }
            else
            {
                --j;
            }
        }

    std::vector<int> scs;

    i = 0, j = 0;

    for(auto kriya : lcs)
    {
        while(alpha[i] != kriya)
        {
            scs.push_back(alpha[i++]);
        }

        while(beta[j] != kriya)
        {
            scs.push_back(beta[j++]);
        }

        scs.push_back(kriya);
        ++i; ++j;
    }

    for(int k = i; k < m; k++)
    {
        scs.push_back(alpha[k]);
    }

    for(int k = j; k < n; k++)
    {
        scs.push_back(beta[k]);
    }

    return scs;
}
```

■

§ Problem 70. *A palindromic Kriya sequence bears the same Kriyas in the corresponding forward and backward directional positions. Determine the total possible number of palindromic Kriya contiguous subsequences for a given Kriya sequence.* ◊

§§ Solution. Let $f_p(i, j)$ represent the possibility of the Kriya sequence $<k_i, k_{i+1}, \cdots, k_{j-1}, k_j>$ being palindromic, using an optimal policy with p-steps.

If $k_i \equiv k_j$, then this sequence is palindromic if

- there is just one Kriya, i.e. $i \equiv j$, the sequence is $<k_i>$. $\therefore j = i$.

- there are just two Kriyas, i.e. these two Kriyas are adjacent ones, the sequence is $<k_i,\ k_{i+1}>$. $\therefore j = i + 1$.
- there is just one Kriya between i and j, i.e. total three Kriyas, the sequence is $<k_i,\ k_{i+1},\ k_{i+2}>$. $\therefore j = i + 2$.
- there is more than one Kriyas between i and j, i.e. $j > i + 2$ and the Kriya contiguous subsequence $<k_{i+1},\ \cdots,\ k_{j-1}>$ is also palindromic, which is represented by $f_{p-1}(i + 1,\ j - 1)$.

$$\therefore f_p(i,\ j) = \begin{cases} true & \text{if } j \equiv i \\ k_i \equiv k_j & \text{if } i < j \leq i + 2 \\ f_{p-1}(i + 1,\ j - 1) & \text{if } k_i \equiv k_j \text{ and } j > i + 2 \end{cases}$$

Algorithm 91 Counting Palindromic Kriya Contiguous Subsequence

```
function palindromickriya(ks[0..n − 1])
    count ← 0
    f[0..n][0..n] ← {0}

    for i ∈ [n − 1, 0] do
        for j ∈ [i, n) do
            f[i][j] ← (ks[i] ≡ ks[j]) and
                        (j ≤ i + 2 or f[i + 1][j − 1])
            if f[i][j] then
                count ← count + 1
            end if
        end for
    end for

    return count
end function
```

Time complexity is $\mathcal{O}(n^2)$. Space complexity is $\mathcal{O}(n^2)$.

```cpp
int palindromickriya(std::vector<int> & ks)
{
    int n = ks.size(); // number of Kriyas

    int count = 0; // number of palindromic
        contiguous subsequences

    std::vector<std::vector<bool>> f(n+1, std::
        vector<bool>(n+1, false));

    for(int i = n-1; i >= 0; --i)
    {
        for(int j = i; j < n; ++j)
        {
            f[i][j] = (ks[i] == ks[j]) and (j <= i
                + 2 or f[i+1][j-1]);
```

```
            if(f[i][j]) ++count;
        }
    }

    return count;
}
```

Kriya Sequence	Count of Palindromic ones
<1, 2, 1>	4 : <1> <2> <1> <1, 2, 1>
<2, 2, 2>	6 : <2> <2> <2> <2, 2> <2, 2> <2, 2, 2>
<1, 2, 3>	3 : <1> <2> <3>

■

§ **Problem 71.** *In § Problem 70, determine the longest possible palindromic Kriya contiguous subsequence.* ◇

§§ **Solution**. Following the solution of § Problem 70 :

Algorithm 92 Longest Palindromic Kriya Contiguous Sub sequences

function longestpalindromickriya($ks[0..n-1]$)
  $is \leftarrow 0$ ▷ Starting Index of the longest palindromic contiguous subsequence
  $len \leftarrow 1$ ▷ Length of the longest palindromic contiguous subsequence
  $f[0..n][0..n] \leftarrow \{0\}$

  for $i \in [n-1,\ 0]$ **do**
    for $j \in [i,\ n)$ **do**
      $f[i][j] \leftarrow (ks[i] \equiv ks[j])$ **and**
   $(j \leq i+2$ **or** $f[i+1][j-1])$
      if $f[i][j]$ and $len < j-i+1$ **then**
        $is \leftarrow i$
        $len \leftarrow j-i+1$
      end if
    end for
  end for

  return $ks[is..is+len]$
end function

Time complexity is $\mathcal{O}(n^2)$. Space complexity is $\mathcal{O}(n^2)$.

```
std::vector<int> longestpalindromickriya(std::
    vector<int> & ks)
{
    int n = ks.size(); // number of Kriyas

```

```cpp
    int is = 0; // starting index of the longest
        palindromic contiguous subsequence
    int len = 1; // length of the longest
        palindromic contiguous subsequence

    std::vector<std::vector<bool>> f(n+1, std::
        vector<bool>(n+1, false));

    for(int i = n-1; i >= 0; --i)
    {
        for(int j = i; j < n; ++j)
        {
            f[i][j] = (ks[i] == ks[j]) and (j <= i
                + 2 or f[i+1][j-1]);

            if(f[i][j] and len < j-i+1)
            {
                is = i;
                len = j-i+1;
            }
        }
    }

    return std::vector<int>(ks.cbegin() + is, ks.
        cbegin() + is + len);
}
```

Kriya Sequence	Longest Palindromic Kriya Contiguous Subsequence
<2, 1, 2, 1, 4>	<2, 1, 2> <1, 2, 1>
<8, 5, 1, 1, 5, 6, 7>	<5, 1, 1, 5>
<3, 2, 2, 4>	<2, 2>

■

§ Problem 72. *In § Problem 71, determine the length of the longest possible palindromic Kriya subsequence.* ◊

§§ Solution. Let $f_p(i,\ j)$ represent the maximum length of the palindromic Kriya sequence
<k_i, k_{i+1}, $\cdots$, k_{j-1}, k_j>, using an optimal policy with p-steps.

$$\therefore f_p(i,\ j) = \begin{cases} 1 & \text{if } i \equiv j \\ 2 + f_{p-1}(i+1,\ j-1) & \text{if } k_i \equiv k_j \text{ and } j > i \\ \text{Max}(f_{p-1}(i+1,\ j),\ f_{p-1}(i,\ j-1)) & \text{Otherwise} \end{cases}$$

Algorithm 93 Maximum Length of Palindromic Kriya Subsequence

function longestpalindromickriya($ks[0..n-1]$)
    $f[0..n-1][0..n-1] \leftarrow \{0\}$

```
    for i ∈ [0, n) do
        f[i][i] ← 1                          ▷ Single Kriya : Unit Length
    end for
    for l ∈ [2, n] do
        for i ∈ [0, n − l) do
            j ← i + l − 1
            if ks[i] ≡ ks[j] then
                f[i][j] ← 2 + f[i + 1][j − 1]
            else
                f[i][j] ← max(f[i + 1][j], f[i][j − 1])
            end if
        end for
    end for

    return f[0][n − 1]
end function
```

Time complexity is $\mathcal{O}(n^2)$. Space complexity is $\mathcal{O}(n^2)$.

```cpp
int longestpalindromickriya(std::vector<int> & ks)
{
    int n = ks.size(); // number of Kriyas

    std::vector<std::vector<int>> f(n, std::vector
        <int>(n, 0));

    for(int i = 0; i < n; ++i)
    {
        f[i][i] = 1; // Single Kriya : Hence
            length is 1
    }

    for(int l = 2; l <= n; ++l)
    {
        for(int i = 0; i <= n-l; ++i)
        {
            int j = i+l-1;

            if(ks[i] == ks[j])
            {
                f[i][j] = 2 + f[i+1][j-1];
            }
            else
            {
                f[i][j] = std::max(f[i+1][j], f[i
                    ][j-1]);
            }
        }
    }

    return f[0][n-1];
}
```

Alternatively:

Algorithm 94 Max Length of Palindromic Kriya Subsequence : Alternative

```
function longestpalindromickriya(ks[0..n − 1])
    f[0..n − 1][0..n − 1] ← {0}

    for i ∈ (n, 0] do
        f[i][i] ← 1
        for j ∈ [i + 1, n) do
            if ks[i] ≡ ks[j] then
                f[i][j] ← 2 + f[i + 1][j − 1]
            else
                f[i][j] ← max(f[i + 1][j], f[i][j − 1])
            end if
        end for
    end for

    return f[0][n − 1]
end function
```

Time complexity is $\mathcal{O}(n^2)$. Space complexity is $\mathcal{O}(n^2)$.

```cpp
int longestpalindromickriya(std::vector<int> & ks)
{
    int n = ks.size(); // number of Kriyas

    std::vector<std::vector<int>> f(n, std::vector
        <int>(n, 0));

    for(int i = n-1; i >= 0; --i)
    {
        f[i][i] = 1;

        for(int j = i+1; j < n; ++j)
        {
            if(ks[i] == ks[j])
            {
                f[i][j] = 2 + f[i+1][j-1];
            }
            else
            {
                f[i][j] = std::max(f[i+1][j], f[i
                    ][j-1]);
            }
        }
    }

    return f[0][n-1];
}
```

Kriya Sequence	Max Length of Palindromic Kriya Subsequence
<2, 1, 2, 1, 4>	3 : <2, 1, 2> <1, 2, 1>
<8, 5, 1, 1, 5, 6, 7>	4 : <5, 1, 1, 5>
<3, 2, 2, 4>	2 : <2, 2>
<2, 2, 2, 1, 2>	4 : <2, 2, 2, 2>

Algorithm 95 Maximum Length of Palindromic Kriya Subsequence : Space Optimization

```
function longestpalindromickriya(ks[0..n − 1])
    f[0..n − 1] ← {0}                          ▷ length l
    g[0..n − 1] ← {0}                          ▷ length l-1
    h[0..n − 1] ← {0}                          ▷ length l-2

    for l ∈ [1, n] do
        for i ∈ [0, n − l) do
            j ← i + l − 1
            if i ≡ j then
                f[i] ← 1
            else if ks[i] ≡ ks[j] then
                f[i] ← 2 + h[i + 1]
            else
                f[i] ← max(g[i + 1], g[i])
            end if
        end for

        exchange(f, g)                         ▷ O(1)
        exchange(h, f)                         ▷ O(1)
    end for

    return g[0]
end function
```

Time complexity is $\mathcal{O}(n^2)$. Space complexity is $\mathcal{O}(n)$.

```
int longestpalindromickriya(std::vector<int> & ks)
{
    int n = ks.size(); // number of Kriyas

    std::vector<int> f(n, 0); // length l
    std::vector<int> g(n, 0); // length l-1
    std::vector<int> h(n, 0); // length l-2

    for(int l = 1; l <= n; ++l)
    {
        for(int i = 0; i <= n-l; ++i)
        {
            int j = i+l-1;

```

```
            if(i == j)
            {
                f[i] = 1;
            }

            else if(ks[i] == ks[j])
            {
                f[i] = 2 + h[i+1];
            }
            else
            {
                f[i] = std::max(g[i+1], g[i]);
            }
        }
        f.swap(g);
        h.swap(f);
    }

    return g[0];
}
```

Alternatively:

Algorithm 96 Max Length of Palindromic Kriya Subsequence : Space Optimization : Alternative

```
function longestpalindromickriya(ks[0..n − 1])
    f[0..n − 1] ← {1}

    for i ∈ (n, 0] do
        len ← 0
        for j ∈ [i + 1, n) do
            t ← f[j]
            if ks[i] ≡ ks[j] then
                f[j] ← 2 + len
            end if
            len ← max(len, t)
        end for
    end for

    return max(f[0..n − 1])
end function
```

Time complexity is $\mathcal{O}(n^2)$. Space complexity is $\mathcal{O}(n)$.

```
int longestpalindromickriya(std::vector<int> & ks)
{
    int n = ks.size(); // number of Kriyas

    std::vector<int> f(n, 1);

    for(int i = n-1; i >= 0; --i)
    {
```

```
        int len = 0;

        for(int j = i+1; j < n; ++j)
        {
            int t = f[j];

            if(ks[i] == ks[j])
            {
                f[j] = 2 + len;
            }

            len = std::max(len, t);
        }
    }

    int maxl = 0;

    for(auto l : f)
    {
        maxl = std::max(maxl, l);
    }

    return maxl;
}
```

■

§ Problem 73. *Determine the total number of ways of formation of a Kriya subsequence β of a given Kriya sequence α.* ◊

§§ Solution. Let $f_p(i,\ j)$ be the number of Kriya subsequences $\equiv <\beta_1,\ \beta_2,\ \cdots,\ \beta_j>$ of the Kriya sequence $<\alpha_1,\ \alpha_2,\ \cdots,\ \alpha_i>$, using an optimal policy with p-steps.

$$\therefore f_p(i,\ j) = \begin{cases} 0 & \text{if } i \equiv 0 \text{, i.e. } \alpha \text{ is empty} \\ 1 & \text{if } j \equiv 0 \text{, i.e. } \beta \text{ is empty} \\ f_{p-1}(i-1,\ j) & \text{if } \alpha_i \neq \beta_j \\ f_{p-1}(i-1,\ j) + f_{p-1}(i-1,\ j-1) & \text{if } \alpha_i \equiv \beta_j \end{cases}$$

Algorithm 97 Count of Distinct Kriya Subsequences

```
function kriyasubseq(α[0..na − 1], β[0..nb − 1])
    f[0..na − 1][0..nb − 1] ← {0}

    for i ∈ [0, na] do
        f[i][0] ← 1                ▷ Empty seq is a subsequence too
    end for
    for i ∈ [1, na] do
        for j ∈ [1, nb] do
            if α[i − 1] ≠ β[j − 1] then
                f[i][j] ← f[i − 1][j]
            else
                f[i][j] ← f[i − 1][j] + f[i − 1][j − 1]
            end if
```

            end for
        end for

        return $f[na][nb]$
    end function

Time complexity is $\mathcal{O}(na \times nb)$. Space complexity is $\mathcal{O}(na \times nb)$.

```cpp
int kriyasubseq(std::vector<int> & alpha, std::vector<int> & beta)
{
    int na = alpha.size();
    int nb = beta.size();

    std::vector<std::vector<int>> f(na+1, std::vector<int>(nb+1, 0));

    for(int i = 0; i <= na; ++i) f[i][0] = 1; // empty seq is a subseq too.

    for(int i = 1; i <= na; ++i)
    {
        for(int j = 1; j <= nb; ++j)
        {
            f[i][j] = f[i-1][j]; // alpha[i-1] not equals beta[j-1]

            if(alpha[i-1] == beta[j-1])
            {
                f[i][j] += f[i-1][j-1];
            }
        }
    }

    return f[na][nb];
}
```

α	β	**Count of distinct β in α**	**Indices of α**
<6, 1, 3, 3, 3, 5, 9>	<6, 1, 3, 3, 5, 9>	3	<0, 1, 2, 3, 5, 6> <0, 1, 3, 4, 5, 6> <0, 1, 2, 4, 5, 6>
<2, 1, 2, 6, 2, 1, 6>	<2, 1, 6>	5	<0, 1, 3> <0, 1, 6> <0, 5, 6> <2, 5, 6> <4, 5, 6>

Algorithm 98 Count of Distinct Kriya Subsequences : Space Optimization

1: **function** kriyasubseq($\alpha[0..na-1]$, $\beta[0..nb-1]$)

$f[0..nb] \leftarrow \{0\}$
$f[0] \leftarrow 1$ ▷ Empty seq is a subsequence too
for $i \in [1,\ na]$ **do**
  for $j \in [nb,\ 1]$ **do**
    if $\alpha[i-1] \equiv \beta[j-1]$ **then**
      $f[j] \leftarrow f[j] + f[j-1]$
    end if
  end for
end for

return $f[nb]$
end function

Time complexity is $\mathcal{O}(na \times nb)$. Space complexity is $\mathcal{O}(nb)$.

```
int kriyasubseq(std::vector<int> & alpha, std::
    vector<int> & beta)
{
    int na = alpha.size();
    int nb = beta.size();

    std::vector<int> f(nb+1, 0);

    f[0] = 1; // empty seq is a subseq too.

    for(int i = 1; i <= na; ++i)
    {
        for(int j = nb; j >= 1; --j)
        {
            if(alpha[i-1] == beta[j-1])
            {
                f[j] += f[j-1];
            }
        }
    }

    return f[nb];
}
```

■

§ **Problem 74.** *Determine the minimum number of operations to transform a Kriya sequence α to β, given addition, removal and replacement as the only operations on a Kriya.* ◊

§§ **Solution**. Let $f_p(i,\ j)$ be the minimum number of operations to transform $<\alpha_1,\ \alpha_2,\ \cdots,\ \alpha_i>$ to $<\beta_1,\ \beta_2,\ \cdots,\ \beta_j>$, using an optimal policy of p-steps.

Following are the choices to transform $<\alpha_1,\ \alpha_2,\ \cdots,\ \alpha_i>$ to $<\beta_1,\ \beta_2,\ \cdots,\ \beta_j>$:

1. If Addition was the last operation then $f_p(i,\ j) \equiv f_{p-1}(i,\ j-1) + 1$.
2. If Removal was the last operation then $f_p(i,\ j) \equiv f_{p-1}(i-1,\ j) + 1$.

3. If Replacement was the last operation then $f_p(i,\ j) \equiv f_{p-1}(i-1,\ j-1) + 1$ and $\alpha_i \neq \beta_j$.
4. If $\alpha_i \equiv \beta_j$, then $f_p(i,\ j) \equiv f_{p-1}(i-1,\ j-1)$.

Note that :

- If $i \equiv 0$, i.e. α is empty, then a sequence of j Additions transforms <> to <$\beta_1,\ \beta_2,\ \cdots,\ \beta_j$>.
- If $j \equiv 0$, i.e. β is empty, then a sequence of i Removals transforms <$\alpha_1,\ \alpha_2,\ \cdots,\ \alpha_i$> to <>.
- If $i \equiv j \equiv 0$, i.e. both α and β are empty, then no operation is required to transform <> to <>.

$$
\begin{aligned}
\therefore f_p(0,\ 0) &\equiv 0 \\
f_p(0,\ j) &\equiv j \\
f_p(i,\ 0) &\equiv i
\end{aligned}
$$

And,

$$
\therefore f_p(i,\ j) = \text{Min}\begin{cases} f_{p-1}(i,\ j-1) + 1 & \text{Addition} \\ f_{p-1}(i-1,\ j) + 1 & \text{Removal} \\ f_{p-1}(i-1,\ j-1) + 1 & \text{Replacement : if } \alpha_i \neq \beta_j \\ f_{p-1}(i-1,\ j-1) & \text{if } \alpha_i \equiv \beta_j \end{cases}
$$

Algorithm 99 Transform Kriya

```
function transformkriya(α[0..na − 1], β[0..nb − 1])
    f[0..na − 1][0..nb] ← {0}
    for i ∈ [0, na] do
        f[i][0] ← i
    end for
    for j ∈ [0, nb] do
        f[0][j] ← j
    end for
    for i ∈ [1, na] do
        for j ∈ [1, nb] do
            if α[i − 1] ≡ β[j − 1] then
                f[i][j] ← f[i − 1][j − 1]
            else
                f[i][j] ← f[i − 1][j − 1] + 1
            end if
            f[i][j] ← min(f[i][j], min{f[i − 1][j], f[i][j − 1]} + 1)
        end for
    end for

    return f[na][nb]
end function
```

Time complexity is $\mathcal{O}(na \times nb)$. Space complexity is $\mathcal{O}(na \times nb)$.

```
int transformkriya(std::vector<int> & alpha, std::
    vector<int> & beta)
```

```
{
    int na = alpha.size();
    int nb = beta.size();

    std::vector<std::vector<int>> f(na+1, std::
        vector<int>(nb+1, 0));

    for(int i = 0; i <= na; ++i) f[i][0] = i;

    for(int j = 0; j <= nb; ++j) f[0][j] = j;

    for(int i = 1; i <= na; ++i)
    {
        for(int j = 1; j <= nb; ++j)
        {
            if(alpha[i-1] == beta[j-1])
            {
                f[i][j] = f[i-1][j-1];
            }
            else
            {
                f[i][j] = f[i-1][j-1] + 1;
            }

            f[i][j] = std::min(f[i][j], std::min(f
                [i-1][j], f[i][j-1]) + 1);
        }
    }

    return f[na][nb];
}
```

Reconstruction of the transformation path from the optimal solution :

Algorithm 100 Print Transformation Path

function printkriya($\alpha[0..na-1],\ \beta[0..nb-1]$)
  $f[0..na-1][0..nb] \leftarrow \{0\}$
  for $i \in [0,\ na]$ **do**
    $f[i][0] \leftarrow i$
  end for
  for $j \in [0,\ nb]$ **do**
    $f[0][j] \leftarrow j$
  end for
  for $i \in [1,\ na]$ **do**
    for $j \in [1,\ nb]$ **do**
      if $\alpha[i-1] \equiv \beta[j-1]$ **then**
        $f[i][j] \leftarrow f[i-1][j-1]$
      else
        $f[i][j] \leftarrow$
    $\mathbf{min}(f[i-1][j-1],\ \mathbf{min}\{f[i-1][j],\ f[i][j-1]\}) + 1$

```
            end if
        end for
    end for

    while na > 0 and nb > 0 do
        if α[na − 1] ≡ β[nb − 1] then
            na ← na − 1
            nb ← nb − 1
        else if na > 0 and nb > 0 and f[na][nb] ≡ f[na − 1][[nb − 1] + 1 then    ▷ Replacement
            print "Replace " α[na − 1] " with " β[nb − 1]
            na ← na − 1
            nb ← nb − 1
        end if
        if na > 0 and f[na][nb] ≡ f[na − 1][nb] + 1 then    ▷ Removal
            print "Remove " α[na − 1]
            na ← na − 1
        end if
        if nb > 0 and f[na][nb] ≡ f[na][nb − 1] + 1 then    ▷ Addition
            print "Add " β[nb − 1]
            nb ← nb − 1
        end if
    end while
end function
```

Time complexity of reconstruction part (while loop) is $\mathcal{O}(\mathbf{min}(na, nb))$.

```
void printkriya(std::vector<int> & alpha, std::
    vector<int> & beta)
{
    int na = alpha.size();
    int nb = beta.size();

    std::vector<std::vector<int>> f(na+1, std::
        vector<int>(nb+1, 0));

    for(int i = 0; i <= na; ++i) f[i][0] = i;

    for(int j = 0; j <= nb; ++j) f[0][j] = j;

    for(int i = 1; i <= na; ++i)
    {
        for(int j = 1; j <= nb; ++j)
        {
            if(alpha[i-1] == beta[j-1])
            {
                f[i][j] = f[i-1][j-1];
            }
            else
            {
```

```
                f[i][j] = f[i-1][j-1] + 1;
            }

            f[i][j] = std::min(f[i][j], std::min(f[i-1][j], f[i][j-1]) + 1);
        }
    }

    while(na > 0 and nb > 0)
    {
        if(alpha[na-1] == beta[nb-1])
        {
            --na;
            --nb;
        }
        else if(na > 0 and nb > 0 and f[na][nb] == f[na-1][nb-1] + 1) // Replacement
        {
            std::cout << "Replace " << alpha[na-1] << " with " << beta[nb-1] << std::endl;
            --na;
            --nb;
        }
        if(na > 0 and f[na][nb] == f[na-1][nb] + 1) // Removal
        {
            std::cout << "Remove " << alpha[na-1] << std::endl;
            --na;
        }
        if(nb > 0 and f[na][nb] == f[na][nb-1] + 1) // Addition
        {
            std::cout << "Add " << beta[nb-1] << std::endl;
            --nb;
        }
    }
    std::cout << "\n\n";
}
```

α	β	Optimal Operations	Count
<5, 10, 15, 16, 1>	<15, 10, 16>	<5,10,15,16> : Remove 1 <5,10,16> : Remove 15 <15, 10, 16> : Replace 5 with 15	3
<3,5,9,2,5,9,3,6,5>	<2,12,2,1,15,9,3,6,5>	<3,5,9,2,5,15,9,3,6,5> : Add 15 <3,5,9,2,1,15,9,3,6,5> : Replace 5 with 1 <3,5,2,1,15,9,3,6,5> : Remove 9 <3,12,2,1,15,9,3,6,5> : Replace 5 with 12 <2,12,2,1,15,9,3,6,5> : Replace 3 with 2	5
<1, 2, 3>	<5, 7>	<1, 2, 7> : Replace 3 with 7 <1, 7> : Remove 2 <5, 7> : Replace 1 with 5	3
<3, 1, 5>	<1, 3, 5>	<3, 5> : Remove 1 <1, 3, 5> : Add 1	2
<3, 9, 7, 2, 9>	<3, 9, 5, 8>	<3, 9, 7, 2, 8> : Replace 9 with 8 <3, 9, 7, 8> : Remove 2 <3, 9, 5, 8> : Replace 7 with 5	3

Algorithm 101 Transform Kriya : Space Optimization

```
function transformkriya(α[0..na − 1], β[0..nb − 1])
    f[0..nb] ← {0}
    for j ∈ [0, nb] do
        f[j] ← j
    end for
    for i ∈ [1, na] do
        prev ← f[0]                                  ▷ f[i − 1][j − 1]
        f[0] ← i
        for j ∈ [1, nb] do
            cur ← f[j]                               ▷ f[i − 1][j]
            if α[i − 1] ≡ β[j − 1] then
                f[j] ← prev
            else
                f[j] ← min(prev, min{f[j], f[j − 1]}) + 1
            end if

            prev ← cur
        end for
    end for

    return f[nb]
end function
```

Time complexity is $\mathcal{O}(na \times nb)$. Space complexity is $\mathcal{O}(nb)$.

```cpp
int transformkriya(std::vector<int> & alpha, std::
    vector<int> & beta)
{
    int na = alpha.size();
    int nb = beta.size();

    std::vector<int> f(nb+1, 0);

    for(int j = 0; j <= nb; ++j) f[j] = j;

    for(int i = 1; i <= na; ++i)
    {
        int prev = f[0]; // f[i-1][j-1]

        f[0] = i;

        for(int j = 1; j <= nb; ++j)
        {
            int cur = f[j]; // f[i-1][j]

            if(alpha[i-1] == beta[j-1])
            {
                f[j] = prev;
            }
            else
            {
```

```
                f[j] = std::min(prev, std::min(f[j], f[j-1])) + 1;
            }

            prev = cur;
        }
    }

    return f[nb];
}
```

Alternatively :

Algorithm 102 Print Operations

```
Operations : None, Add, Remove, Replace
function printop(α[0..na − 1], β[0..nb − 1], i, j, op)
    if op ≡ Add then
        print " Add " β[j − 1]
    else if op ≡ Remove then
        print " Remove " α[i − 1]
    else if op ≡ Replace then
        print " Replace " α[i − 1] " with " β[j − 1]
    end if
end function
```

Time complexity is $\mathcal{O}(1)$. Space complexity is $\mathcal{O}(1)$.

```
enum class Op : int
{
    None, Add, Remove, Replace
}; // None = 0, Add = 1, Remove = 2, Replace = 3

void printop(std::vector<int> & alpha, std::vector<int> & beta, int i, int j, int op)
{
    if(op == static_cast<int>(Op::Add))
    {
        std::cout << " Add " << beta[j-1];
    }
    else if(op == static_cast<int>(Op::Remove))
    {
        std::cout << " Remove " << alpha[i-1];
    }
    else if(op == static_cast<int>(Op::Replace))
    {
        std::cout << " Replace " << alpha[i-1] << " with " << beta[j-1];
    }
}
```

Algorithm 103 Reconstruct Operations

```
function reconstructops(g[0..na][0..nb], α[0..na−1], β[0..nb−1], i, j)
    if i ≡ 0 and j ≡ 0 then
        return
    end if
    printop(α, β, i, j, g[i][j])
    if g[i][j] ≡ None or g[i][j] ≡ Replace then
        i ← i − 1
        j ← j − 1
    else if g[i][j] ≡ Add then
        j ← j − 1
    else if g[i][j] ≡ Remove then
        i ← i − 1
    end if

    reconstructops (g, α, β, i, j)
end function
```

Time complexity is $\mathcal{O}(\mathbf{min}(i,\ j))$. Space complexity is $\mathcal{O}(1)$.

```
void reconstructops(std::vector<std::vector<int>>& g, std::vector<int>& alpha, std::vector<int>& beta, int i, int j)
{
    if(i == 0 and j == 0) return;

    printop(alpha, beta, i, j, g[i][j]);

    if(g[i][j] == static_cast<int>(Op::None) or g[i][j] == static_cast<int>(Op::Replace))
    {
        i = i-1;
        j = j-1;
    }
    else if(g[i][j] == static_cast<int>(Op::Add))
    {
        j = j-1;
    }
    else if(g[i][j] == static_cast<int>(Op::Remove))
    {
        i = i-1;
    }

    reconstructops(g, alpha, beta, i, j);
}
```

Algorithm 104 Transform Kriya and Reconstruct Operations

```
function transformkriya(α[0..na − 1], β[0..nb − 1])
```

$f[0..na][0..nb] \leftarrow \{\infty\}$ ▷ store optimal count of operations
$g[0..na][0..nb] \leftarrow \{0\}$ ▷ store operations used in optimal way

for $i \in [0,\ na]$ **do**
  $f[i][0] \leftarrow i$
  $g[i][0] \leftarrow Remove$
end for
for $j \in [0,\ nb]$ **do**
  $f[0][j] \leftarrow j$
  $g[0][j] \leftarrow Add$
end for
for $i \in [1,\ na]$ **do**
  for $j \in [1,\ nb]$ **do**
    if $\alpha[i-1] \equiv \beta[j-1]$ **then**
      $f[i][j] \leftarrow f[i-1][j-1]$
      $g[i][j] \leftarrow None$
    else if $f[i-1][j-1]+1 < f[i][j]$ **then**
      $f[i][j] \leftarrow f[i-1][j-1]+1$
      $g[i][j] \leftarrow Replace$
    else if $f[i][j-1]+1 < f[i][j]$ **then**
      $f[i][j] \leftarrow f[i][j-1]+1$
      $g[i][j] \leftarrow Add$
    else if $f[i-1][j]+1 < f[i][j]$ **then**
      $f[i][j] \leftarrow f[i-1][j]+1$
      $g[i][j] \leftarrow Remove$
    end if
  end for
end for

reconstructops $(g,\ \alpha,\ \beta,\ na,\ nb)$
print "Optimal Count of Operations : "
return $f[na][nb]$
end function

Time complexity is $\mathcal{O}(na \times nb)$. Space complexity is $\mathcal{O}(na \times nb)$.

```
int transformkriya(std::vector<int> & alpha, std::
    vector<int> & beta)
{
    int na = alpha.size();
    int nb = beta.size();

    // store optimal count of operations
    std::vector<std::vector<int>> f(na+1, std::
        vector<int>(nb+1, std::numeric_limits<int
        >::max()));

    // store operations used in optimal way
    std::vector<std::vector<int>> g(na+1, std::
```

```
        vector<int>(nb+1, 0));

    for(int i = 0; i <= na; ++i)
    {
        f[i][0] = i;
        g[i][0] = static_cast<int>(Op::Remove);
    }

    for(int j = 0; j <= nb; ++j)
    {
        f[0][j] = j;
        g[0][j] = static_cast<int>(Op::Add);
    }

    for(int i = 1; i <= na; ++i)
    {
        for(int j = 1; j <= nb; ++j)
        {
            if(alpha[i-1] == beta[j-1])
            {
                f[i][j] = f[i-1][j-1];
                g[i][j] = static_cast<int>(Op::
                    None);
            }
            else if(f[i-1][j-1] + 1 < f[i][j])
            {
                f[i][j] = f[i-1][j-1] + 1;
                g[i][j] = static_cast<int>(Op::
                    Replace);
            }

            if(f[i][j-1] + 1 < f[i][j])
            {
                f[i][j] = f[i][j-1] + 1;
                g[i][j] = static_cast<int>(Op::Add
                    );
            }

            if(f[i-1][j] + 1 < f[i][j])
            {
                f[i][j] = f[i-1][j] + 1;
                g[i][j] = static_cast<int>(Op::
                    Remove);
            }
        }
    }

    reconstructops(g, alpha, beta, na, nb);

    std::cout << "\n Optimal Count of Operations :
        ";

    return f[na][nb];
}
```

α	β	**Optimal Operations**	**Count**
<5, 10, 15, 16, 1>	<15, 10, 16>	<5,10,15,16> : Remove 1 <5,10,16> : Remove 15 <15, 10, 16> : Replace 5 with 15	3
<3,5,9,2,5,9,3,6,5>	<2,12,2,1,15,9,3,6,5>	<3,5,9,2,15,9,3,6,5> : Replace 5 with 15 <3,5,9,1,15,9,3,6,5> : Replace 2 with 1 <3,5,2,1,15,9,3,6,5> : Replace 9 with 2 <3,12,2,1,15,9,3,6,5> : Replace 5 with 12 <2,12,2,1,15,9,3,6,5> : Replace 3 with 2	5
<1, 2, 3>	<5, 7>	<1, 2, 7> : Replace 3 with 7 <1, 5, 7> : Replace 2 with 5 <5, 7> : Remove 1	3
<3, 1, 5>	<1, 3, 5>	<3, 3, 5> : Replace 1 with 3 <1, 3, 5> : Replace 3 with 1	2
<3, 9, 7, 2, 9>	<3, 9, 5, 8>	<3, 9, 7, 2, 8> : Replace 9 with 8 <3, 9, 7, 5, 8> : Replace 2 with 5 <3, 9, 5, 8> : Remove 7	3

Note that there can be more than one optimal set of operations (with same count). ■

§ Problem 75. *Determine the solution if adjacent transposition is also allowed as an operation in § Problem 74.* ◊

§§ Solution. Assuming single operation on resulting contiguous subsequences :

the fourth choice to transform $<\alpha_1, \alpha_2, \cdots, \alpha_i>$ to $<\beta_1, \beta_2, \cdots, \beta_j>$ is :

> If (adjacent) Transpose was the last operation then $f_p(i, j) \equiv f_{p-1}(i-2, j-2)+1$ and $\alpha_i \equiv \beta_{j-1} \wedge \alpha_{i-1} \equiv \beta_j$.

$$\therefore f_p(i, j) = \text{Min} \begin{cases} f_{p-1}(i, j-1)+1 & \text{Addition} \\ f_{p-1}(i-1, j)+1 & \text{Removal} \\ f_{p-1}(i-1, j-1)+1 & \text{Replacement : if } \alpha_i \neq \beta_j \\ f_{p-1}(i-1, j-1) & \text{if } \alpha_i \equiv \beta_j \\ f_{p-1}(i-2, j-2)+1 & \text{Transpose : } \alpha_i \equiv \beta_{j-1} \wedge \alpha_{i-1} \equiv \beta_j \end{cases}$$

Algorithm 105 Print Operations

Operations : *None*, *Add*, *Remove*, *Replace*, *Transpose*
function printop($\alpha[0..na-1]$, $\beta[0..nb-1]$, i, j, op)
  if $op \equiv Add$ **then**
    print " Add " $\beta[j-1]$
  else if $op \equiv Remove$ **then**
    print " Remove " $\alpha[i-1]$
  else if $op \equiv Replace$ **then**
    print " Replace " $\alpha[i-1]$ " with " $\beta[j-1]$
  else if $op \equiv Transpose$ **then**
    print " Transpose " $\alpha[i-2]$ " with " $\alpha[i-1]$
  end if
end function

Time complexity is $\mathcal{O}(1)$. Space complexity is $\mathcal{O}(1)$.

```cpp
enum class Op : int
{
    None, Add, Remove, Replace, Transpose
}; // None = 0, Add = 1, Remove = 2, Replace = 3,
    Transpose = 4

void printop(std::vector<int> & alpha, std::vector
    <int> & beta, int i, int j, int op)
{
    if(op == static_cast<int>(Op::Add))
    {
        std::cout << " Add " << beta[j-1];
    }
    else if(op == static_cast<int>(Op::Remove))
    {
        std::cout << " Remove " << alpha[i-1];
    }
    else if(op == static_cast<int>(Op::Replace))
    {
        std::cout << " Replace " << alpha[i-1] <<
            " with " << beta[j-1];
    }
    else if(op == static_cast<int>(Op::Transpose))
    {
        std::cout << " Transpose " << alpha[i-2]
            << " and " << alpha[i-1];
    }
}
```

Algorithm 106 Reconstruct Operations

```
function reconstructops(g[0..na][0..nb], α[0..na − 1], β[0..nb − 1], i, j)
    if i ≡ 0 and j ≡ 0 then
        return
    end if
    printop(α, β, i, j, g[i][j])
    if g[i][j] ≡ None or g[i][j] ≡ Replace then
        i ← i − 1
        j ← j − 1
    else if g[i][j] ≡ Add then
        j ← j − 1
    else if g[i][j] ≡ Remove then
        i ← i − 1
    else if g[i][j] ≡ Transpose then
        i ← i − 2
        j ← j − 2
    end if

    reconstructops (g, α, β, i, j)
end function
```

Time complexity is $\mathcal{O}(\textbf{min}(i,\ j))$. Space complexity is $\mathcal{O}(1)$.

```
void reconstructops(std::vector<std::vector<int>>
    & g, std::vector<int> & alpha, std::vector<int
    > & beta, int i, int j)
{
    if(i == 0 and j == 0) return;

    printop(alpha, beta, i, j, g[i][j]);

    if(g[i][j] == static_cast<int>(Op::None) or g[
        i][j] == static_cast<int>(Op::Replace))
    {
        i = i-1;
        j = j-1;
    }
    else if(g[i][j] == static_cast<int>(Op::Add))
    {
        j = j-1;
    }
    else if(g[i][j] == static_cast<int>(Op::Remove
        ))
    {
        i = i-1;
    }
    else if(g[i][j] == static_cast<int>(Op::
        Transpose))
    {
        i = i-2;
        j = j-2;
    }

    reconstructops(g, alpha, beta, i, j);
}
```

Algorithm 107 Transform Kriya and Reconstruct Operations

---

function transformkriya($\alpha[0..na-1]$, $\beta[0..nb-1]$)
    $f[0..na][0..nb] \leftarrow \{\infty\}$ ▷ store optimal count of operations
    $g[0..na][0..nb] \leftarrow \{0\}$ ▷ store operations used in optimal way

    for $i \in [0,\ na]$ **do**
        $f[i][0] \leftarrow i$
        $g[i][0] \leftarrow Remove$
    end for
    for $j \in [0,\ nb]$ **do**
        $f[0][j] \leftarrow j$
        $g[0][j] \leftarrow Add$

end for
for $i \in [1,\ na]$ **do**
for $j \in [1,\ nb]$ **do**
if $\alpha[i-1] \equiv \beta[j-1]$ **then**
$f[i][j] \leftarrow f[i-1][j-1]$
$g[i][j] \leftarrow None$
else if $f[i-1][j-1]+1 < f[i][j]$ **then**
$f[i][j] \leftarrow f[i-1][j-1]+1$
$g[i][j] \leftarrow Replace$
else if $f[i][j-1]+1 < f[i][j]$ **then**
$f[i][j] \leftarrow f[i][j-1]+1$
$g[i][j] \leftarrow Add$
else if $f[i-1][j]+1 < f[i][j]$ **then**
$f[i][j] \leftarrow f[i-1][j]+1$
$g[i][j] \leftarrow Remove$
else if $i > 1$ and $j > 1$ and $\alpha[i-1] \equiv \beta[j-2]$ and $\alpha[i-2] \equiv \beta[j-1]$ and $f[i-2][j-2]+1 < f[i][j]$ **then**
$f[i][j] \leftarrow f[i-2][j-2]+1$
$g[i][j] \leftarrow Transpose$
end if
end for
end for

reconstructops $(g,\ \alpha,\ \beta,\ na,\ nb)$
print "Optimal Count of Operations : "
return $f[na][nb]$
end function

Time complexity is $\mathcal{O}(na \times nb)$. Space complexity is $\mathcal{O}(na \times nb)$.

```cpp
int transformkriya(std::vector<int> & alpha, std::
    vector<int> & beta)
{
    int na = alpha.size();
    int nb = beta.size();

    // store optimal count of operations
    std::vector<std::vector<int>> f(na+1, std::
        vector<int>(nb+1, std::numeric_limits<int
        >::max()));

    // store operations used in optimal way
    std::vector<std::vector<int>> g(na+1, std::
        vector<int>(nb+1, 0));

    for(int i = 0; i <= na; ++i)
    {
        f[i][0] = i;
        g[i][0] = static_cast<int>(Op::Remove);
    }

    for(int j = 0; j <= nb; ++j)
```

```
    {
        f[0][j] = j;
        g[0][j] = static_cast<int>(Op::Add);
    }

    for(int i = 1; i <= na; ++i)
    {
        for(int j = 1; j <= nb; ++j)
        {
            if(alpha[i-1] == beta[j-1])
            {
                f[i][j] = f[i-1][j-1];
                g[i][j] = static_cast<int>(Op::
                    None);
            }
            else if(f[i-1][j-1] + 1 < f[i][j])
            {
                f[i][j] = f[i-1][j-1] + 1;
                g[i][j] = static_cast<int>(Op::
                    Replace);
            }

            if(f[i][j-1] + 1 < f[i][j])
            {
                f[i][j] = f[i][j-1] + 1;
                g[i][j] = static_cast<int>(Op::Add
                    );
            }

            if(f[i-1][j] + 1 < f[i][j])
            {
                f[i][j] = f[i-1][j] + 1;
                g[i][j] = static_cast<int>(Op::
                    Remove);
            }

            if((i > 1) and (j > 1) and
                (alpha[i-1] == beta[j-2]) and
                (alpha[i-2] == beta[j-1]) and
                (f[i-2][j-2] + 1 < f[i][j]))
            {
                f[i][j] = f[i-2][j-2] + 1;
                g[i][j] = static_cast<int>(Op::
                    Transpose);
            }
        }
    }

    reconstructops(g, alpha, beta, na, nb);

    std::cout << "\n Optimal Count of Operations :
        ";

    return f[na][nb];
```

```
}
```

α	β	**Optimal Operations**	**Count**
<3, 1>	<1, 3>	Transpose 3 and 1	1
<2, 3, 1>	<4, 1, 3>	Transpose 3 and 1 Replace 2 with 4	2
<3, 1>	<1, 2, 3>	Replace 1 with 3 Replace 3 with 2 Add 1	3
<1, 2, 3, 4, 5>	<1, 2, 4, 3, 8>	Replace 5 with 8 Transpose 3 and 4	2

Note that : to transform <3, 1> to <1, 2, 3> : if Transpose of 3 and 1 is allowed then <3, 1> becomes <1, 3>. Now it is not allowed to transform the resulting contiguous subsequence <1, 3> again, hence Add 2 is not allowed here, i.e. due to this restriction, count of 2 is allowed though being an optimal one.

If there is no restriction on number of transformations on the resulting contiguous subsequences:

Algorithm 108 Transform Kriya : Unrestricted Operations

```
function transformkriya(α[0..na − 1], β[0..nb − 1])
    maxsize ← na + nb
    da[0..maxsize − 1] ← 0
    f[0..na][0..nb] ← {∞}                ▷ store optimal count of operations
    f[0][0] ← ∞

    for i ∈ [0, na] do
        f[i + 1][1] ← i
        f[i + 1][0] ← ∞
    end for
    for j ∈ [0, nb] do
        f[1][j + 1] ← j
        f[0][j + 1] ← ∞
    end for
    for i ∈ [1, na] do
        db ← 0
        for j ∈ [1, nb] do
            i1 ← da[β[j − 1]]
            j1 ← db
            if α[i − 1] ≡ β[j − 1] then
                c ← 0
            else
                c ← 1
            end if
```

if $c \equiv 0$ **then**
    $db \leftarrow j$
end if

$f[i+1][j+1] \leftarrow$ Min(f[i][j] + c, f[i+1][j] + 1, f[i][j+1] + 1, f[i1][j1] + (i-i1-1) + 1 + (j-j1-1))
end for
$da[\alpha[i-1]] \leftarrow i$
end for

return $f[na+1][nb+1]$
end function

Time complexity is $\mathcal{O}(na \times nb)$. Space complexity is $\mathcal{O}(na \times nb)$.

```
int transformkriya(std::vector<int> & alpha, std::
    vector<int> & beta)
{
    int na = alpha.size();
    int nb = beta.size();

    int maxsize = na + nb;

    std::vector<int> da(maxsize, 0);

    int infinity = std::numeric_limits<int>::max()
        /2;

    // store optimal count of operations
    std::vector<std::vector<int>> f(na+2, std::
        vector<int>(nb+2, infinity));

    f[0][0] = infinity;

    for(int i = 0; i <= na; ++i)
    {
        f[i+1][1] = i;
        f[i+1][0] = infinity;
    }

    for(int j = 0; j <= nb; ++j)
    {
        f[1][j+1] = j;
        f[0][j+1] = infinity;
    }

    for(int i = 1; i <= na; ++i)
    {
        int db = 0;

        for(int j = 1; j <= nb; ++j)
        {
            int i1 = da[beta[j-1]];
            int j1 = db;
```

```
            int c = ((alpha[i-1] == beta[j-1]) ? 0 : 1);

            if(c == 0) db = j;

            f[i+1][j+1] = std::min(f[i][j] + c, std::min(f[i+1][j] + 1, std::min(f[i][j+1] + 1, f[i1][j1] + (i-i1-1) + 1 + (j-j1-1))));
        }

        da[alpha[i-1]] = i;
    }

    return f[na+1][nb+1];
}
```

α	β	**Optimal Operations**	**Count**
<3, 1>	<1, 2, 3>	Transpose 1 with 3 Add 2	2

■

§ Problem 76. *Revisit the solution if Copy and Finish are also allowed as transformation operations in § Problem 75, where Finish, being the final operation, processes all the remaining Kriyas in α and each operation bears a specific cost for the transformation in action.* ◊

§§ Solution. $<\alpha_1, \alpha_2, \cdots, \alpha_m> \implies <\beta_1, \beta_2, \cdots, \beta_n>$

Extending the previous solution leads to :

$$\therefore f_p(i,\ j) = \text{Min} \begin{cases} f_{p-1}(i-1,\ j-1) + cost_{Copy} & \text{Copy : if } \alpha_i \equiv \beta_j \\ f_{p-1}(i-1,\ j-1) + cost_{Replace} & \text{Replacement : if } \alpha_i \not\equiv \beta_j \\ f_{p-1}(i-2,\ j-2) + cost_{Transpose} & \text{Transpose : if } i,j \geq 2 \text{ and } \alpha_i \equiv \beta_{j-1} \wedge \alpha_{i-1} \equiv \beta_j \\ f_{p-1}(i-1,\ j) + cost_{Remove} & \text{Removal : Always} \\ f_{p-1}(i,\ j-1) + cost_{Add} & \text{Addition : Always} \\ \underset{i \in [0,\ m)}{\text{Min}} \{f_{p-1}(i,\ n)\} + cost_{Finish} & \text{Finish : if } i \equiv m \text{ and } j \equiv n. \end{cases}$$

Algorithm 109 Edit Distance : Print Operations with Copy and Finish

Operations : *Copy*, *Replace*, *Transpose*, *Remove*, *Add*, *Finish*
OP : op (operation), e (entity : value or index)
function printop($\alpha[0..na-1]$, $\beta[0..nb-1]$, i, j, op)
  if $op \equiv Copy$ **then**
    print " Copy " $\alpha[i-1]$
  else if $op \equiv Replace$ **then**
    print " Replace " $\alpha[i-1]$ " with " $\beta[j-1]$
  else if $op \equiv Transpose$ **then**
    print " Transpose " $\alpha[i-2]$ " with " $\alpha[i-1]$
  else if $op \equiv Remove$ **then**
    print " Remove " $\alpha[i-1]$
  else if $op \equiv Add$ **then**

```
            print " Add " β[j − 1]
        else if op ≡ Finish then
            print " Finish "
        end if
    end function
```

Time complexity is $\mathcal{O}(1)$. Space complexity is $\mathcal{O}(1)$.

```cpp
enum Cost {Copy, Replace, Transpose, Remove, Add,
    Finish};

struct OP
{
    int op;
    char e;
};

void printop(std::string & alpha, std::string &
    beta, int i, int j, int op)
{
    if(op == Copy)
    {
        std::cout << " Copy " << alpha[i-1];
    }
    else if(op == Replace)
    {
        std::cout << " Replace " << alpha[i-1] <<
            " with " << beta[j-1];
    }
    else if(op == Transpose)
    {
        std::cout << " Transpose " << alpha[i-2]
            << " and " << beta[j-2];
    }
    else if(op == Remove)
    {
        std::cout << " Remove " << alpha[i-1];
    }
    else if(op == Add)
    {
        std::cout << " Add " << beta[j-1];
    }
    else if(op == Finish)
    {
        std::cout << " Finish ";
    }
}
```

Algorithm 110 Edit Distance : Print Custom Operations with Reconstruct Operations

```
function reconstructops(op[0..m][0..n], α[0..m−1], β[0..n−1], i, j)
    if i ≡ 0 and j ≡ 0 then
        return
    end if
    i1 ← i
    j1 ← j

    if op[i][j].op ≡ Copy or op[i][j].op ≡ Replace then
        i1 ← i − 1
        j1 ← j − 1
    else if op[i][j].op ≡ Transpose then
        i1 ← i − 2
        j1 ← j − 2
    else if op[i][j].op ≡ Remove then
        i1 ← i − 1
        j1 ← j
    else if op[i][j].op ≡ Add then
        i1 ← i
        j1 ← j − 1
    else                                    ▷ Finish : i ≡ m and j ≡ n
        assert(op[i][j].op ≡ Finish)
        k ← op[i][j].e

        i1 ← k
        j1 ← j
    end if

    reconstructops (op, α, β, i1, j1)
    printop(α, β, i, j, op[i][j].op)
end function
```

Time complexity is $\mathcal{O}(\mathbf{min}(i,\ j))$. Space complexity is $\mathcal{O}(1)$.

```
void reconstructops(std::vector<std::vector<OP>> &
      op, std::string & alpha, std::string & beta,
    int i, int j)
{
    if(i == 0 and j == 0) return;

    int i1 = i, j1 = j;

    if(op[i][j].op == Copy or op[i][j].op ==
          Replace)
    {
        i1 = i-1;
        j1 = j-1;
    }
    else if(op[i][j].op == Transpose)
    {
        i1 = i-2;
        j1 = j-2;
```

```
    }
    else if(op[i][j].op == Remove)
    {
        i1 = i-1;
        j1 = j;
    }
    else if(op[i][j].op == Add)
    {
        i1 = i;
        j1 = j-1;
    }
    else // Finish, i == m, j == n
    {
        assert(op[i][j].op == Finish);
        int k = op[i][j].e;

        i1 = k;
        j1 = j;
    }

    reconstructops(op, alpha, beta, i1, j1);

    printop(alpha, beta, i, j, op[i][j].op);
}
```

Algorithm 111 Edit Distance : Transform Kriya and Reconstruct Custom Operations

function transformkriya($\alpha[0..m-1]$, $\beta[0..n-1]$, $cost[0..5]$)
  $f[0..m][0..n] \leftarrow \{\infty\}$ ▷ store optimal count of operations
  $g[0..m][0..n] \leftarrow \{\}$ ▷ store operations used in optimal way

  for $i \in [0,\ m]$ **do**
    $f[i][0] \leftarrow i \times cost[Remove]$
    $g[i][0].op \leftarrow Remove$
  end for
  for $j \in [0,\ n]$ **do**
    $f[0][j] \leftarrow j \times cost[Add]$
    $g[0][j].op \leftarrow Add$
  end for
  for $i \in [1,\ m]$ **do**
    for $j \in [1,\ n]$ **do**
      if $\alpha[i-1] \equiv \beta[j-1]$ **then**
        $f[i][j] \leftarrow f[i-1][j-1] + cost[Copy]$
        $g[i][j].op \leftarrow Copy$
      end if
      if $\alpha[i-1] \neq \beta[j-1]$ and $f[i-1][j-1]+cost[Replace] < f[i][j]$ **then**

$f[i][j] \leftarrow f[i-1][j-1] + cost[Replace]$
$g[i][j] \leftarrow \{Replace,\ \beta[j-1]\}$ ▷ by $\beta[j-1]$
end if
if $i \geq 2$ and $j \geq 2$ and $\alpha[i-1] \equiv \beta[j-2]$ and $\alpha[i-2] \equiv \beta[j-1]$ and $f[i-2][j-2] + cost[Transpose] < f[i][j]$ **then**
$f[i][j] \leftarrow f[i-2][j-2] + cost[Transpose]$
$g[i][j].op \leftarrow Transpose$
end if
if $f[i-1][j] + cost[Remove] < f[i][j]$ **then**
$f[i][j] \leftarrow f[i-1][j] + cost[Remove]$
$g[i][j].op \leftarrow Remove$
end if
if $f[i][j-1] + cost[Add] < f[i][j]$ **then**
$f[i][j] \leftarrow f[i][j-1] + cost[Add]$
$g[i][j] \leftarrow \{Add,\ \beta[j-1]\}$
end if
end for
end for

for $i \in [0,\ m]$ **do**
if $f[i][n] + cost[Finish] < f[m][n]$ **then**
$f[m][n] \leftarrow f[i][n] + cost[Finish]$
$g[m][n] \leftarrow \{Finish,\ i\}$
end if
end for

reconstructops $(g,\ \alpha,\ \beta,\ m,\ n)$
print "Optimal Count of Operations : "
return $f[na][nb]$
end function

Time complexity is $\mathcal{O}(m \times n)$. Space complexity is $\mathcal{O}(m \times n)$.

```
int transformkriya(std::string & alpha, std::string & beta, std::vector<int> & cost)
{
    int m = alpha.size();
    int n = beta.size();

    std::vector<std::vector<int>> f(m+1, std::vector<int>(n+1, std::numeric_limits<int>::max()));
    std::vector<std::vector<OP>> g(m+1, std::vector<OP>(n+1));

    for(int i = 0; i <= m; ++i)
    {
        f[i][0] = i * cost[Remove];
        g[i][0].op = Remove;
    }

    for(int j = 0; j <= n; ++j)
```

```
    {
        f[0][j] = j * cost[Add];
        g[0][j].op = Add;
    }

    for(int i = 1; i <= m; ++i)
    {
        for(int j = 1; j <= n; ++j)
        {
            if(alpha[i-1] == beta[j-1])
            {
                f[i][j] = f[i-1][j-1] + cost[Copy];
                g[i][j].op = Copy;
            }

            if((alpha[i-1] != beta[j-1]) and f[i-1][j-1] + cost[Replace] < f[i][j])
            {
                f[i][j] = f[i-1][j-1] + cost[Replace];
                g[i][j] = {Replace, beta[j-1]};
            }

            if((i >= 2) and (j >= 2) and
               (alpha[i-1] == beta[j-2]) and
               (alpha[i-2] == beta[j-1]) and
               (f[i-2][j-2] + cost[Transpose] < f[i][j]))
            {
                f[i][j] = f[i-2][j-2] + cost[Transpose];
                g[i][j].op = Transpose;
            }

            if(f[i-1][j] + cost[Remove] < f[i][j])
            {
                f[i][j] = f[i-1][j] + cost[Remove];
                g[i][j].op = Remove;
            }

            if(f[i][j-1] + cost[Add] < f[i][j])
            {
                f[i][j] = f[i][j-1] + cost[Add];
                g[i][j] = {Add, beta[j-1]};
            }
        }
    }

    for(int i = 0; i <= m; ++i)
    {
        if(f[i][n] + cost[Finish] < f[m][n])
```

```
        {
            f[m][n] = f[i][n] + cost[Finish];
            g[m][n] = {Finish, static_cast<char>(i
                )};
        }
    }

    reconstructops(g, alpha, beta, m, n);

    return f[m][n];
}
```

α	β	**Cost**	**Optimal Operations**	**Count**
algorithm	altruistic	Copy : 1 Replace : 1 Transpose : 1 Remove : 1 Add : 1 Finish : 1	Add a Replace a with l Replace l with t Replace g with r Replace o with u Replace r with i Replace i with s Copy t Replace h with i Replace m with c	10

■

§ Problem 77. *Determine the optimal alignment of two Kriya sequences allowing introduction of gaps to equalize the lengths such that there are no two gaps in the similar ordered positions followed by additive scoring of matched/unmatched Kriyas in respective ordered positions such that optimal aligned ones score highest.* ◊

§§ Solution. Let $f_p(i,\ j)$ be the optimal score for aligning $<\alpha_1,\ \alpha_2,\ \cdots,\ \alpha_i>$ to $<\beta_1,\ \beta_2,\ \cdots,\ \beta_j>$.

$$\therefore f_p(i,\ j) = \text{Max}\begin{cases} f_{p-1}(i-1,\ j-1) + score_{\alpha_i,\ \beta_j} & \text{cf. Copy/Replace} \\ f_{p-1}(i,\ j-1) + score_{gap,\ \beta[j-1]} & \text{cf. Addition of gap in } \alpha \\ f_{p-1}(i-1,\ j) + score_{\alpha[i-1],\ gap} & \text{cf. Removal from } \alpha : \text{Addition of gap in } \beta \end{cases}$$

where

$$score_{\alpha_i,\ \beta_j} = \begin{cases} score_{matched} & \text{if } \alpha_i \equiv \beta_j : \text{cf. Copy} \\ score_{unmatched} & \text{if } \alpha_i \neq \beta_j : \text{cf. Replace} \end{cases}$$

Let the Kriya sequences be sequences of characters (i.e. strings) for the sake of simplicity and

$$score_{\alpha[i-1],\ gap} \equiv score_{gap,\ \beta[j-1]} \equiv -2$$
$$score_{matched} \equiv 0$$
$$score_{unmatched} \equiv -1$$

Algorithm 112 Reconstruct and Print Aligned Kriya Sequences

$Directions\ :\ Diagonal,\ Left,\ Up$

function printaligned($g[0..m][0..n]$, $\alpha[0..m-1]$, $\beta[0..n-1], i, j$)
  if $i \equiv 0$ or $j \equiv 0$ **then**
    return
  end if
  if $g[i][j] \equiv Diagonal$ **then**
    printaligned(g, α, β, $i-1$, $j-1$)
    print $\alpha[i-1]$ " " $\beta[j-1]$
  else if $g[i][j] \equiv Left$ **then**
    printaligned(g, α, β, i, $j-1$)
    print "- " $\beta[j-1]$
  else if $g[i][j] \equiv Up$ **then**
    printaligned(g, α, β, $i-1$, j)
    print $\alpha[i-1]$ " -"
  end if
end function

Time complexity is $\mathcal{O}(m+n)$. Space complexity is $\mathcal{O}(1)$.

```cpp
enum Dir {Diagonal, Left, Up};

void printaligned(std::vector<std::vector<int>> & g, std::string & alpha, std::string & beta, int i, int j)
{
    if(i == 0 or j == 0) return;

    if(g[i][j] == Diagonal)
    {
        printaligned(g, alpha, beta, i-1, j-1);
        std::cout << alpha[i-1] << " " << beta[j-1] << "\n";
    }
    else if(g[i][j] == Left)
    {
        printaligned(g, alpha, beta, i, j-1);
        std::cout << "-" << " " << beta[j-1] << "\n";
    }
    else if(g[i][j] == Up)
    {
        printaligned(g, alpha, beta, i-1, j);
        std::cout << alpha[i-1] << " " << "-" << "\n";
    }
}
```

Algorithm 113 Generate Aligned Kriya Sequences

function alignkriya($\alpha[0..m-1]$, $\beta[0..n-1]$)
  $f[0..m][0..n] \leftarrow \{\infty\}$ ▷ Store optimal total scores

```
    g[0..m][0..n] ← {∞}    ▷ Store directions as per f-matrix
    for i ∈ [0, m] do
        f[i][0] ← i × −2
        g[i][0] ← Up
    end for
    for i ∈ [0, n] do
        f[0][j] ← j × −2
        g[0][j] ← Left
    end for
    for i ∈ [1, m] do
        for j ∈ [1, n] do
            if α[i − 1] ≡ β[j − 1] then
                f[i][j] ← f[i − 1][j − 1]
                g[i][j] ← Diagonal
            else if f[i][j] < f[i − 1][j − 1] − 1 then
                f[i][j] ← f[i − 1][j − 1] − 1
                g[i][j] ← Diagonal
            else if f[i][j] < f[i][j − 1] − 2 then
                f[i][j] ← f[i][j − 1] − 2
                g[i][j] ← Left
            else if f[i][j] < f[i − 1][j] − 2 then
                f[i][j] ← f[i − 1][j] − 2
                g[i][j] ← Up
            end if
        end for
    end for
                    ▷ reconstruction of aligned kriya sequences
    printaligned(g, α, β, m, n)
    return f[m][n]
end function
```

Time complexity is $\mathcal{O}(mn)$. Space complexity is $\mathcal{O}(mn)$.

```cpp
int alignkriya(std::string & alpha, std::string & beta)
{
    int m = alpha.size();
    int n = beta.size();

    std::vector<std::vector<int>> f(m+1, std::vector<int>(n+1, std::numeric_limits<int>::min()));
    std::vector<std::vector<int>> g(m+1, std::vector<int>(n+1, std::numeric_limits<int>::min()));

    for(int i = 0; i <= m; ++i)
    {
        f[i][0] = i * -2;
        g[i][0] = Up;
    }

    for(int j = 0; j <= n; ++j)
```

```
    {
        f[0][j] = j * -2;
        g[0][j] = Left;
    }

    for(int i = 1; i <= m; ++i)
    {
        for(int j = 1; j <= n; ++j)
        {
            if(alpha[i-1] == beta[j-1])
            {
                f[i][j] = f[i-1][j-1];
                g[i][j] = Diagonal;
            }

            else if(f[i][j] < f[i-1][j-1] - 1)
            {
                f[i][j] = f[i-1][j-1] - 1;
                g[i][j] = Diagonal;
            }

            if(f[i][j] < f[i][j-1] - 2)
            {
                f[i][j] = f[i][j-1] - 2;
                g[i][j] = Left;
            }

            if(f[i][j] < f[i-1][j] - 2)
            {
                f[i][j] = f[i-1][j] - 2;
                g[i][j] = Up;
            }
        }
    }
    // reconstruction of aligned kriya sequences
        from g-matrix
    printaligned(g, alpha, beta, m, n);

    return f[m][n];
}
```

$$\alpha : AACAGTTACC$$
$$\beta : TAAGGTCA$$
$$gap : -$$

Aligned α	A	A	C	A	G	T	T	A	C	C
Aligned β	T	A	–	A	G	G	T	–	C	A
Score	-1	0	-2	0	0	-1	0	-2	0	-1

Total Score : -7

Alternatively :

Algorithm 114 Generate & Reconstruct Aligned Kriya Sequences

```
function alignkriya(α[0..m − 1], β[0..n − 1])
    f[0..m][0..n] ← {∞}                ▷ Store optimal total scores
    for i ∈ [0, m] do
        f[i][0] ← i × −2
    end for
    for j ∈ [0, n] do
        f[0][j] ← j × −2
    end for
    for i ∈ [1, m] do
        for j ∈ [1, n] do
            if α[i − 1] ≡ β[j − 1] then
                score ← 0
            else
                score ← 1
            end if
            f[i][j] ← max(f[i − 1][j − 1] + score, f[i][j − 1] − 2, f[i − 1][j] − 2)
        end for
    end for
                        ▷ reconstruction of aligned kriya sequences
    i ← m
    j ← n
    while i > 0 and j > 0 do
        if α[i − 1] ≡ β[j − 1] then
            score ← 0
        else
            score ← 1
        end if
        if f[i][j] ≡ f[i − 1][j − 1] + score then
            α_aligned ← α_aligned + α[i − 1]
            β_aligned ← β_aligned + β[j − 1]
            i ← i − 1
            j ← j − 1
        else if f[i][j] ≡ f[i][j − 1] − 2 then
            α_aligned ← α_aligned + '−'
            β_aligned ← β_aligned + β[j − 1]
            j ← j − 1
        else if f[i][j] ≡ f[i − 1][j] − 2 then
            α_aligned ← α_aligned + α[i − 1]
            β_aligned ← β_aligned + '−'
            i ← i − 1
        end if
    end while
    α_aligned ← α_aligned + α[0..i]
    β_aligned ← β_aligned + "−[i]"          ▷ Append i times −
    α_aligned ← α_aligned + "−[i]"
```

$\beta_{aligned} \leftarrow \beta_{aligned} + \beta[0..j]$

reverse$(\alpha_{aligned})$
reverse$(\beta_{aligned})$

print $\alpha_{aligned}$ and $\beta_{aligned}$
return $f[m][n]$
end function

Time complexity is $\mathcal{O}(mn)$. Space complexity is $\mathcal{O}(mn)$.

```
int alignkriya(std::string & alpha, std::string & beta)
{
    int m = alpha.size();
    int n = beta.size();

    std::vector<std::vector<int>> f(m+1, std::vector<int>(n+1, std::numeric_limits<int>::min()));

    for(int i = 0; i <= m; ++i)
    {
        f[i][0] = i * -2;
    }

    for(int j = 0; j <= n; ++j)
    {
        f[0][j] = j * -2;
    }

    for(int i = 1; i <= m; ++i)
    {
        for(int j = 1; j <= n; ++j)
        {
            int score = ((alpha[i-1] == beta[j-1]) ? 0 : -1);

            f[i][j] = std::max({f[i-1][j-1] + score, f[i][j-1] - 2, f[i-1][j] - 2});
        }
    }


    // reconstruction of aligned kriya sequences from f-matrix
    std::string alpha_aligned, beta_aligned;

    alpha_aligned.reserve(m+n);
    beta_aligned.reserve(m+n);

    int i = m, j = n;

    while(i > 0 and j > 0)
    {
```

```
        int score = ((alpha[i-1] == beta[j-1]) ? 0 : -1);
        if(f[i][j] == f[i-1][j-1] + score)
        {
            alpha_aligned += alpha[i-1];
            beta_aligned += beta[j-1];
            --i; --j;
        }
        else if(f[i][j] == f[i][j-1] - 2)
        {
            alpha_aligned += '_';
            beta_aligned += beta[j-1];
            --j;
        }
        else if(f[i][j] == f[i-1][j] - 2)
        {
            alpha_aligned += alpha[i-1];
            beta_aligned += '_';
            --i;
        }
    }

    alpha_aligned += alpha.substr(0, i);
    beta_aligned += std::string(i, '_');

    alpha_aligned += std::string(j, '_');
    beta_aligned += beta.substr(0, j);

    std::reverse(alpha_aligned.begin(), alpha_aligned.end());
    std::reverse(beta_aligned.begin(), beta_aligned.end());

    std::cout << "Aligned Kriya Sequences are" << std::endl;
    std::cout << alpha_aligned << std::endl;
    std::cout << beta_aligned << std::endl;

    return f[m][n];
}
```

■

§ Problem 78. *Determine the minimal possible sum of removed Kriyas to render the given two Kriya sequences identical.* ◊

§§ Solution. Let $f_p(i,\ j)$ be the minimal possible sum of removed Kriyas to render the Kriya sequence $<\alpha_1,\ \alpha_2,\ \cdots,\ \alpha_i>$ identical to the Kriya sequence $<\beta_1,\ \beta_2,\ \cdots,\ \beta_j>$, using an optimal sequence of p-steps.

$$\therefore f_p(i,\ j) = \begin{cases} f_{p-1}(i-1,\ j-1) & \text{if } \alpha[i-1] \equiv \beta[j-1] \\ \text{Min}[f_{p-1}(i,\ j-1),\ f_{p-1}(i-1,\ j)] & \text{Otherwise.} \end{cases}$$

Algorithm 115 Identical Kriya Sequences

```
function identicalkriya(α[0..m − 1], β[0..n − 1])
    f[0..m][0..n] ← {∞}    ▷ Stores optimal sum of removed Kriyas
    for i ∈ [1, m] do
        f[i][0] ← f[i − 1][0] + α[i − 1]    ▷ β is empty : remove Kriyas from α one by one
    end for
    for j ∈ [1, n] do
        f[0][j] ← f[0][j − 1] + β[j − 1]    ▷ α is empty : remove Kriyas from β one by one
    end for
    for i ∈ [1, m] do
        for j ∈ [1, n] do
            if α[i − 1] ≡ β[j − 1] then
                f[i][j] ← f[i − 1][j − 1]
            else
                f[i][j] ← min(f[i][j − 1] + β[j − 1], f[i − 1][j] + α[i − 1])
            end if
        end for
    end for
    return f[m][n]
end function
```

Time complexity is $\mathcal{O}(mn)$. Space complexity is $\mathcal{O}(mn)$.

```cpp
int identicalkriya(std::vector<int> & alpha, std::vector<int> & beta)
{
    int m = alpha.size();
    int n = beta.size();

    std::vector<std::vector<int>> f(m+1, std::vector<int>(n+1, 0));

    // beta is empty : remove Kriyas from alpha one by one
    for(int i = 1; i <= m; i++)
    {
        f[i][0] = f[i-1][0] + alpha[i-1];
    }

    // alpha is empty : remove Kriyas from beta one by one
    for(int j = 1; j <= n; j++)
    {
        f[0][j] = f[0][j-1] + beta[j-1];
    }

    for(int i = 1; i <= m; i++)
```

```
    {
        for(int j = 1; j <= n; j++)
        {
            if(alpha[i-1] == beta[j-1])
            {
                f[i][j] = f[i-1][j-1];
            }
            else
            {
                f[i][j] = std::min(
                        f[i][j-1] + beta[j-1], // remove Kriya from beta or
                        f[i-1][j] + alpha[i-1] // remove Kriya from alpha
                        );
            }
        }
    }

    return f[m][n];
}
```

Algorithm 116 Identical Kriya Sequences with Reconstruction

function identicalkriya($\alpha[0..m-1]$, $\beta[0..n-1]$)
  $f[0..m][0..n] \leftarrow \{\infty\}$ ▷ Stores optimal sum of removed Kriyas
  for $i \in [1,\ m]$ **do**
    $f[i][0] \leftarrow f[i-1][0] + \alpha[i-1]$ ▷ β is empty : remove Kriyas from α one by one
  end for
  for $j \in [1,\ n]$ **do**
    $f[0][j] \leftarrow f[0][j-1] + \beta[j-1]$ ▷ α is empty : remove Kriyas from β one by one
  end for
  for $i \in [1,\ m]$ **do**
    for $j \in [1,\ n]$ **do**
      if $\alpha[i-1] \equiv \beta[j-1]$ **then**
        $f[i][j] \leftarrow f[i-1][j-1]$
      else
        $f[i][j] \leftarrow$ **min**$(f[i][j-1] + \beta[j-1],\ f[i-1][j] + \alpha[i-1])$
      end if
    end for
  end for ▷ Reconstruction
  while $i > 0$ or $j > 0$ **do**
    if $\alpha[i-1] \equiv \beta[j-1]$ **then**
      $i \leftarrow i-1$

        $j \leftarrow j - 1$
    else if $f[i][j] \leftarrow f[i][j-1] + \beta[j-1]$ **then**
        print "Remove " $\beta[j-1]$
        $j \leftarrow j - 1$
    else if $f[i][j] \leftarrow f[i-1][j] + \alpha[i-1]$ **then**
        print "Remove " $\alpha[i-1]$
        $i \leftarrow i - 1$
    end if
  end while
  return $f[m][n]$
end function

Time complexity is $\mathcal{O}(mn)$. Space complexity is $\mathcal{O}(mn)$. Time complexity of reconstruction part (while loop) is $\mathcal{O}(m+n)$.

```cpp
int identicalkriya(std::vector<int> & alpha, std::vector<int> & beta)
{
    int m = alpha.size();
    int n = beta.size();

    std::vector<std::vector<int>> f(m+1, std::vector<int>(n+1, 0));

    // beta is empty : remove Kriyas from alpha one by one
    for(int i = 1; i <= m; i++)
    {
        f[i][0] = f[i-1][0] + alpha[i-1];
    }

    // alpha is empty : remove Kriyas from beta one by one
    for(int j = 1; j <= n; j++)
    {
        f[0][j] = f[0][j-1] + beta[j-1];
    }

    for(int i = 1; i <= m; i++)
    {
        for(int j = 1; j <= n; j++)
        {
            if(alpha[i-1] == beta[j-1])
            {
                f[i][j] = f[i-1][j-1];
            }
            else
            {
                f[i][j] = std::min(
                        f[i][j-1] + beta[j-1], // remove Kriya from beta or
                        f[i-1][j] + alpha[i-1] //
```

```
                                        remove Kriya from alpha
                                                  );
                }
            }
        }

        // Reconstruction
        int i = m;
        int j = n;

        while(i > 0 or j > 0)
        {
            if(alpha[i-1] == beta[j-1])
            {
                --i; --j;
            }
            else if(f[i][j] == f[i][j-1] + beta[j-1])
            {
                std::cout << "Remove beta[" << (j-1)
                    << "] : " << beta[j-1] << "\n";
                --j;
            }
            else if(f[i][j] == f[i-1][j] + alpha[i-1])
            {
                std::cout << "Remove alpha[" << (i-1)
                    << "] : " << alpha[i-1] << "\n";
                --i;
            }
        }

        return f[m][n];
}
```

α	β	**Removal Steps**	**Optimal Sum**	**Equalized Kriya Seq**
<7, 4, 1>	<4, 1, 8>	Remove $\beta[2]:8$ Remove $\alpha[0]:7$	(7+8 =) 15	<4, 1>
<4, 5, 8, 5, 9, 5>	<8, 5, 5, 9>	Remove $\alpha[5]:5$ Remove $\beta[1]:5$ Remove $\alpha[1]:5$ Remove $\alpha[0]:4$	(4+5+5+5 =) 19	<8, 5, 9>

Alternatively :

Algorithm 117 Identical Kriya Sequences : Reconstruction (Recursive)

function reconstructkriya($f[0..m][0..n]$, $\alpha[0..m-1]$, $\beta[0..n-1]$, i, j)
  if $i \equiv 0$ and $j \equiv 0$ **then**
    return
  end if
  if $\alpha[i-1] \equiv \beta[j-1]$ **then**
    reconstructkriya(f, α, β, $i-1$, $j-1$)
  else if $f[i][j] \equiv f[i][j-1] + \beta[j-1]$ **then**
    reconstructkriya(f, α, β, i, $j-1$)
    print "Remove " $\beta[j-1]$
  else if $f[i][j] \equiv f[i-1][j] + \alpha[i-1]$ **then**
    reconstructkriya(f, α, β, $i-1$, j)
    print "Remove " $\alpha[i-1]$
  end if
end function

Time complexity is $\mathcal{O}(m+n)$. Space complexity is $\mathcal{O}(1)$.

```
void reconstructkriya(std::vector<std::vector<int
    >> & f, std::vector<int> & alpha, std::vector<
    int> & beta, int i, int j)
{
    if(i == 0 and j == 0) return;

    if(alpha[i-1] == beta[j-1])
    {
        reconstructkriya(f, alpha, beta, i-1, j-1)
            ;
    }
    else if(f[i][j] == f[i][j-1] + beta[j-1])
    {
        reconstructkriya(f, alpha, beta, i, j-1);
        std::cout << "Remove beta[" << (j-1) << "]
            : " << beta[j-1] << "\n";
    }
    else if(f[i][j] == f[i-1][j] + alpha[i-1])
    {
        reconstructkriya(f, alpha, beta, i-1, j);
        std::cout << "Remove alpha[" << (i-1) << "
            ] : " << alpha[i-1] << "\n";
    }
}
```

Algorithm 118 Generate Identical Kriya Sequences with Reconstruction (Recursive)

function identicalkriya($\alpha[0..m-1]$, $\beta[0..n-1]$)

$f[0..m][0..n] \leftarrow \{\infty\}$ ▷ Stores optimal sum of removed Kriyas
  for $i \in [1,\ m]$ **do**
    $f[i][0] \leftarrow f[i-1][0] + \alpha[i-1]$ ▷ β is empty : remove Kriyas from α one by one
  end for
  for $j \in [1,\ n]$ **do**
    $f[0][j] \leftarrow f[0][j-1] + \beta[j-1]$ ▷ α is empty : remove Kriyas from β one by one
  end for
  for $i \in [1,\ m]$ **do**
    for $j \in [1,\ n]$ **do**
      if $\alpha[i-1] \equiv \beta[j-1]$ **then**
        $f[i][j] \leftarrow f[i-1][j-1]$
      else
        $f[i][j] \leftarrow \mathbf{min}(f[i][j-1] + \beta[j-1],\ f[i-1][j] + \alpha[i-1])$
      end if
    end for
  end for ▷ Reconstruction
  reconstructkriya$(f,\ \alpha,\ \beta,\ m,\ n)$
  return $f[m][n]$
end function

Time complexity is $\mathcal{O}(mn)$. Space complexity is $\mathcal{O}(mn)$.

```
int identicalkriya(std::vector<int> & alpha, std::
    vector<int> & beta)
{
    int m = alpha.size();
    int n = beta.size();

    std::vector<std::vector<int>> f(m+1, std::
        vector<int>(n+1, 0));

    // beta is empty : remove Kriyas from alpha
        one by one
    for(int i = 1; i <= m; i++)
    {
        f[i][0] = f[i-1][0] + alpha[i-1];
    }

    // alpha is empty : remove Kriyas from beta
        one by one
    for(int j = 1; j <= n; j++)
    {
        f[0][j] = f[0][j-1] + beta[j-1];
    }

    for(int i = 1; i <= m; i++)
    {
        for(int j = 1; j <= n; j++)
        {
```

```
            if(alpha[i-1] == beta[j-1])
            {
                f[i][j] = f[i-1][j-1];
            }
            else
            {
                f[i][j] = std::min(
                        f[i][j-1] + beta[j-1], // remove Kriya from beta or
                        f[i-1][j] + alpha[i-1] // remove Kriya from alpha
                             );
            }
        }
    }

    // Reconstruction
    reconstructkriya(f, alpha, beta, m, n);

    return f[m][n];
}
```

Algorithm 119 Generate Identical Kriya Sequences : Optimal Space

function identicalkriya($\alpha[0..m-1]$, $\beta[0..n-1]$)
  $f[0..n] \leftarrow \{\infty\}$ ▷ Stores optimal sum of removed Kriyas
  for $j \in [1, n]$ **do**
    $f[j] \leftarrow f[j-1] + \beta[j-1]$ ▷ α is empty : remove Kriyas from β one by one
  end for
  for $i \in [1, m]$ **do**
    $prev \leftarrow f[0]$
    $f[0] \leftarrow f[0] + \alpha[i-1]$
    for $j \in [1, n]$ **do**
      $cur \leftarrow f[j]$
      if $\alpha[i-1] \equiv \beta[j-1]$ **then**
        $f[j] \leftarrow prev$
      else
        $f[j] \leftarrow \mathbf{min}(f[j-1] + \beta[j-1],\ f[j] + \alpha[i-1])$
      end if
    end for
  end for ▷ Reconstruction
  reconstructkriya(f, α, β, m, n)
  return $f[n]$
end function

Time complexity is $\mathcal{O}(mn)$. Space complexity is $\mathcal{O}(n)$.

```
int identicalkriya(std::vector<int> & alpha, std::
    vector<int> & beta)
{
    int m = alpha.size();
    int n = beta.size();

    std::vector<int> f(n+1, 0);

    for(int j = 1; j <= n; j++)
    {
        f[j] = f[j-1] + beta[j-1];
    }

    for(int i = 1; i <= m; i++)
    {
        int prev = f[0];

        f[0] += alpha[i-1];

        for(int j = 1; j <= n; j++)
        {
            int cur = f[j];

            if(alpha[i-1] == beta[j-1])
            {
                f[j] = prev;
            }
            else
            {
                f[j] = std::min(
                        f[j-1] + beta[j-1], //
                            remove Kriya from
                            beta or
                        f[j] + alpha[i-1]    //
                            remove Kriya from
                            alpha
                            );
            }

            prev = cur;
        }
    }

    return f[n];
}
```

■

§ Problem 79. *Determine the maximum possible sum of δ removed Kriyas from the head and tail of a given Kriya sequence* $<\alpha_1, \alpha_2, \cdots, \alpha_n>$. ◊

§§ Solution. There are three choices for removing δ Kriyas :

1. All of δ Kriyas are removed from the tail, or
2. All of δ Kriyas are removed from the head, or

3. λ Kriyas are removed from the head and the remaining $\delta-\lambda$ Kriyas are removed from the tail. Let $f(\lambda)$ be the maximum possible sum in this case.

$$
\begin{aligned}
\therefore f(0) &= \alpha_{n-(\delta-1)} + \alpha_{n-(\delta-2)} + \cdots + \alpha_{n-2} + \alpha_{n-1} + \alpha_n \\
f(1) &= \alpha_1 + \alpha_{n-(\delta-2)} + \cdots + \alpha_{n-2} + \alpha_{n-1} + \alpha_n \\
&= f(0) + \alpha_1 - \alpha_{n-(\delta-1)} \\
f(2) &= \alpha_1 + \alpha_2 + \alpha_{n-(\delta-3)} + \cdots + \alpha_{n-2} + \alpha_{n-1} + \alpha_n \\
&= f(1) + \alpha_2 - \alpha_{n-(\delta-2)} \\
\therefore f(\lambda) &= f(\lambda-1) + \alpha_\lambda - \alpha_{n-(\delta-\lambda)}\ \forall\lambda \in [1,\ \delta] \\
f(\delta-1) &= \alpha_1 + \alpha_2 + \cdots + \alpha_{\delta-1} + \alpha_n \\
\therefore f(\delta) &= \alpha_1 + \alpha_2 + \cdots + \alpha_{\delta-1} + \alpha_\delta \\
&= f(\delta-1) + \alpha_\delta - \alpha_n
\end{aligned}
$$

Let $f_p(\lambda)$ be the maximum possible sum using an optimal policy with p-steps.

$$
\therefore f_p(\lambda) = \begin{cases} \sum\limits_{\theta=n-(\delta-\lambda)}^{n} \alpha_\theta & \text{if } \lambda \equiv 0 \\ \text{Max}\left[f_{p-1}(\lambda-1) + \alpha_\lambda - \alpha_{n-(\delta-\lambda)}\right] & \forall\lambda \in [1,\ \delta]. \end{cases}
$$

Algorithm 120 Optimal Removed Kriyas

function maxkriya($\alpha[0..m-1],\ \beta[0..n-1]$)
    $f[0..\delta-1] \leftarrow \{0\}$ ▷ Stores optimal sum of removed Kriyas
    for $\lambda \in [n-\delta,\ n)$ **do** ▷ start from all δ-Kriyas being at rightmost locations
        $f[0] \leftarrow f[0] + \alpha[\lambda]$
    end for
    $maxsum \leftarrow f[0]$
    for $\lambda \in [1,\ \delta)$ **do**
        $f[\lambda] \leftarrow f[\lambda-1] + \alpha[\lambda-1] - \alpha[n-(\delta-\lambda)-1]$
        $maxsum \leftarrow$ **max**($maxsum,\ f[\lambda]$)
    end for
    return $maxsum$
end function

Time complexity is $\mathcal{O}(\delta)$. Space complexity is $\mathcal{O}(\delta)$.

```
int maxkriya(std::vector<int> & alpha, int delta)
{
    int n = alpha.size();

    std::vector<int> f(delta, 0);

    // start from all delta-Kriyas being at
        rightmost locations
    for(int lambda = n-delta; lambda < n; lambda
        ++)
    {
        f[0] += alpha[lambda];
```

```
    }

    int maxsum = f[0];

    // sliding window
    for(int lambda = 1; lambda < delta; lambda++)
    {
        // include one from left, exclude one from right
        f[lambda] = f[lambda-1] + alpha[lambda-1] - alpha[n-(delta-lambda)-1];
        maxsum = std::max(maxsum, f[lambda]);
    }

    return maxsum;
}
```

α	δ	**Removal Steps**	**Optimal Sum**
<1,4,5,8,7,6,3,2>	4	Remove <1,4,5,8> from head or Remove <7,6,3,2> from tail	18
<1,4,5,8,7,6,3,2>	5	Remove <8,7,6,3,2> from tail	26
<1,10,100,1,1,500,1>	2	Remove <500, 1> from tail	501
<1,10,100,1,1,500,1>	3	Remove <1,500, 1> from tail, or Remove <1> from head and <500,1> from tail	502
<1,10,100,1,1,500,1>	4	Remove <500, 1> from tail and Remove <1,10> from head	512

■

Chapter 15

Kriya Catalysis

§ Problem 80. *Linear scan of a Kriya sequence, having α Kriyas, for searching the maximal Kriya β, invokes exactly γ favorable comparisons. Determine the total possible number of Kriya sequences for a given set of α, β and γ.* $\diamond$

§§ Solution. Let $f_p(count,\ kriya,\ numcomp)$ be the number of ways to construct a Kriya sequence having $count$ Kriyas with $kriya$ as the maximum Kriya found with γ comparisons, using an optimal policy with p-steps.

Any Kriya $\in [1,\ kriya]$ can be added at the end of a Kriya sequence having $count - 1$ Kriyas with $kriya$ as the maximum Kriya found with $numcomp$ comparisons, i.e.

$$f_p(count,\ kriya,\ numcomp) = kriya \times f_{p-1}(count - 1,\ kriya,\ numcomp)$$

Similarly, the maximum Kriya $kriya$ can be added at the end of a Kriya sequence having $count - 1$ Kriyas with maximum Kriya being strictly less than $kriya$ found with $numcomp-1$ comparisons, i.e.

$$f_p(count,\ kriya,\ numcomp) = \sum_{k\equiv 1}^{kriya-1} f_{p-1}(count - 1,\ k,\ numcomp - 1)$$

$$\therefore f_p(count, kriya, numcomp) = \begin{cases} 1 & \text{if } count \equiv numcomp \equiv 1 \\ kriya \times f_{p-1}(count - 1, kriya, numcomp) & \text{Append any} \in [1,\ kriya] \\ \sum\limits_{k\equiv 1}^{kriya-1} f_{p-1}(count - 1, k, numcomp - 1) & \text{Append max } kriya \end{cases}$$

Algorithm 121 Kriya Sequence Generation : Count Ways : Constraints of Favourable Comparisons

```
function countks(α, β, γ)
    f[0..α][0..β][0..γ] ← {0}
    for kriya ∈ [1, β] do
        f[1][kriya][1] ← 1    ▷ unit length Kriya sequence : 1 way
    end for
    for count ∈ [1, α] do
        for kriya ∈ [1, β] do
            for numcomp ∈ [1, γ] do
                f[count][kriya][numcomp] ←
      f[count][kriya][numcomp]+f[count−1][kriya][numcomp]× kriya    ▷ append any Kriya in [1, kriya]
                for k ∈ [1, kriya − 1] do
                    f[count][kriya][numcomp] ←
      f[count][kriya][numcomp] + f[count − 1][k][numcomp − 1]    ▷ append the max Kriya kriya
                end for
            end for
        end for
    end for
    ways ← 0
    for kriya ∈ [1, β] do
        ways ← ways + f[α][kriya][γ]
    end for
    return ways
end function
```

Time complexity is $\mathcal{O}(\alpha\beta^2\gamma)$. Space complexity is $\mathcal{O}(\alpha\beta\gamma)$.

```
int countks(int alpha, int beta, int gamma)
{
    std::vector<std::vector<std::vector<int>>> f(
        alpha+1, std::vector<std::vector<int>>(
        beta+1, std::vector<int>(gamma+1, 0)));

    for(int kriya = 1; kriya <= beta; kriya++)
    {
        f[1][kriya][1] = 1; // unit length
            sequence : 1 way
    }

    for(int count = 1; count <= alpha; count++)
    {
        for(int kriya = 1; kriya <= beta; kriya++)
        {
            for(int numcomp = 1; numcomp <= gamma;
                numcomp++)
            {
                // append any Kriya in [1, kriya]
                    at the end
                f[count][kriya][numcomp] += f[
                    count-1][kriya][numcomp] *
```

```
                              kriya;

                    // append the Kriya "kriya" at the end
                    for(int k = 1; k < kriya; k++)
                    {
                        f[count][kriya][numcomp] += f[count-1][k][numcomp-1];
                    }
                }
            }
        }

        int ways = 0;

        for(int kriya = 1; kriya <= beta; kriya++)
        {
            ways += f[alpha][kriya][gamma];
        }

        return ways;
}
```

α	β	γ	**ways**	**count**
1	2	1	<1> <2>	2
2	2	1	<1, 1> <2, 1> <2, 2>	3
2	3	1	<1, 1> <2, 1> <2, 2> <3, 1> <3, 2> <3, 3>	6
2	1	1	<1, 1>	1
2	2	2	<1, 2>	1
1	2	2	-	0

■

§ Problem 81. *Each Sadhak has her own preference of practicing Kriyas. Determine the total number of ways of practicing α distinct Kriyas by β ($< \alpha$) Sadhaks given a sequence of $kriyas$ such that $kriyas[sadhak]$ represents the Kriya sequence preferred by the $sadhak$.* ◊

§§ Solution. Let $f_p(kriya,\ subset)$ be the number of ways of practicing the preferred the first $kriya$ Kriyas by each sadhak from the subset.

Since the number of Sadhaks is less than the number of Kriyas, hence it is helpful to build the reverse mapping, i.e. Kriya to list of Sadhaks, such that $sadhaks[kriya]$ represents the list of Sadhaks who prefer a given kriya.

There are two parts to build the subset of sadhaks : the subset of sadhaks practice the first $kriya - 1$ Kriyas, i.e. the Kriya marked as $kriya$ is left out. One Sadhak from the subset practices the Kriya marked as $kriya$ and other Sadhaks practice from the remainig $kriya - 1$ Kriyas, i.e. $sadhak$ prefers $kriya$ and belongs to the subset.

$$\therefore f_p(kriya,\ subset) = f_{p-1}(kriya - 1,\ subset)$$

$$+ \sum_{sadhak \in sadhaks[kriya]} f_{p-1}(kriya - 1,\ subset \hat{} (1 << sadhak))$$

Algorithm 122 Preferred Kriya Practice : Count Ways

function practicekriyas($kriyas[0..\beta-1][],\ \alpha$)
  $sadhaks[0..\alpha][] \leftarrow \{0\}$
  for $sadhak \in [0,\ \beta]$ **do**
    for $kriya \in kriyas[sadhak]$ **do**
      $sadhaks[kriya].append(sadhak)$ ▷ $kriya \implies sadhaks$
    end for
  end for
  $subsetsadhaks \leftarrow 1 << \beta$
  $f[0..\alpha][0..subsetsadhaks-1] \leftarrow \{0\}$
  $f[0][0] \leftarrow 1$
  for $kriya \in [1,\ \alpha]$ **do**
    for $subset \in [0,\ subsetsadhaks)$ **do**
      $f[kriya][subset] \leftarrow f[kriya][subset] + f[kriya-1][subset]$ ▷ using first $kriya-1$ Kriyas
      for $sadhak \in sadhaks[kriya]$ **do**
        if $subset \& (1 << sadhak) \neq 0$ **then**
          $f[kriya][subset] \leftarrow f[kriya][subset] + f[kriya-1][subset \hat{} (1 << sadhak)]$
        end if
      end for
    end for
  end for
  return $f[\alpha][subsetsadhaks-1]$
end function

Time complexity is $\mathcal{O}(\alpha 2^{\beta} \beta)$. Space complexity is $\mathcal{O}(\alpha 2^{\beta})$.

```
int practicekriyas(std::vector<std::vector<int>> &
    kriyas, int alpha)
{
    int beta = kriyas.size(); // count of sadhaks

    // sadhaks => kriyas
    // kriyas[sadhak-1] => <kriyas> preferred by a
        given sadhak
    //
    // kriyas => sadhaks
    // sadhaks[kriya-1] => <sadhaks> who prefer a
        given kriya
    std::vector<std::vector<int>> sadhaks(alpha +
        1);

    for(int sadhak = 0; sadhak < beta; sadhak++)
    {
```

```
        for(auto kriya : kriyas[sadhak])
        {
            sadhaks[kriya].emplace_back(sadhak);
        }
    }

    const int count_subset_sadhaks = 1 << beta;

    // f[kriya][subset] : number of ways
    // each sadhak from the subset practice
    // her preferred Kriya from [1..kriya].
    std::vector<std::vector<int>> f(alpha+1, std::vector<int>(count_subset_sadhaks, 0));

    f[0][0] = 1; // there is only one way : no sadhak has any Kriya

    for(int kriya = 1; kriya <= alpha; kriya++)
    {
        for(int subset = 0; subset < count_subset_sadhaks; subset++)
        {
            // using first (kriya-1) Kriyas
            f[kriya][subset] += f[kriya-1][subset];

            // one sadhak from the subset practices the Kriya (kriya)
            // other sadhaks practice from the remaining (kriya-1) Kriyas
            // i.e. sadhak prefers kriya and belongs to the subset
            for(const auto sadhak : sadhaks[kriya])
            {
                const int mask = 1 << sadhak;

                if((subset & mask) != 0)
                {
                    f[kriya][subset] += f[kriya-1][subset ^ mask];
                }
            }
        }
    }

    return f[alpha][count_subset_sadhaks - 1];
}
```

Algorithm 123 Preferred Kriya Practice : Count Ways : Space Optimization

```
function practicekriyas(kriyas[0..β − 1][], α)
    sadhaks[0..α][] ← {0}
    for sadhak ∈ [0, β] do
        for kriya ∈ kriyas[sadhak] do
            sadhaks[kriya].append(sadhak)                ▷ kriya ⟹ sadhaks
        end for
    end for
    f[0..(1 << β) − 1] ← {0}
    f[0] ← 1                                   ▷ one way : empty set
    for kriya ∈ [0, α) do
        for subset ∈ [(1 << β) − 1, 0] do
            for sadhak ∈ sadhaks[kriya] do
                if subset&(1 << sadhak) ≠ 0 then
                    f[subset] ← f[subset]+f[subset^(1 << sadhak)]
                end if
            end for
        end for
    end for
    return f[(1 << β) − 1]
end function
```

Time complexity is $\mathcal{O}(\alpha 2^{\beta}\beta)$. Space complexity is $\mathcal{O}(2^{\beta})$.

```cpp
int practicekriyas(std::vector<std::vector<int>> & kriyas, int alpha)
{
    int beta = kriyas.size(); // count of sadhaks

    // sadhaks => kriyas
    // kriyas[sadhak-1] => <kriyas> preferred by a given sadhak
    //
    // kriyas => sadhaks
    // sadhaks[kriya-1] => <sadhaks> who prefer a given kriya
    std::vector<std::vector<int>> sadhaks(alpha);

    for(int sadhak = 0; sadhak < beta; sadhak++)
    {
        for(auto kriya : kriyas[sadhak])
        {
            sadhaks[kriya-1].emplace_back(sadhak);
        }
    }

    // f[subset] : number of ways
    // each sadhak from the subset practice
    // her preferred Kriya from [1..kriya].
    std::vector<int> f(1 << beta, 0);

    f[0] = 1; // there is only one way : no sadhak has any Kriya

```

```
    for(int kriya = 0; kriya < alpha; kriya++)
    {
        for(int subset = (1 << beta) - 1; subset
            >= 0; --subset)
        {
            for(const auto sadhak : sadhaks[kriya
                ])
            {
                if((subset & (1 << sadhak)) != 0)
                {
                    f[subset] += f[subset ^ (1 <<
                        sadhak)];
                }
            }
        }
    }

    return f[(1 << beta) - 1];
}
```

sequence of kriyas	Count of Kriyas : β	ways	count
< <2, 4, 1>, <1, 4> >	5	<2, 1> <2, 4> <4, 1> <1, 4>	4
< <2, 4, 1>, <1, 4>, <2> >	10	<4, 1, 2> <1, 4, 2>	2

■

§ Problem 82. *Determine the number of ways of splitting a rectangular Kriya Grid bearing binary values (i.e. 1 or 0) into δ regions using $\delta - 1$ split lines : each split line being either horizontal or vertical : such that each region contains at least one Kriya labeled* 1. ◊

§§ Solution. Treating the topmost left vertex as the origin $(0,\ 0)$ and the bottom right vertex as $(r-1,\ c-1)$, let $f_p(split,\ i,\ j)$ be the number of ways of splitting the $grid[i..r-1][j..c-1]$ into $split$ regions.

Let $countk(i,\ j)$ be the count of Kriya bearing 1 in the $grid[0..i][0..j]$. Pre-summation for all the possible regions in the grid :

$$\begin{aligned}\therefore countk(i,\ j) &= grid(i,\ j)\\ &+ countk(i+1,\ j)\\ &+ countk(i,\ j+1)\\ &- countk(i+1,\ j+1) \quad \forall i \in [r-1,\ 0] \wedge j \in [c-1,\ 0]\end{aligned}$$

Let $testk(r_1,\ c_1,\ r_2,\ c_2)$ represent the state if there exists at least one Kriya bearing 1 in the region $grid[r_1..c_1][r_2..c_2]$.

$$\begin{aligned}\therefore testk(r_1,\ c_1,\ r_2,\ c_2) = countk[r1][c1] &- countk[r2+1][c1]\\ &- countk[r1][c2+1]\\ &+ countk[r2+1][c2+1] \geq 1\end{aligned}$$

$$\therefore f_p(split,\ i,\ j) = \begin{cases} 1 & \text{if } countk(i,\ j) \geq 1 \wedge split \equiv 0 \\ 0 & \text{if } countk(i,\ j) < 1 \wedge split \equiv 0 \\ f_{p-1}(split-1,\ i_1,\ j) & i_1 \in [i+1..r-1] \wedge testk(i,\ j,\ i_1-1,\ c-1) \\ f_{p-1}(split-1,\ i,\ j_1) & j_1 \in [j+1..c-1] \wedge testk(i,\ j,\ r-1,\ j_1-1) \end{cases}$$

Algorithm 124 Binary Split Kriyas : Count Ways

```
function performkriya(grid[0..r − 1][0..c − 1], δ)
    countk[0..r][0..c] ← {0}    ▷ count[i][j] : count of Kriya 1 in grid[0..i][0..j]
    for i ∈ [r − 1, 0] do
        for j ∈ [c − 1, 0] do
            countk[i][j] ← grid[i][j]+countk[i+1][j]+countk[i][j+1] − countk[i + 1][j + 1]
        end for
    end for
    f[0..δ − 1][0..r − 1][0..c − 1] ← {0}
    for i ∈ [0..r) do
        for j ∈ [0..c) do
            if countk[i][j] ≥ 1 then
                f[0][i][j] ← 1
            else
                f[0][i][j] ← 0
            end if
        end for
    end for
    for split ∈ [1, δ) do
        for i ∈ [0, r) do
            for j ∈ [0, c) do                                ▷ horizontal split
                for i1 ∈ [i + 1, r) do
                    if countk[i][j] − countk[i1][j] − countk[i][c] + countk[i1][c] > 0 then
                        f[split][i][j] ← f[split][i][j]+f[split−1][i1][j]
                    end if
                end for                                      ▷ vertical split
                for j1 ∈ [j + 1, c) do
                    if countk[i][j] − countk[r][j] − countk[i][j1] + countk[r][j1] > 0 then
                        f[split][i][j] ← f[split][i][j]+f[split−1][i][j1]
                    end if
                end for
            end for
        end for
    end for
    return f[δ − 1][0][0]
end function
```

Time complexity is $\mathcal{O}(\delta rc(r+c))$. Space complexity is $\mathcal{O}(\delta rc)$.

```
int performkriya(std::vector<std::vector<int>> &
    grid, int delta)
```

```
{
    int r = grid.size();
    int c = grid[0].size();

    // grid[i][j] is either 0 or 1
    // countk[i][j] : count of kriyas labelled as 1 in grid[0..i][0..j]
    std::vector<std::vector<int>> countk(r+1, std::vector<int>(c+1, 0));

    for(int i = r-1; i >= 0; --i)
    {
        for(int j = c-1; j >= 0; --j)
        {
            countk[i][j] = grid[i][j] + countk[i+1][j] + countk[i][j+1] - countk[i+1][j+1];
        }
    }

    std::vector<std::vector<std::vector<int>>> f(delta, std::vector<std::vector<int>>(r, std::vector<int>(c, 0)));

    for(int i = 0; i < r; ++i)
    {
        for(int j = 0; j < c; ++j)
        {
            f[0][i][j] = ((countk[i][j] >= 1) ? 1 : 0);
        }
    }

    for(int split = 1; split < delta; split++)
    {
        for(int i = 0; i < r; ++i)
        {
            for(int j = 0; j < c; ++j)
            {
                // horizontal split
                for(int i1 = i+1; i1 < r; ++i1)
                {
                    if(countk[i][j] - countk[i1][j] - countk[i][c] + countk[i1][c] > 0)
                    {
                        f[split][i][j] += f[split-1][i1][j];
                    }
                }

                // vertical split
                for(int j1 = j+1; j1 < c; ++j1)
                {
```

```
                if(countk[i][j] - countk[r][j]
                    - countk[i][j1] + countk[
                    r][j1] > 0)
                {
                    f[split][i][j] += f[split
                        -1][i][j1];
                }
            }
        }
    }
}

    return f[delta-1][0][0];
}
```

Kriya Grid	Count of Split Regions : δ	ways	count
$\begin{array}{ccc}1&0&0\\1&1&1\\0&0&0\end{array}$	3	$\begin{array}{ccc}1&0&0\\\hline 1&1&1\\0&0&0\end{array} \Longrightarrow \begin{array}{c\|cc}1&1&1\\0&0&0\end{array}$ $\begin{array}{ccc}1&0&0\\\hline 1&1&1\\0&0&0\end{array} \Longrightarrow \begin{array}{cc\|c}1&1&1\\0&0&0\end{array}$ $\begin{array}{c\|cc}1&0&0\\1&1&1\\0&0&0\end{array} \Longrightarrow \begin{array}{c\|c}0&0\\1&1\\0&0\end{array}$	3
$\begin{array}{cccc}0&1&0&1\\1&0&0&1\\0&1&1&0\\1&1&1&1\end{array}$	1	$\begin{array}{cccc}0&1&0&1\\1&0&0&1\\0&1&1&0\\1&1&1&1\end{array}$	1
$\begin{array}{cccc}0&1&0&1\\1&0&0&1\\0&1&1&0\\1&1&1&1\end{array}$	2		6
$\begin{array}{cccc}0&1&0&1\\1&0&0&1\\0&1&1&0\\1&1&1&1\end{array}$	3		24
$\begin{array}{ccc}1&0&0\\1&1&0\\0&0&0\end{array}$	3	$\begin{array}{ccc}1&0&0\\\hline 1&1&0\\0&0&0\end{array} \Longrightarrow \begin{array}{c\|cc}1&1&0\\0&0&0\end{array}$	1

■

§ Problem 83. *Determine the number of ways of organizing a Kriya Grid $n \times 3$ using unlimited instances of three Kriyas : α, β and γ such that no two adjacent grid-cells have the same Kriya.* ◊

§§ Solution. Grid has $n > 1$ rows and 3 columns. There are two possibilities for a given row, it may contain :

1. three distinct Kriyas, say <α, β, γ> : 6 ways. The possibilities for the next row are :
   a) <β, γ, α>
   b) <γ, α, β>
   c) <β, α, β>
   d) <γ, α, γ>

   Note that the first two have 3 distinct Kriyas whereas the last two have 2 distinct Kriyas.

2. two distinct Kriyas, say <α, β, α> : 6 ways. The possibilities for the next row are :
   a) <β, α, γ>
   b) <γ, α, β>
   c) <β, α, β>
   d) <β, γ, β>
   e) <γ, α, γ>
   Note that the first two have 3 distinct Kriyas whereas the last two have 2 distinct Kriyas.

Let $f_p^3(i)$ be the number of ways to populate i rows with i^{th} row bearing 3 distinct Kriyas and $f_p^2(i)$ be the number of ways to populate i rows with i^{th} row bearing 2 distinct Kriyas.

$$\therefore f_p^3(i) = \begin{cases} 6 & \text{if } i \equiv 1 \\ 2f_{p-1}^3(i-1) + 2f_{p-1}^2(i-1) & \text{if } i > 1 \end{cases}$$

$$\therefore f_p^2(i) = \begin{cases} 6 & \text{if } i \equiv 1 \\ 2f_{p-1}^3(i-1) + 3f_{p-1}^2(i-1) & \text{if } i > 1 \end{cases}$$

Let $f_p(i)$ be the number of ways to populate i rows :

$$\therefore f_p(i) = f_p^3(i) + f_p^2(i)$$

Algorithm 125 Organize Kriyas : Ways of Non-adjacent ones

function organizekriya(n)
  $f_p^3[0..n] \leftarrow \{0\}$
  $f_p^2[0..n] \leftarrow \{0\}$

  $f_p^3[1] \leftarrow 6$
  $f_p^2[1] \leftarrow 6$

  for $i \in [2, n]$ **do**
    $f_p^3[i] \leftarrow 2f_p^3[i-1] + 2f_p^2[i-1]$
    $f_p^2[i] \leftarrow 2f_p^3[i-1] + 3f_p^2[i-1]$
  end for
  return $\left(f_p^3[n] + f_p^2[n]\right)$
end function

Time complexity is $\mathcal{O}(n)$. Space complexity is $\mathcal{O}(n)$.

```
int organizekriya(int n)
{
    std::vector<int> f3(n+1, 0);
    std::vector<int> f2(n+1, 0);

    f3[1] = f2[1] = 6;

    for(int i = 2; i <= n; ++i)
```

```
    {
        f3[i] = 2 * f3[i-1] + 2 * f2[i-1];
        f2[i] = 2 * f3[i-1] + 3 * f2[i-1];
    }

    return (f3[n] + f2[n]);
}
```

n	Count
1	12
2	54
3	246
4	5118

■

§ Problem 84. *Given an ordered Kriya sequence, two Sadhaks, Ram and Shyam starts practicing Kriyas in the given order. Selected Kriyas are not available anymore. Each Sadhak is allowed to select 1, 2 or 3 Kriyas at a time from the remaining Kriyas in the sequence. Determine the difference between the maximum possible sums of Kriyas of each Sadhak.* ◊

§§ Solution. Let $f_p(i)$ be the difference between the maximal sums of Kriyas of the present Sadhak and other in the ith selection from a Kriya sequence $ks[0..n-1]$, using an optimal policy of p-steps.

$$\therefore f_p(i) = \text{Max} \begin{cases} 0 & \text{if } i \equiv n \\ ks[i] - f_{p+1}(i+1) & \text{if } i \equiv n-1 \\ ks[i] + ks[i+1] - f_{p+1}(i+2) & \text{if } i < n-1 \\ ks[i] + ks[i+1] + ks[i+2] - f_{p+1}(i+3) & \text{if } i < n-2 \end{cases}$$

Algorithm 126 Select Kriyas Alternately : Optimal Difference

function diffkriya($ks[0..n-1]$)
  $f_p[0..n] \leftarrow 0$
  for $i \in [n-1,\ 0]$ **do**
    $f_p[i] \leftarrow ks[i] - f_p[i+1]$
    if $i < n-1$ **then**
      $f_p[i] \leftarrow \textbf{max}(f_p[i],\ ks[i] + ks[i+1] - f_p[i+2])$
    end if
    if $i < n-2$ **then**
      $f_p[i] \leftarrow$
   $\textbf{max}(f_p[i],\ ks[i] + ks[i+1] + ks[i+2] - f_p[i+3])$
    end if
  end for
  return $f_p(0)$
end function

Time complexity is $\mathcal{O}(n)$. Space complexity is $\mathcal{O}(n)$.

```
int diffkriya(std::vector<int> & ks)
{
    int n = ks.size();

    // f[i] : diff between the maximum sum of kriyas of
    // the current Sadhak and the other in the ith turn
    std::vector<int> f(n+1, 0);

    for(int i = n-1; i >= 0; --i)
    {
        f[i] = ks[i] - f[i+1];

        if(i < n-1)
        {
            f[i] = std::max(f[i], ks[i] + ks[i+1] - f[i+2]);
        }

        if(i < n-2)
        {
            f[i] = std::max(f[i], ks[i] + ks[i+1] + ks[i+2] - f[i+3]);
        }
    }

    return f[0];
}
```

Kriya Sequence	1st Sadhak's Kriyas	2nd Sadhak's Kriyas	Diff
<2, 5, 9, 20>	<2, 5, 9>	<20>	-4 (2+5+9-20)
<2, 5, 9, 2, 10>	<2, 5, 9>	<2, 10>	4 (2+5+9-(2+10))
<2, 5, 9, 2, 10, 4>	<2, 5, 9>	<2, 10, 4>	0 (2+5+9-(2+10+4))
<2, -5, 9, 2, 10, 4>	<2> <10, 4>	<-5, 9, 2> <>	10 (2+10+4-(-5+9+2))

■

§ **Problem 85.** *A Kriya (integer $\in [1, \ \lambda]$) sequence is encoded as a digits sequence $ds[0..n-1]$. Determine the number of ways to decode ds as potential Kriya sequence(s).* ◊

§§ **Solution**. Let $f_p(i)$ be the number of ways to decode a digits sequence $ds[i..n-1]$, using an optimal policy of p-steps.

$$\therefore f_p(i) = \begin{cases} 1 & \text{if } i \equiv n : \text{one way : empty kriya seq} \\ \sum\limits_{\substack{1 \le ds[i..j] \le \lambda \\ j \in [i+1, \ n]}} f_{p-1}(j) & \text{if } i \in [0, \ n-1] \end{cases}$$

Algorithm 127 Decode Kriya Sequence from Digits Sequence

function reconskriya($ds[0..n-1], \ \lambda$)
    $f_p[0..n] \leftarrow 0$

    $f_p[n] \leftarrow 1$ ▷ One way to construct an empty kriya sequence
    for $i \in [n-1,\ 0]$ **do**
        $kriya \leftarrow ds[i]$
        for $j \in [i+1, n]$ **do**
            if $kriya > 0$ and $kriya \le \lambda$ **then**
                $f_p[i] \leftarrow f_{p-1}[i] + f_{p-1}[j]$
                if $j < n$ **then**
                    $kriya \leftarrow 10 \times kriya + ds[j]$
                end if
            end if
        end for
    end for
    return $f_p(0)$
end function

Time complexity is $\mathcal{O}(n \log \lambda)$. Space complexity is $\mathcal{O}(n)$.

```cpp
int reconskriya(std::vector<int> ds, int lambda)
{
    int n = ds.size();

    std::vector<int> f(n+1, 0);

    f[n] = 1;

    for(int i = n-1; i >= 0 ; --i)
    {
        int kriya = ds[i];

        for(int j = i+1; j < n+1; ++j)
        {
            if(kriya > 0 and kriya <= lambda)
            {
                f[i] += f[j];

                if(j < n)
                {
                    kriya = kriya * 10 + ds[j];
                }
            }
        }
    }

    return f[0];
}
```

Digits Sequence	λ	Ways	Count
<1, 0, 9, 0>	100	<10, 90>	1
<1, 2, 3>	200	<123> <12, 3> <1, 23> <1, 2, 3>	4

■

§ Problem 86. *Given an ordered sorted integer sequence of Kriyas* $<k_1,\ k_2,\ \cdots,\ k_n>$ *and time to practice any Kriya being same* τ*, the transduction quotient* TQ *of a given Kriya is defined as the product of that Kriya and time taken to practice all the previous Kriyas including the given Kriya. Determine the maximum possible sum of* TQ*s given that Sadhak is allowed to discard any Kriya(s).* ◊

§§ Solution. Let $f_p(i,\ j)$ be the maximum sum of TQs for practicing j Kriyas out of first i Kriyas.

$$\therefore f_p(i,\ j) = \begin{cases} 0 & \text{if } i \equiv j \equiv 0 \\ f_{p-1}(i-1,\ 0) & \text{if } j \equiv 0 \\ \text{Max}[f_{p-1}(i-1,\ j),\ f_{p-1}(i-1,\ j-1) + j\tau k_i] & \text{Otherwise} \end{cases}$$

Algorithm 128 Sorted Kriya Sequence : Transduction Quotient

function transducekriya($<k_1,\ k_2,\ \cdots,\ k_n>,\ \tau$)
  $f_p[0..n][0..n] \leftarrow \infty$
  $f_p[0][0] \leftarrow 0$
  for $i \in [1,\ n]$ **do**
    $f_p(i,\ 0) \leftarrow f_{p-1}(i-1,\ 0)$
    for $j \in [1,\ i]$ **do**
      $f_p(i,\ j) \leftarrow$
   max$(f_{p-1}(i-1,\ j),\ f_{p-1}(i-1,\ j-1) + j\tau k_i)$
    end for
  end for
  $maxsum \leftarrow -\infty$
  for $j \in [0,\ n]$ **do**
    $maxsum \leftarrow$ **max**$\{maxsum,\ f_p(n,\ j)\}$
  end for
  return $maxsum$
end function

Time complexity is $\mathcal{O}(n^2)$. Space complexity is $\mathcal{O}(n^2)$.

```
int transducekriya(std::vector<int> & ks, int tau
    = 1)
{
    int n = ks.size();

    std::vector<std::vector<int>> f(n+1, std::
        vector<int>(n+1, std::numeric_limits<int
        >::min()));

    f[0][0] = 0;

    for(int i = 1; i <= n; ++i)
    {
        f[i][0] = f[i-1][0];

        for(int j = 1; j <= i; ++j)
```

```
        {
            f[i][j] = std::max(f[i-1][j], f[i-1][j-1] + j * tau * ks[i-1]);
        }
    }

    int maxsum = std::numeric_limits<int>::min();

    for(int j = 0; j <= n; ++j)
    {
        maxsum = std::max(maxsum, f[n][j]);
    }

    return maxsum;
}
```

Kriya Sequence	τ	Optimal Ways	Optimal Sum
<-10, -9, 9, 10>	1	$1\times -10+2\times -9+3\times 9+4\times 10$	39
<-10, -9, -1, 0, 10>	2	$1\times 2\times -9+2\times 2\times -1+3\times 2\times 0+4\times 2\times 10$	58

■

§ Problem 87. *Cross Kriya Potential CKP is the inner product of all the possible two non-empty Kriya subsequences, having same number of Kriyas in each, for given two Kriya Sequences. Determine the maximum possible CKP.* ◊

§§ Solution. Let $f_p(i,\ j)$ be maximum CKP for the two Kriya sequences $<\alpha_1,\ \alpha_2,\ \cdots,\ \alpha_i>$ and $<\beta_1,\ \beta_2,\ \cdots,\ \beta_j>$, using an optimal policy of p-steps.

$$\therefore f_p(i,\ j) = \text{Max}\begin{cases} f_{p-1}(i-1,\ j) & \alpha_i \text{ is excluded} \\ f_{p-1}(i,\ j-1) & \beta_j \text{ is excluded} \\ f_{p-1}(i-1,\ j-1)+\alpha_i\times\beta_j & \text{if } f_{p-1}(i-1,\ j-1)>0 \\ \alpha_i\times\beta_j & \text{if } f_{p-1}(i-1,\ j-1)\le 0 \end{cases}$$

Algorithm 129 Cross Kriya Potential

function crosskriya($<\alpha_1,\ \alpha_2,\cdots,\ \alpha_m>,\ <\beta_1,\ \beta_2,\cdots,\ \beta_n>$)
  $f_p[0..m][0..n] \leftarrow -\infty$
  for $i\in[1,\ m]$ **do**
    for $j\in[1,\ n]$ **do**
      $f_p(i,\ j)\leftarrow$ **max**
$\{f_{p-1}(i-1,\ j),\ f_{p-1}(i,\ j-1),\ \mathbf{max}[0,\ f_{p-1}(i-1,\ j-1)]+\alpha_i\beta_j\}$
    end for
  end for
  return $f_p(m,\ n)$
end function

Time complexity is $\mathcal{O}(mn)$. Space complexity is $\mathcal{O}(mn)$.

```
int crosskriya(std::vector<int> & alpha, std::vector<int> & beta)
{
```

```
    int m = alpha.size();
    int n = beta.size();

    std::vector<std::vector<int>> f(m+1, std::
        vector<int>(n+1, std::numeric_limits<int
        >::min()/2));

    for(int i = 1; i <= m; ++i)
    {
        for(int j = 1; j <= n; ++j)
        {
            f[i][j] = std::max(
                    {
                      f[i-1][j],
                      f[i][j-1],
                      std::max(0, f[i-1][j-1]) +
                          alpha[i-1] * beta[j
                        -1]
                    }
                    );
        }
    }

    return f[m][n];
}
```

$<\alpha_1, \cdots>$	$<\beta_1, \cdots>$	**Optimal Subsequences**	**Optimal CKP**
<5, -5, 6, -6>	<4, -4, 3, -3>	<5, -5, 6, -6> × <4, -4, 3, -3>	76
<5, -5, 6, -6>	<4, 3, 5, 2>	<5, 6> × <4, 5>	50
<5, -5, 6, -6>	<4, 6, 1, 2>	<5, 6> × <4, 6>	56
<5, -5, -1, -4>	<4, 6, 1, 1>	<5> × <6>	30

■

§ Problem 88. *There are $m = 3n (n > 0)$ Kriyas in a circular sequence. Once a Kriya is selected for practice, it gets vanished after practice along with it's (two) immediate neighbors. Determine the maximum possible sum of Kriyas practiced.* ◊

§§ Solution. Optimal sum of n non-adjacent Kriyas is required. Circular sequence is equivalent to a linear sequence $<k_1, k_2, \cdots, k_{m-1}, k_m>$ where k_m and k_1 are adjacent to each other, hence cannot be selected together. So the problem is equivalent to finding the maximum of the optimal sum of n non-adjacent Kriyas in the two linear sequences $<k_1, k_2, \cdots, k_{m-1}>$ and $<k_2, \cdots, k_{m-1}, k_m>$.

Let $f_p(i, j)$ be the maximum sum corresponding to practicing j Kriyas out of i Kriyas $<k_1, k_2, \cdots, k_{i-1}, k_i>$.

$$\therefore f_p(i, j) = \text{Max} \begin{cases} 0 & \text{if } j \equiv 0 \\ 0 & \text{if } i \equiv 0 \\ k_1 & \text{if } i \equiv 1 \\ f_{p-1}(i-1, j) & k_i \text{ is not selected for practice} \\ f_{p-1}(i-2, j-1) + k_i & k_i \text{ is selected, } \therefore k_{i-1} \text{ can't be selected} \end{cases}$$

Algorithm 130 Maximum Sum : Linear and Circular Kriya Sequence

function slinearkriya($<k_1, k_2, \cdots, k_{m-1}, k_m>$, n)
    $f_p(0..m,\ 0..n) \leftarrow -\infty$ ▷ $f_p(i,\ j)$: maximum sum for practicing j out of i Kriyas
    for $i \in [0,\ m]$ **do**
        $f_p(i,\ 0) \leftarrow 0$ ▷ no Kriya is selected
    end for
    for $j \in [0,\ n]$ **do**
        $f_p(0,\ j) \leftarrow 0$ ▷ no Kriya is available
    end for
    for $i \in [1,\ m]$ **do**
        for $j \in [1,\ n]$ **do**
            if $i \equiv 1$ **then** ▷ single Kriya
                $f_p(i,\ j) \leftarrow k_1$
            else
                $f_p(i,\ j) \leftarrow$
        max$\{f_{p-1}(i-1,\ j),\ f_{p-1}(i-2,\ j-1) + k_i\}$
            end if
        end for
    end for
    return $f_p(m,\ n)$
end function

function maxsumcircularkriya($<k_1, k_2, \cdots, k_{m-1}, k_m>$)
    $n \leftarrow \frac{m}{3}$
    return max[
slinearkriya($<k_1, k_2, \cdots, k_{m-1}>$, n),
slinearkriya($<k_2, \cdots, k_{m-1}, k_m>$, n)]
end function

Time complexity is $\mathcal{O}(mn \approx m^2)$. Space complexity is $\mathcal{O}(mn \approx m^2)$.

```cpp
int maxsumlinearkriya(std::vector<int> ks, int n)
{
    int m = ks.size();

    // f[i][j] : maximum sum for practicing j out
        of i Kriyas
    std::vector<std::vector<int>> f(m+1, std::
        vector<int>(n+1, std::numeric_limits<int
        >::min()));

    // no Kriya is selected
    for(int i = 0; i <= m; ++i)
    {
        f[i][0] = 0;
    }

```

```
    // no Kriya is available
    for(int j = 0; j <= n; ++j)
    {
        f[0][j] = 0;
    }

    for(int i = 1; i <= m; ++i)
    {
        for(int j = 1; j <= n; ++j)
        {
            if(i == 1) // single Kriya
            {
                f[i][j] = ks[0];
            }
            else
            {
                f[i][j] = std::max(
                                  // ith Kriya is selected
                                  f[i-1][j],
                                  // ith Kriya is not selected
                                  // (i-1)th Kriya cannot be selected
                                  f[i-2][j-1] + ks[i-1]
                                  );
            }
        }
    }

    return f[m][n];
}


int maxsumcircularkriya(std::vector<int> ks)
{
    int n = ks.size()/3;

    return std::max(maxsumlinearkriya(std::vector<int>(ks.begin(), ks.end()-1), n), maxsumlinearkriya(std::vector<int>(ks.begin()+1, ks.end()), n));
}
```

$<k_1, k_2, \cdots, k_{m-1}, k_m>$	**Optimal Sum**
<1, 9, 2, 8, 3, 7>	17(=9+8)
<1, 2, 3, 4, 5, 6, 7, 8, 9>	21(=5+7+9)
<9, 15, 9, 5, 1, 2>	20(=15+5)
<7, 8, 7, 5, 1, 2>	14(=7+7)

■

ॐ ॐ ॐ

Bibliography

[1] Richard E. Bellman, *Dynamic Programming*. Princeton University Press, 1957.

[2] Chandra Shekhar Kumar, *Advanced C++ FAQs*. Ancient Science Publishers, 2014.

[3] Richard E. Bellman and Stuart E. Dreyfus, *Applied Dynamic Programming*. Princeton University Press, 1962.

[4] Chandra Shekhar Kumar, *Conceptual Solutions to (CLRS) Introduction to Algorithms (Part II : Sorting and Order Statistics)*. Ancient Science Publishers, 2014.

[5] Richard E. Bellman, Stuart E. Dreyfus and Averill M. Law, *The Art and Theory of Dynamic Programming*. Academic Press, 1977.

[6] W. A. Whitworth and Chandra Shekhar Kumar, *Concepts, Problems and Solutions in Permutations, Combinations and Probability*. Ancient Science Publishers, 2020.

[7] David Gries, *The Science of Programming(Monographs in Computer Science)*. Springer (February 1, 1987).

[8] Sergei Nakariakov, *Cracking Programming Interviews*. Ancient Science Publishers, 2014.

[9] Lev Tarasov and Chandra Shekhar Kumar, *Concepts, Problems and Solutions in School Calculus*. Ancient Science Publishers, 2020.

[10] Leslie Lamport, *LaTeX: A Document Preparation System*. Addison Wesley, Massachusetts, 2nd Edition, 1994.

[11] Chandra Shekhar Kumar, *Conceptual Kinematics*. Ancient Science Publishers, 2017.

Index

ॐ ॐ ॐ

This page is intentionally left blank.